SONG
OF THE
SHEPHERDESS

GWENDOLYN HERTZLER

© 2017 by TGS International, a wholly owned subsidiary of Christian Aid Ministries, Berlin, Ohio.

All rights reserved. No part of this book may be used, reproduced, or stored in any retrieval system, in any form or by any means, electronic or mechanical, without written permission from the publisher except for brief quotations embodied in critical articles and reviews.

ISBN: 978-1-947319-00-4

Sheep photo: stock.adobe.com

Map on page IV: Gavin Miles

Second printing: December 2017

Printed in the USA

Published by:
TGS International
P.O. Box 355, Berlin, Ohio 44610 USA
Phone: 330-893-4828
Fax: 330-893-2305
www.tgsinternational.com

TGS001593

DEDICATION

This story is dedicated to the Shepherd's scattered sheep.

"In returning and rest shall ye be saved; in quietness and in confidence shall be your strength. . . . He will be very gracious unto thee at the voice of thy cry; when he shall hear it, he will answer thee" (Isaiah 30:15, 19).

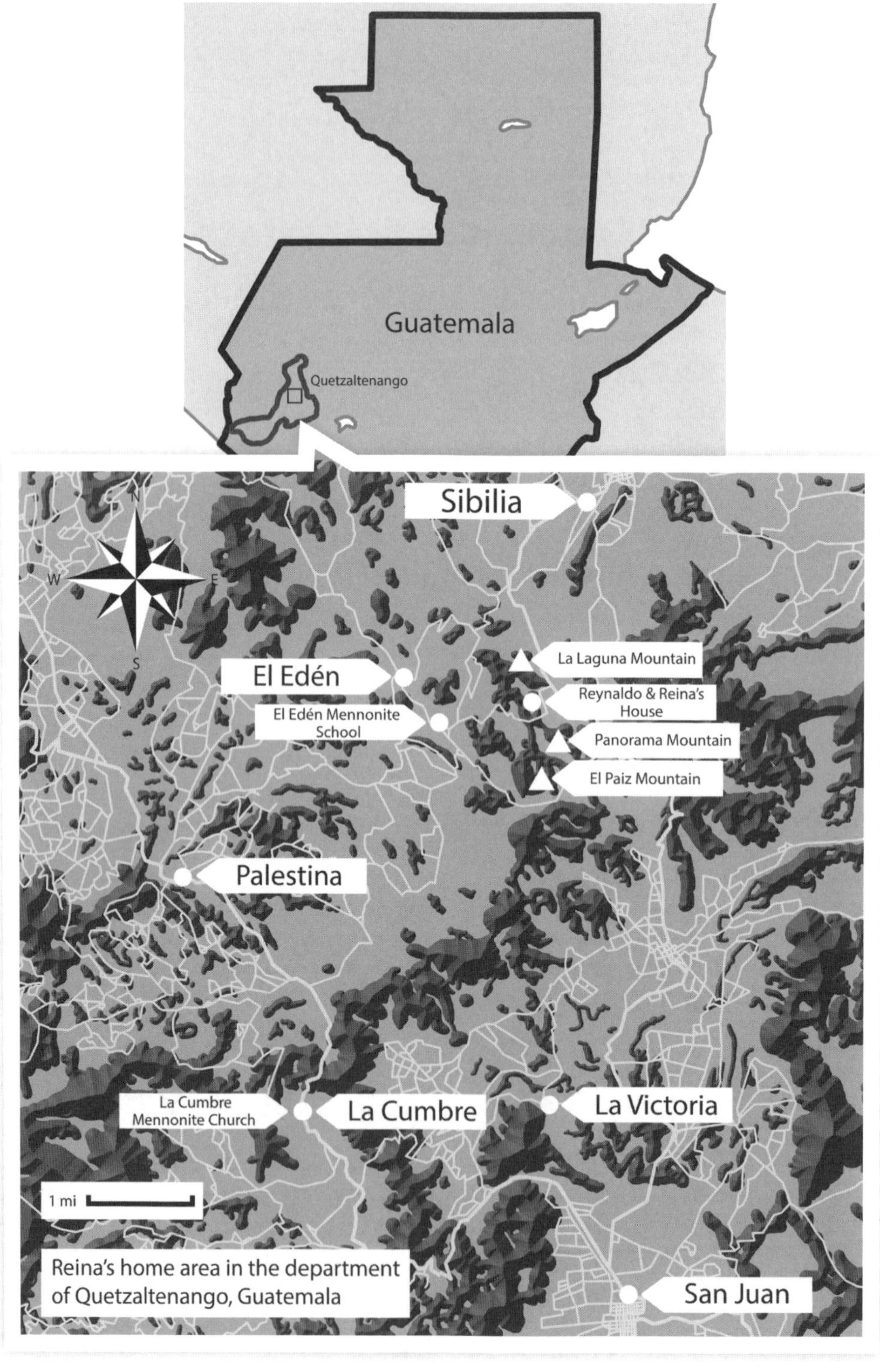

Reina's home area in the department of Quetzaltenango, Guatemala

TABLE OF CONTENTS

	Dedication	3
	Preface	7
	Prologue	9
Chapter 1	Bacilio Dies	11
Chapter 2	A Beggar	17
Chapter 3	Carlos Moves In	21
Chapter 4	God Is Light	27
Chapter 5	Diverted Dahlias	33
Chapter 6	Coyotes or Carlos?	39
Chapter 7	A Gift and an Attack	45
Chapter 8	Yanet's Escape	51
Chapter 9	Market Day	57
Chapter 10	Wedding Day	65
Chapter 11	The Still and the Strife	71
Chapter 12	Prince of Peace	75
Chapter 13	A Guest from the City	79
Chapter 14	The Demon Returns	83
Chapter 15	The Mennonites	89
Chapter 16	The Decision	93
Chapter 17	The Baptism	101
Chapter 18	Reynaldo Goes Missing	109
Chapter 19	Attack at the Mill	119
Chapter 20	The Making of a Man	125
Chapter 21	Benjamín	131
Chapter 22	Suffering and Triumph	135
Chapter 23	Night Patrol	141
Chapter 24	Jailed	147
Chapter 25	More Church Problems	153
Chapter 26	Crumbling Hopes	159
Chapter 27	Joel	163
Chapter 28	Homeless	169
Chapter 29	A New Normal	175
Chapter 30	Churchyard Showdown	183

Chapter 31	Papa Leaves	191
Chapter 32	The Kiss of Belonging	195
Chapter 33	The Wrong Army	199
Chapter 34	A Solution	209
Chapter 35	New Beginning	217
Chapter 36	Los Angeles	221
Chapter 37	Temptation	229
Chapter 38	Out on the Mountains Cold	235
Chapter 39	Hope Gone	243
Chapter 40	Hamit	247
Chapter 41	Los Angeles for Jesus	255
Chapter 42	Home at Last?	261
Chapter 43	Starting Over	269
Chapter 44	Going Home	277
Chapter 45	Life at La Laguna	283
Chapter 46	Another Return	289
Chapter 47	Interrogations	293
Chapter 48	The Next Step	299
Chapter 49	Family Again	307
Chapter 50	Two Rings	313
Chapter 51	Wedding Day	321
Chapter 52	Counting the Cost	327
Chapter 53	Seeking	335
Chapter 54	Starting Over—Again	339
Chapter 55	Getting Settled	345
Chapter 56	A Clue	353
Chapter 57	Two Searches	359
Chapter 58	Along a Country Road	365
Chapter 59	Vicenta Goes Home	371
Chapter 60	Blessed Are the Meek	375
Chapter 61	This Is My Body	381
	Epilogue	384
	Afterword	386
	Acknowledgments	390
	Pronunciation Guide	392
	About the Author	395

PREFACE

It was late September 2010. Above the clatter of supper dishes, I heard my husband, Henry, talking on the phone.

After he hung up, he came to me in the kitchen. "A Guatemalan lady showed up at the Sunday morning meeting in Perkins three weeks ago. She has attended every week since then." He said it slowly, as if trying to make sense of it. "Her story sounds exactly like Reynalda Barrios, but her name is Luisa. Could two women have such similar stories? Could it possibly be Reynalda?"

He had my full attention. I strained to remember.

I pictured Reynalda sitting on the plaid couch in our living room in Shedd, Oregon. She had come for supper. In her lap sat a bright-eyed, round-cheeked baby boy. "If his father won't let him go with me to Guatemala, will you keep my baby? I want him to be raised in a Christian home." Reynalda's request had unnerved me then. But that had been twenty years and two thousand miles before. I had always supposed that she and her baby returned to Guatemala.

Before Reynalda left our house in Shedd that day, she had signed my guest book, "Luisa Barrios, October 10, 1990."

"Luisa is Reynalda," I said to Henry now.

My mind traveled back further, ten more years and another thousand miles. Henry was driving. We were rattling over rural Guatemala's rutted, dusty roads. On my lap I cradled the damp limpness of a starving newborn boy.

Both babies, the round-cheeked boy in Shedd and the starving newborn in Guatemala, were Reynalda's babies—Luisa's babies.

Connecting the dots now as I stood in our cabin in northeastern Oklahoma, I felt we were treading on holy ground.

In March of 1992, after the last time we had said goodbye to Reynalda Luisa Barrios and her children, we had wound through a maze of dingy halls lined with silent doors, down creaking stairways strewn with trash, back to our locked Dodge Colt waiting on an L.A. street.

I had curled up in the front seat and wept into my journal: "O Shepherd, with your great heart of love for these scattered sheep, will you show us the meaning of this journey? How can we retreat into the great walled fold and forget this revelation?"

The questions had haunted me for twenty-three years.

This story is my attempt to hear the Shepherd's answer—my attempt to understand the meaning.

Gwendolyn Hertzler
June 2015
Oaks, Oklahoma

PROLOGUE

Perhaps each pilgrimage reaches a passage where going back seems right but impossible, and going forward seems wrong but imperative. In this point of pressure, a small, dark-eyed woman picked her way down a bluff, stepping from stone to stone. On her back was a fat, bright-eyed baby, the son of a man she didn't trust. Wind wrapped her skirt around her legs and whiffled and snapped a U.S. flag that beckoned her from a tattered past into a lonely future. That flag, not far off now, marked the roof of the garish market building where she had been told to go. Pigeons lined one edge of its red tile roof, and trash skidded around its crumbling first course of adobe blocks. Behind that market's facade, a brisk business thrived, assisting pilgrims in this painful and desperate passage.

Several miles to the east, a skinny, frightened girl in overalls ducked under a fence, clutching a worn dress in a grocery bag. The girl was a page of the small, dark-eyed woman's past, only one of many loose pages that fluttered out, demanding to be read and reckoned with, though the cover of the book was irreversibly closed and the binding irreparably broken.

Torn between two great missions—driving missions she could never seem to reconcile—the woman had already been blown across this divide and back by winds of misunderstanding and confusion. This time the winds that drove her were a lawyer's mistake and a man's determination to keep his son. She would never quit hoping and praying, but today she must do what she had to do.

She glanced again at the U.S. flag above the red tile roof. She no longer harbored any illusions about the freedom it promised. But it did promise food for her family, and that was something. Everything, maybe.

Trying to look casual, she picked her way down the north side of the bluffs.

CHAPTER 1

Bacilio Dies

A coyote's shrill cry rang from the mountain behind the adobe hut and echoed among the surrounding hills. A skinny dog howled back. Cornfields, barely visible in foggy moonlight, fell away from the little house toward the river at the bottom of the hill.

Chilolo's[1] body sagged against the door frame as he gazed toward the dim outline of mountains towering all around this valley—his home from birth. The last trace of sunset had disappeared, and a half moon hovered behind the trees. He hugged his thin coat tighter around him. At ten thousand feet, the night air was cold.

Behind him, inside the house, he heard the burble of water in a bowl as his mother dunked a rag and wrung it out. All evening she had been trying to cool his father's head, but the sick man still groaned.

Chilolo squeezed his eyes shut, as if that would stop the bothersome tears. He couldn't stop anything these days—not the lightning that scorched his father's forty sheep, not the wheeling of the vultures above the hill where the rotting carcasses still sprawled, not the strangling of the cattle, not the hopelessness in Mama's eyes, not the agony that wracked Papa's body. And

[1] For pronunciations of Spanish words, see page 392.

without Papa's help, how could he stop the relentless creeping of grass into the cornfields?

It was too much to do alone. He was only thirteen. He needed Papa. And Mama. Chilolo tried not to think of the calf he had found that afternoon, tried not to think of its rolled-back eyes, its upthrust chin, and its outstretched neck. That calf was the third loss from their small herd in three months.

The dog barked, and Chilolo glanced along the front of the house toward the wooded hillside that encircled their little shelf of land. He straightened himself and rounded the corner of the house. He could hear them before they came into view, stepping out of the trees into the watery moonlight and crossing the path that ran by the house. It was his mother's brother Lencho and, close behind him, the witch doctor.

"Quiet, Chico!" Chilolo ordered the excited dog, and he hurried to meet the visitors.

"Good evening," he said, bowing.

"Good evening," they answered, pausing to shake his hand before continuing toward the house. Chilolo hurried ahead to open the door for them. Following them in, he shivered and yanked the door shut. Night crouched over the house.

The medicine man glanced around the small room. On a dirty mat in one corner sat a wide-eyed eight-year-old girl. Her baby sister slept beside her under a tangle of dark hair. In the other corner was a mat for the boy. A few clothes and tools hung on the walls. The sick man lay on a mat across the room from the little girls. His stomach was swollen and he was vomiting. His wife held a bloodstained rag under his mouth.

The medicine man knew the story of the strangled cows and the lightning-blasted sheep. Bacilio, the sick man, had come to him often in recent months, seeking his help and advice. Bacilio's wife, Vicenta, was the witch doctor's cousin. She lifted pleading eyes to his.

The witch doctor walked to the middle of the room. With the tip of his machete, he scratched a circle in the middle of the hard earthen floor. He

Bacilio Dies

called the family around the circle and began a sing-song chant. Then he turned to Chilolo. "Blow out the candles."

Chilolo hurried to obey, and the semi-darkness deepened. He paused and glanced at the witch doctor for confirmation. Should he blow out the candle that flickered in the face of the holy saint on the corner shelf? Yes, that one too.

In the blackness, the front door creaked as it crept open. Chilolo gaped at the widening shaft of moonlight on the floor. No one was near the door. A dark package hurtled through the open doorway and landed at Chilolo's feet. Vicenta gasped.

"Ahh!" smiled the witch doctor. "This is what has troubled you. All these bad things are happening to you because this thing has cursed you. Pick it up and open it."

With trembling hands, Chilolo lifted the tarp-wrapped bundle. As he unwrapped it, three smaller packages fell out. Candles. Automatically he counted them—nine in each package, twenty-seven in all.

"Burn them," said the witch doctor. "That will be the end of your trouble. Your father will get well." His job finished, the man rose and collected his things to go.

Chilolo left Vicenta and the girls and Bacilio in the sala[2] and carried the bundle of candles across the courtyard to the kitchen. The top half of the door was open, and he could see a glimmer of coals between the three cooking stones. He stepped inside, into the warmth of the room and the familiar lingering scent of wood smoke, tamales,[3] and coffee.

Squatting, he stirred the coals with a stick. Carefully he piled the twenty-seven candles on the bright coals. Flames burst upward from the wax, glaring on the adobe walls and on the clay dishes and pots arranged on a rough plank table in the corner. Sooty tails of smoke swirled and hovered under the ceiling thatch.

---

[2] A room that served for both sleeping and visiting, usually a separate building across a courtyard from the kitchen.

[3] A corn-based dough filled with meat, wrapped in a corn husk or other leaf.

SONG OF THE SHEPHERDESS

Chilolo could hardly wait for the candles to finish burning. Would this really be the end of the trouble? When the last shimmering drops of wax were gone, he slipped back across the courtyard to the room where his family slept.

"Mama, they're gone! I burned them all," he whispered.

Bacilio moaned again. "Don't worry, son," Vicenta said. "The magic hasn't had time to work."

Chilolo sank onto his mat and fell asleep.

Morning came too soon. As Chilolo milked the cows, tethered them on fresh grass, and hoed the corn, three-year-old Reina toddled behind him, her bright, trusting eyes and sweet chatter the only thing untouched by the disaster that hounded them. All Chilolo could think of was Papa. Surely Papa would be better soon. Surely the magic would work.

Bacilio was worse that night, vomiting blood and racked with pain. The next morning Chilolo found another calf strangled on its tether.

Someone ran to summon the witch doctor. This time he ordered Chilolo to cut off the head of the dead calf. The thought of more blood made Chilolo sick, but he would do whatever it took to make Papa well, to see him laugh with little Reina, to see Mama smile again.

Oh, what wouldn't he do to see Papa swing an *azadón*[4] again, smooth and steady, cultivating the deep, loamy soil in little terraces up and down their steep fields? He could picture him out there among the young stalks of corn, his skin brown and leathery, not that horrible sickly yellow. He could almost hear the crunching *chop-chop* of the *azadón,* and the small metallic *clink* when the sharp edge found a stone.

Chilolo severed the calf's head with a machete and presented it to the witch doctor.

Once they had the calf's head, Uncle Lencho and Chilolo followed the wiry little witch doctor down across the river, then up the mountain called Panorama. It was a steep twenty-minute hike, but it was easy for Chilolo. He had come this way often in happier times, for high on the side of Panorama

---

[4] A hand tool shaped roughly like a wide, heavy hoe.

Bacilio Dies

was the place where Bacilio made and sold whiskey.

The still was far from any main roads, accessible only by a steep path, and closed in on all sides by bushes, ferns, and trees. It was hidden from the police but familiar to the locals, especially the Indians who came out of the mountains at night to fill their jugs, leaving their coins with Bacilio.

Whiskey, or *cusha*,[5] made good money for Bacilio. It was only one of his many projects, for he worked hard and was an enterprising man. He often traveled down to the coast and hauled back huge bags of fish to sell in the local markets. Twice a year buyers came from the city to shear Bacilio's sheep, and they paid him well for the wool. Before the latest troubles started, he had owned a herd of ten cows, and from their milk Vicenta made cheese to sell at the market in San Juan.

Why was there so little to show for all the money Papa had made? Could the witch doctor be right? Was Papa trapped by a powerful curse?

The three soon reached the high shelf where the still was hidden. The gurgle of spring water and the trill of evening songbirds blended with the *chunk-chunk* of Uncle Lencho's *azadón* as he dug the hole the witch doctor had ordered. Across the canyon, toward the slopes of La Laguna, the sun was sinking in a blaze of purple and orange behind the pink-tinged outlines of endless mountains.

Uncle Lencho stepped back. The witch doctor settled the calf's bloody head into the hole and then fished a book from the pocket of his ill-fitting jacket. He opened the book and handed it to Chilolo, pointing to the place where he should read.

Chilolo squinted at the page. He had learned to read a little in the months he had managed to sneak away to school when Papa thought he was watching the sheep in the mountains. He took a deep breath and began to sound out the weird, meaningless words of the incantation.

A sudden vibration thrilled his bare feet. He jerked his head up. A deep

---

[5] In Guatemala, the word *cusha* generally refers to a homemade distilled liquor based on fruit. However, the corn-based drink Bacilio and his descendants brewed was also referred to as *cusha,* at least by locals.

roar rose from the belly of the mountain as the ground heaved and shook. The two men turned from the clearing and fled downhill. Chilolo bolted after them, crashing through briars and stumbling over rocks. Around them, trees swayed with the writhing mountain.

When the ground was finally steady again under their feet, they stopped, dazed and gasping. None of them recognized the place they had come to. The sun was setting, and no one wanted to return to the unfinished job by the still, so they picked their way down the mountain, leaving the unseeing eyes in the calf's head to stare at the sky until the vultures came to pick them out.

When they reached the path again, they parted, Uncle Lencho and the witch doctor to their homes and Chilolo back to his home on La Laguna.

No one but baby Reina slept that night. Bacilio kept groaning and throwing up blood, oblivious to the presence of Vicenta, Chilolo, and Angela, who sat helplessly on their mats and watched his ragged breathing.

Vicenta kept the candle burning in front of the saint on the corner shelf. Sometimes she got up, walked to the shelf, and stood there gazing at the little image. She crossed herself, and her lips moved. As the long night dragged on, Bacilio's retching quieted down, but his gasping breaths and soft groans continued.

Chilolo peered at the key-wound clock hanging crookedly on the wall by the window. It was two in the morning. Papa missed a breath. Mama leaned closer. Outside the stuffy adobe hut, the night was quiet.

A long pause, then another faint breath. They watched the feeble thumping in Papa's gaunt chest slow, then stop.

In the dead calm, the door creaked. Chilolo spun around, staring as it slowly swung open, charging the room with cold moonlight.

Papa's spirit was gone.

CHAPTER 2

A Beggar

After Bacilio died, Vicenta sold all but one or two of the remaining cows. With the money from their sale, she bought the seventeen acres of land she and Bacilio had been renting from the government. She would miss the income from the cows, but she was sure her decision would prove sound. With land of their own, she and the children could surely find some way to survive.

Now, however, the last year's corn crop was gone except for the bit Vicenta had saved to keep the chickens alive. It would be several weeks before this year's crop could be harvested, and until then, there was nothing to feed the children.

Vicenta was out of options. They had to eat. She picked up her empty market basket and walked purposefully down the path along the tall corn, across the river in the valley, and into the mountains of El Paiz.

Had it been only thirteen years since she and Bacilio had come here from her parents' home? How promising life had looked at twenty-eight years old! This remote location and their scanty resources had not worried them then.

The older folks, especially Vicenta's mother, had clucked and shaken their heads. There was a baby on the way, and the life Vicenta and Bacilio were choosing was rugged and unpredictable. They had all agreed that Vicenta's parents would keep four-year-old Mariano and two-year-old Cornelia.

Bacilio and Vicenta had moved to their seventeen rented acres and had built a small adobe hut, nestled between four living trees that served as corner posts. The house snuggled against the lower slopes of a mountain known as La Laguna, in honor of a long-extinct lake. When the family arrived, the deep, fertile fields were mostly clear and ready to farm. The spring gave plenty of fresh water for all their needs. They had been in their new home for only a few weeks when Chilolo was born.

As the river disappeared behind her, Vicenta hiked up the steep trail with her empty basket, continuing her reverie.

Bacilio had been ambitious and enterprising, and by the time Adelma was born, two years after Chilolo, the farm was doing well. They had the cows, the sheep, their two youngest children, and each other, and life was good—until the day Vicenta entered the house to find one-year-old Adelma sitting beside a basket of eggs, choking on a mouthful of eggshells. Vicenta snatched the baby off the floor and tried in vain to open her airway. Ten minutes later her baby lay limp and quiet in her arms. Adelma was gone. It was the first great sorrow to touch the little home.

A year later Angela was born, and three years after that, Yanet. When Yanet was less than two years old, Vicenta's mother came to visit. Watching the long hours Vicenta spent working the fields and seeing that another child would be born soon, the grandmother declared that Yanet should go home with her. Remembering what had happened to Adelma, Vicenta agreed. Weary as she was, it was too easy to let Yanet go.

Though Vicenta's arms had ached for her little girl in the weeks that followed, the birth of Luisa Reynalda—Reina, they called her—took the edge off the longing. Somehow as the months turned to years, Yanet had never returned home. Vicenta suspected that by now her mother had become too attached to her granddaughter to let Yanet go. Besides, Vicenta could hardly feed the children she had, which was why she was now trudging along the mountain trail.

A Beggar

Her destination was in sight now—Feliciano Escobar's well-kept homestead. It was just as well her memories were interrupted. She didn't want to remember the past year: the strangled cattle, the charred sheep, the disease that had wasted her husband's body, the hunger of her children.

Thirteen years ago, she never would have imagined it could come to this. Timidly she called at the wrought-iron gate, "Good afternoon!"

A patter of small feet was followed by the creaking of the gate as it swung open. A child looked up at her, then bowed low, thrusting back his small hands until the cupped palms faced upward on either side of him. Were those dimples in the backs of his little elbows? The child let her in and ran to call his mother. Vicenta waited in a neat courtyard surrounded by flowers.

When Feliciano's wife arrived, Vicenta showed her the empty basket. "Please, my children are hungry. Do you have any corn to spare?" She felt weak and tired. Bright, scrubbed children's faces peered at her from doorways—six of them. Vicenta had six children too. What would it be like to have them all at home, well-fed and cared for?

Vicenta's basket was heavy as she settled it on her head a few minutes later. Murmuring her thanks, she turned, holding her head just a little higher than necessary, and hurried back down the trail.

It was the first of many such journeys to beg food from neighbors.

The weary years passed. Angela could help more now, and Chilolo worked like a man. When the corn in Vicenta's fields was ready, she and Chilolo and Angela worked long hours to harvest it. Then, at least, they had plenty of corn for a few months.

Vicenta took in laundry for people from nearby Sibilia. She lugged heavy baskets of soiled clothes down the hill to the river, scrubbing each garment on the rocks, beating it with a thick, heavy root. As she beat, the root released a milky, soapy substance on the clothes, leaving them fresh and clean. After the clothes were scrubbed, she wrung out each garment by hand and draped it over the bushes or spread it on the grass to dry.

Washing didn't pay well, but it provided a little cash for the weekly trip to the San Juan market where she purchased sugar, coffee, and tomatoes, staples that would not grow at their high elevation.

Whenever Vicenta could buy enough corn and sugar to make *cusha*, she and Chilolo would load down the horse late at night and make the steep, winding journey down into the river bottom, then up and up into the beautiful, endless hills of Panorama, where she hoped the law would not find her. There on the large flat rock in the clearing where cold spring water flowed out through a cut in the bank—the same clearing where she and Bacilio had worked together so many nights—she would set corn mash to sour. After it soured, she cooked the fermented concoction, patiently distilling it into potent *cusha*.

It took most of the nights of a full week to get a batch brewed to perfection. On the final night, when the *cusha* flowed strong and clear and dangerous, she would wait by the rock while the Indians from far back in the hills slipped out singly or in twos and threes to fill their bottles under the copper spout protruding from the big cooking vat.

The darkness and the wooded mountain hid her for now from the eyes of the law, but they would never hide her from the loving eyes of the great Shepherd who wept for the lost sheep gathered at that rock.

CHAPTER 3

Carlos Moves In

The year was 1955, three years after Bacilio's death. Vicenta's son Mariano, who had been raised by his grandmother, had served his two years in the Guatemalan army along with his cousin Carlos. At the end of their service, the boys moved in with the family in the little adobe house at the foot of La Laguna. Vicenta welcomed them: Mariano, her own firstborn, and Carlos, the son of her deceased sister. For six-year-old Reina, home would never be the same.

Mariano and Carlos had grown up like brothers in their grandparents' home, which was perched on the top edge of the bank along the road that twisted and rolled among the hills between El Edén and La Laguna. Life at their grandparents' house had not been easy. Relationships among the aunts, uncles, and cousins who lived there had often been rugged, and they had been poor, like most of their relatives in that remote hill country. But there had always been food to eat, and Grandma had been kind and motherly.

Mariano and Carlos had joined the army soon after Bacilio's death, and they were still in the service when they received word that their beloved grandma had died. No one on the army base cared about the pain of that loss in the hearts of two lonely boys from the hills beyond El Edén.

SONG OF THE SHEPHERDESS

When the boys were released to go home after their two years of military service, they hardly knew where home was anymore. With their grandmother gone, they saw no point in returning to the quarrelsome aunts and distant grandfather. Since no other option presented itself, they decided to move in with Mariano's mother.

It was awkward for Mariano, the oldest son, to be a newcomer in his own family. Since his father's death, his younger brother had become the man of the house. Mariano did his best to help where he could and worked alongside Chilolo.

For Carlos it was worse. Embittered by the brutality of two years in the army and never having known the warmth of a real family, he vented his frustrations on his six-year-old cousin, Reina. He could tolerate Angela, and something about good-natured Chilolo commanded his respect, but he hated snappy-eyed Reina, the apple of her mother's eye and the embodiment of the security and acceptance he had never known.

Reina lay on her mat, staring at the grass thatch above her. What was this deadness inside, this dread? A lizard crawled up the adobe wall and disappeared in the dusty thatch—a fleeting distraction—and then she remembered. She pressed her hands against her eyelids, hot tears running down over her ears. Why had Mama believed Carlos? Reina had never stolen his fruit. As if it weren't enough for Carlos to beat her when her mother wasn't around, now he made up stories and got her mother to spank her too.

If Papa were here, he wouldn't let Carlos beat me. If Papa were here, he would believe me. If Papa were here . . . But Papa isn't here.

She could not even remember her father, but when Vicenta spoke about him, Reina knew he was someone special. "Oh, Reina child, your papa was good and kind. We never fought or argued when your papa was here."

Reina rubbed her face on the coarse dry fabric of her mat. Vicenta was getting up now, and Reina didn't want to be seen crying.

In the semi-darkness Reina watched her mother brush her hair. Her quick fingers whisked the tails of shining hair into long, thin braids. She tied the ends with bits of string, then stepped over the forms of her sleeping family. The door squeaked as she opened it. Vicenta stopped in the doorway, her willowy form silhouetted against the muted orange of sunrise. Then she yawned and went out, leaving the door standing open.

Vicenta would be stirring the coals in the kitchen now to heat water for coffee. Reina had gathered wood the night before, so she knew her mother had plenty. After finishing her coffee and tortilla, Vicenta would lug tubs of clothes down to the river. *If Papa were here,* Reina thought, *Mama wouldn't have to work so hard scrubbing clothes all morning for the neighbors. If Papa were here, I would get him to bring Yanet home from Grandpa's house. Then the aunts wouldn't talk so mean to her and make her work like a slave.*

Compassion for her sister loomed bigger in her mind than her own misery and helped her focus her wandering thoughts. She had just enough time to wash and comb herself before Yanet would come by on her way to school.

Reina closed her eyes in the dimness of the little house and repeated the prayer she always prayed before she got up in the morning. It was the same prayer she prayed before she went to sleep at night. She guessed she had prayed those sweet lines since she was about the same size as the new lambs—at least, she couldn't remember when she had learned them from Mama.

With God I go to sleep,
With God I wake again,
He is light, He is grace,
And the Holy Spirit. Amen.

The words made her feel peaceful and loved. Mama had taught her about the Trinity: the Father, the Son, and the Holy Spirit. Even though Papa had died, Reina knew she had a heavenly Father who was light and grace.

Reina rolled up her wheat straw mat and propped it against Mama's in the corner. She braided her hair as neatly as she could, but she was sure she could never make her fingers fly as quickly as Mama's or make her braids so smooth.

Outside the door in the crisp cold, Reina leaned over a red clay washbowl set on a rough bench and splashed water over her face. Then she rubbed her tingly cheeks with a length of *manta cantel*.[1]

She didn't stop for breakfast. When she got to school, a thin oatmeal drink would be served to all the mountain children.

When the joyous yapping of the dog signaled Yanet's arrival, Reina skipped to join her. School meant ten minutes to walk beside her sister and best friend—and five blissful hours free from the critical eyes of Carlos. Reina hardly felt the sting of frost on her bare feet.

For Yanet it was different. She had started half an hour before, in the dark, when the frozen earth was like a million needles, stinging her feet with every step. She was almost limping on her numb, swollen feet. It would have been easier and shorter for Yanet to walk the opposite direction from Grandpa's house, to the school in El Edén. Instead she endured the long walk to the school in Sibilia for the opportunity to travel partway with her little sister.

Together the little girls followed the dirt path that skirted the base of the mountain. Then with the agility of young goats, they climbed the back border of the steep, bare cornfield. Before they disappeared under the tall trees, they could see the miniature shapes of several other children on the ridge above. Behind them on the lower trail, more toy-like figures hurried upward.

"Reina, I'm afraid to take the reading test," Yanet confided. "I can't read all those words. What if the aunts find out and tell Mama I am not studying hard enough? What if Mama makes me stop going to school the very first year I've finally managed to go?"

For a few minutes they climbed silently up the slope in the shadow of the trees. Reina was thinking hard. "Yanet! I've got it! I'll read those pages to you every day, and you can memorize them. You're three years older than I, and smarter too. You should have started school before me. So I'll just give

---

[1] A rough muslin cloth used for sugar sacks.

you some of my learning that should have been yours anyway."

Yanet was doubtful, but her misgivings soon melted in the sizzle of Reina's enthusiasm.

At the top of the narrow footpath, the girls entered the main road that wound along the top of the ridge. They hurried past a man bent almost double with a huge load of hay on his back. Ahead of them, a bus belching black smoke growled down the mountain, taking people to San Juan or Xela or beyond. Ten minutes after they met at Reina's house, they reached the schoolhouse. Here, where life was safe and predictable, Reina could immerse herself in her studies—until one o'clock.

On the way home, as she and Yanet broke out of the woods, Reina saw far below them the cluster of little adobe buildings surrounded by wide, terraced fields, all snuggled against the mountain's breast. Had there really been a time when she would rather have been in that little house than anywhere else in the world? Now, if it weren't for her mother, she would rather be almost anywhere else than in that house.

Reina loved her mother. She knew Mama would never leave her, but she did not understand why Mama let Carlos stay. To Reina, love meant solving problems, not merely enduring them.

"Let's see if Mama will let you come to Grandpa's house tonight." Yanet's voice broke into her thoughts.

"Great idea!" Reina answered. "Then we can get started with that reading right away."

When the girls reached the house, Vicenta was washing dishes in the *pila*.[2] Reina danced up to her and hugged her. "Can I go to Grandpa's house and sleep with Yanet after I bring the sheep home tonight?"

It wasn't hard to get Vicenta to say yes. She liked to see Reina happy.

As the girls turned to go after the sheep, Mama reached out and pulled Yanet tenderly against her. She leaned down to kiss her daughter, but Yanet stiffened and turned her face away.

---

[2] A large outdoor concrete sink.

SONG OF THE SHEPHERDESS

What right did Mama have to kiss me? Yanet thought. Where had Mama been when she had wept beside Grandma's grave at seven years old, longing to throw her little body into the cool pit with Grandma and let the men shovel dirt over them both?

No, she guessed, Mama had never wanted her. Even when Grandma was buried, Mama had taken no notice of her pain, nor offered to take Yanet home with her. Mama was nothing to her now. She shrugged out of Vicenta's hug and hurried after Reina without looking back.

Together the girls took the sheep out to the hills for a few hours. Afterward Reina would help Yanet with her evening chores at Grandpa's house, and in the remaining time they would work on Yanet's "reading."

The day the officials conducted the reading tests, Yanet could hardly wait for the dismissal bell to ring. As soon as she and Reina managed to break away from the crowd of children surging out of the schoolhouse, Yanet's laughter tinkled into the clear mountain air. "It worked, Reina! I just held the book in front of me, looked at it, and said it all by heart, everything you read to me. When I got done, the man said, 'Congratulations! You did very well.'" Imitating the duped official, Yanet made her voice gruff, and both girls burst into giggles.

Though she could almost forget it in the relief of the moment, Yanet longed to really read, not just bluff the test. Someday, somehow, she would find a way to study to her heart's content.

CHAPTER 4

God Is Light

Mama's breathing was rhythmic and steady. Reina smiled. She slipped out from under her blanket, took a long step over the end of her mother's mat, and tiptoed past Carlos, the sleeping lion.

It was only the three of them at home these days. Chilolo was working in the city. He was always working to support Mama and Reina and Carlos. Angela had moved away to her boyfriend's house, and Mariano had married and now lived with his wife in a little house he had built down at the corner of the cornfield.

Reina stepped out into the bracing cold of the highland night. A moonlit mist rose from the canyons between the dimly outlined mountains, and wisps of wood smoke hung in the air from the dying kitchen fire. A branch creaked in the breeze. The night throbbed with beauty. Surely no spot on earth could compare with this valley.

Reina combed her long, wavy hair again and again until she was sure it was perfectly smooth and shiny. She smoothed her dress, wishing she could wear something prettier than this sugar sack cloth. It was a dull, straw-white color, made even duller by months of use and weekly washings. Most of the girls in school wore the same plain, rough *manta cantel,* but Reina often looked longingly at the soft print fabrics worn by the few rich girls. She had often seen bolts and bolts of it in glorious displays in the Xela market.

Really, she thought, *it doesn't matter. What matters is that I am going to church to hear the preacher explain God's Holy Scriptures.*

From time to time when she was younger, Reina had visited the Catholic church with her mother. She remembered how small and confused she had always felt standing beside Vicenta under the high domed ceilings. She had never liked the cold, heavy air. She did not like the flickering candles and chanted prayers. She did not like when the priest sprinkled the poor little grumbling babies with water. She did not like to see Mama dutifully paying her precious centavos[1] to the priest. Mama worked hard for each little coin, and Reina was sure her mother needed them more than the priest did.

Reina hated to say no when Mama wanted her to go to church with her, but now that she was twelve years old and big enough to think it through, she stayed away from the cold stone building with its stiff stone statues as much as she could. Mama had taught her to trust and love a God who could hear a little girl pray in her bed, who was light and grace and the Holy Spirit.

Tonight as Reina stood in the moonlight, a great longing swelled inside her. Yanet had told her she had found Jesus in the Presbyterian church in El Edén. Some of the neighbors had invited her to go with them to revival meetings, and after the sermon, the preacher had said that all those who wanted to receive Jesus into their hearts should raise their hands. Yanet had wanted to know Jesus for as long as she could remember, and that night she had wanted Jesus more than anything else. So she had raised her hand, and they had prayed with her, and she had asked Jesus to come into her heart.

Reina didn't suppose she was a real Christian like Yanet. Nobody had helped her pray or say the right things. But she knew that God heard her prayers. Ever since one day two years before, she had known it without the slightest doubt.

Reina remembered it like yesterday. While the sheep had grazed in the

---

[1] One hundred centavos equal one quetzal, the basic unit of currency in Guatemala.

mountains behind the house, she had sat in the shade, embroidering little blue flowers around the edge of one of the tablecloths she and her mother made to sell at the San Juan market. When it was time to head home, Reina had tucked the tablecloth into her bag and called the sheep together. She had followed them down the trail, watching their shorn backs ripple above swirling puffs of dust.

At the place where the trail entered the woods, the path narrowed and the sheep adjusted their formation, snaking down the trail and around a curve. On her left, ferns and orchids touched Reina as she passed. On her right, the same wild garden sloped away under the trees to the valley far below.

Reina jumped as a sudden haze descended on her like a greenish cloud. Confused, she squinted to keep the sheep in sight. Then, as suddenly as the green haze had come, it was gone again. Everything was gone.

Reina stopped short, straining to see. It was no use. Nothing! She blinked. She rubbed her eyes. Blackness!

Suddenly Reina became aware that the tinkling of the bell on the neck of the leading ewe was fading as the distance between them increased. She heard the muffled tapping of many little hooves on the narrow, twisting trail. She must follow that sound now, or she would be lost.

As tears of frustration squeezed from her useless eyes, a picture forced its way behind them. She fought to shut it out—the vacant eyes and sad face of a blind beggar she'd once seen sitting beside the road to San Juan, clad in rags.

Stumbling down the trail, Reina struggled to keep up with the hoofbeats. To her relief, the sometimes troublesome sheep stayed on the trail all the way home. On their own, they found the open shed door and crowded inside. Groping, Reina closed the door and fastened the familiar latch.

A terrifying thought struck her: how would she eat supper with her family? Carlos would never believe she couldn't see, and if Mama wasn't around, he would beat her for pretending.

Trembling, Reina headed toward the house. Hearing no one, she slipped through the open doorway and made her way to the corner of the room, where she set her bag on a low shelf. Unrolling her mat, she lay down. She was tired, so tired, and around her was only black. This problem would have been too big even for Papa, she was sure.

Cold with dread, Reina began whispering her prayer:

> *With God I go to sleep,*
> *With God I wake again.*
> *He is light . . .*

She stopped as the meaning blazed through her. *God is here, and God is light. Light!* For the first time, a prayer formed of her own words welled up from her desperate heart. *God, please! Please help me see! It's so dark I can't even see where to walk. Please God! You are light, and I need you!*

In the dark of her corner, peace filled Reina's heart, and she was sure she felt angels around her as she slipped into sleep.

When Reina awoke the next morning to the rustle of Mama rolling up her mat, one thought consumed her. *God, will I see? Will I see?* She pled with her heavenly Father just as she would have pled with her papa—had he been there. She waited. She opened one eye just a little.

Glory! Both eyes popped open. Glory! The faint glow of a new day filled the window. During the night, a spider had built a web in the top left corner of the opening. On the shelf beside Reina, trailing out of her woven bag, were the little blue flowers scattered along the edge of the tablecloth. Her eyes welled with tears, and her heart filled with the greatest love she had ever known.

Reina rose off her mat in a glow. *There is a God in heaven—a God who hears when I call!* She thrilled at the knowledge that her God was light—light that could open blind eyes—and that He really was with her when she went to sleep and when she awoke.

Though everything inside her was shouting and singing that morning, Reina did not tell her story to Mama or Yanet. No one would believe it. But she knew, and God knew, and that was enough.

Ever since that morning, Reina had longed to know more of this God of light. Tonight was her chance. Shoving her comb into her pocket, Reina stepped around the dark corner of the house. A faint glow flickered through the trees by the trail. She scurried down the path from the house to meet the little group of neighbors, their faces sculpted by the light of a torch, a kerosene-soaked rag held high on a stick by Juan Lopez. Yanet looked up, pleased, as Reina joined them, and everyone exchanged quiet greetings.

CHAPTER 5

Diverted Dahlias

Reina's thoughts were busy as the group climbed quietly through the darkness together. Her mother wouldn't like it if she knew where Reina was. Reina didn't like keeping secrets from Mama. But Mama didn't like when Juan came to read the Bible either, and it was Juan's faithful reading that had taught Reina much of what she knew about God.

Once each week for the past couple of years, Juan had come to their house carrying his Bible in a bright woven bag slung over his shoulder. He usually brought some little gift for them: a pile of fresh watercress, a few cookies, or some other treat. In his quiet, confident way he would offer to read to them, and Vicenta would politely invite him in. What else could she do? Juan was a neighbor and friend. He had cared for Bacilio's sheep when he was just a young boy, before Reina was born.

While Juan read, Vicenta would sit in her chair, gazing down at her laundry-chapped hands, then out the window toward the mountains, then out the door toward the cornfield, then at Juan for a moment, then down at her fidgeting hands again. But Reina drank in the holy words. She felt as if she could never get enough.

There was something unusual about Juan—a peace and sincerity Reina had never seen in any other young man. Since he had become a Christian four years before, he never went to fiestas anymore. At twenty-six, he was still unmarried, maybe because he never flirted with the neighborhood girls like the other boys did. Whenever his farm work was caught up, Juan went from village to village reading the Bible in any home that would let him in. A lot of people didn't like it. The Presbyterians were dangerous, they warned, and ought to be buried with their heads down.

Reina almost shivered with anticipation as she walked beside Yanet and the others, following the same steep path to the high road that she walked every day to school. The main road was strange and empty at night. Sometimes an animal crashed into the brush ahead of them.

At one place a neighbor lay half on and half off the road, and one of the men in the group of churchgoers stopped to pull the limp form to one side. Reina cringed to think that Mama's *cusha* might be the reason this man was out here sprawled unconscious in the road instead of home with his wife and children. *Well,* she told herself, *people don't have to drink so much. Don*[1] *Feliciano drinks a little sometimes, but he doesn't lie drunk in the road.*

At the La Laguna schoolhouse, their party met others. Together they continued along the top of the mountain, entering sleepy Sibilia half an hour later. Candlelight flickered in some of the windows, and people could be seen going about their business inside, but most of the houses were dark.

Reina had often seen the Presbyterian church in daylight, a modest block building up a little hill at the end of the street. Tonight its row of high windows glowed in its dark block walls. As she stepped through the door, the glare of the gas lights hurt her eyes. A few people were already seated on the backless benches. Along the wall by the benches was a row of nails. The men took off their hats and hung them there, running their fingers through their thick black hair. They looked different here, hardly like the grimy farmers Reina saw working in their fields or passing on the road. Though they wore work clothes, everyone was combed, scrubbed, and hatless, with an air of

---

[1] "Sir." A title used for an older, mature, respectable man.

reverent anticipation. Reina and Yanet walked to the front of the room and sat among the other youth.

Few people besides Juan Lopez and the visiting preacher had complete Bibles, but one of the ladies made sure each person had a New Testament to follow along. The preacher stood and read. Then he launched into his message, earnestly warning the small group of mountain folk about the practices of the Catholic Church.

"The priests cannot forgive your sins," the pastor told them, "and Mary can't either. Only God can forgive sins, and He does it freely through Jesus." He explained that it was evil to make people pay the priests, hoping to have their sins forgiven. "Nothing like that is taught in the Bible," he said, "and the Bible is where we learn the will of God." On and on he preached about the idolatry of the images, candles, and holy days.

The reverent atmosphere of the sermon was broken only by an occasional cough or the hiss of a bug colliding with a gas lamp. Reina remained perched on the hard bench until nearly ten o'clock, and she would not have minded a bit had it been longer.

There was a lot to think about on the walk home that night. Reina wished her mother could have heard what the preacher had said. She would tell her all about it tomorrow.

At breakfast the next morning, Vicenta fumed, "I don't understand why you girls want to go and listen to that big-mouthed preacher!"

Reina winced, pinching another little piece off her tortilla. She picked up her clay mug and washed the bite down with sweet coffee. It hurt to disappoint Mama. Reina knew Mama loved God too and wanted to do what was right.

Again she tried to explain. "But Mama, the preacher said that after Mary loaned her body to God to give birth to Jesus, she was only an ordinary woman. He says she can never forgive our sins. The priest can't forgive our sins either, no matter how much we pay him. Only Jesus can forgive and take away our sins, and we can talk to Him directly in prayer."

"That is blasphemy, child. How can you say such things about the Holy

Mother and about the priests? Something bad will happen to us for sure."

Vicenta reached for the large market basket that stood on the floor near the door. "Here, take this up to the woods and fill it full of dahlias. Take them to the Catholic church in Sibilia and put them on the altar among the candles. Maybe then the Holy Mother will have mercy on you, and Christ will forgive you."

Reina knew it was no use arguing. Meekly she picked up the basket and headed toward the woods. Sunlight streamed down, making the dewy grass sparkle, burning the chill off the morning. The woods were cool and peaceful. Reina loved picking dahlias, but take them to the Catholic church and put them among the candles? Never! Still, she filled the basket and ran to the house to show Mama.

"They are beautiful, darling. I'm sure the Holy Mother will be pleased. After you leave them at the church, get a loaf of bread at the market and bring it home. You can beat the rain if you hurry."

Reina climbed the hill again, the bright heads of the dahlias bobbing with every step. Mama's shrewd request for the bread would ensure that she went all the way to Sibilia. Whatever would she do with all these flowers?

"Good morning, Reina!" It was a woman she knew, coming toward her on the road. "Oh, child, where did you find all those beautiful, beautiful dahlias?" she squealed. "Aren't they just too lovely?"

Reina laughed. "Here, would you like some? You can have all you want. They would make a lovely bouquet for your table." She held out the basket.

"Why, thank you, child, I would love to have some." The woman selected several blooms, arranging their long stems into a bouquet. "Thank you very much, Reina. These are so pretty! It is sweet of you, but I don't want to take them all." She hurried on down the road.

A little later Reina met an old lady, her back horizontal beneath a load of kindling. "Would you like some flowers?" Reina asked.

"Thank you, thank you, but no, I don't need any," the old lady answered.

"They are free. You can just have some," Reina said.

The old lady beamed up at her, showing two snaggled rows of teeth.

"Thank you, thank you, child, God bless you!" she said as Reina handed her a cluster of dahlias.

By the time Reina heard the vendors chanting in the Sibilia market and saw the great stone spires of the Catholic church looming above her, only a few blooms snuggled in the bottom of her basket. She gathered them up and shoved them at a little girl, who stuffed a sucker into her mouth and reached out a sticky hand with a giggle.

Reina bought a crusty loaf of bread from the same stall Vicenta frequented. Distant thunder rumbled against the mountain, and Reina pulled a cloth over the bread in the basket. Two cool splashes of rain landed on her wrist and cheek. She glanced up at the Presbyterian church at the end of the street and smiled. Yes, she would be a faithful daughter in every way she could, but she would return to the Presbyterian church. Tonight.

CHAPTER 6

Coyotes or Carlos?

Groaning and sobbing, Reina leaned into her mother's shoulder. At twelve years old, she was too big for Mama's lap, but she would never outgrow Mama's arms, nor her comforting scent of wood smoke, sweat, and cooking grease.

"My poor, poor child," Vicenta crooned. "You suffer too much, my child."

Vicenta had rushed into the house when she heard Reina screaming. She had found her, eyes wide with terror, jumping and dodging while Carlos, crazy with rage, flailed her with a horsewhip.

"Carlos, stop that! Stop it now! Have mercy, Carlos!" Vicenta shouted at him. He lowered his arm, scowling at her. "Carlos, nothing she could possibly have done deserves such cruelty. You are making her life unbearable. Have you no heart?"

Carlos stomped past the bowl of potatoes sitting on the floor where Reina had abandoned it, peels scattered about and a knife lying a few feet away. He slammed the door and headed for the woods.

"Mama, he is horrid, horrid!" Reina sobbed. "I can't stand Carlos, and I wish he wouldn't live here. I was just sitting there cutting potatoes and he brought in a big rat. I think he found it in the cow trough. He told—told me to cut out the rat's—the rat's . . ." she lowered her voice to a faint whisper. "He said I had to cut out its organs." She burst into a fresh torrent of tears, and Mama swayed back and forth, holding her close and patting her. "I wouldn't do it, Mama. I shouldn't have to do it. Carlos got mad and grabbed the horsewhip, and—oh, Mama, I hate him! I hate him! I wish he had died in the army!"

It was after one of these beatings that Reina decided she'd had enough. Mama wasn't doing anything to stop Carlos, and every day seemed worse than the one before. Sometimes she wished she could just die.

A couple of years ago, the witch doctor had tied a rope around his neck, hanged himself in a tree, and died just as the calf had died last year when the rope got too tight around its neck. Everyone talked quietly and seriously about it and supposed he must have carried a terrible secret. Well, it was no secret what was troubling Reina.

Reina found a rope and studied the trees near the house. She chose a branch high enough to look impressive. After several tosses, the rope snaked over the branch and dangled on the other side.

She fastened the near end of the rope to the trunk of the tree among the ferns. Leaping to grab the dangling end, she tugged and calculated until she was quite sure she could sag convincingly when Mama appeared after milking the cows. She would have to close her eyes or roll them back into her head. It was a pity she had to do anything deathly with her eyes; she wanted to see her mother's face when she found her precious daughter hanging from a tree. Twelve years old and too miserable to live! Mama would make Carlos leave for sure.

When Vicenta found Reina, she was not impressed. She explained to Reina that it was wrong to pretend such an evil thing to try to make people pity you. In the end, all Reina got for her trouble was a good whipping from Mama.

To avoid the house, Reina began staying on the mountain at night. Vicenta worried and told her scary stories about the cats and coyotes that roamed the hills in the dark, but Reina loved the mountains, and nothing out there could be as bad as going home to Carlos. Sometimes she woke up chilly at

Coyotes or Carlos?

Reina felt safer spending nights on the mountain than in her house.

eleven or twelve, roused the sheep, and walked down the long, narrow trail in the dark. By then Carlos was snoring, so she could creep into the house and lie down undetected. But some nights she didn't come home at all.

In the spring, when the neighbor's corn was pushing through the soil, Reina had another reason to stay in the hills. When she brought the sheep home at night, they loved to break away from the road for a bedtime snack of tender young corn greens. She always tried to herd them past on the other side of the road, but when they saw the corn, the flock would lose all dignity, kicking their hooves up behind them like a bunch of frolicking lambs.

When they broke away like that, she ran after them as fast as she could. Her heart pounded in her chest like the pounding of their wicked little hooves. She knew what would happen when Carlos found out, as he always did. But her bare feet, though tough as leather, couldn't move as quickly over the sharp stones and thorns as the hooves of the wayward sheep. Over the years, those brief detours into the neighbor's corn had earned Reina more beatings than she could remember.

Often Reina left home early in the morning while the dew was still on the grass and the sun was coming up over the trees. She did not bother with eating breakfast or packing a lunch. The mountains were full of food. Long ago, she had learned to forage for fruits, berries, and mushrooms and to dig wild potatoes and orchid roots.

Among the hills where Reina watched the sheep, the local Indians made charcoal in pits, about a foot and a half wide. They built a fire in a pit, added small chunks of wood until the pit was full, then covered the pit with leaves and earth, sealing out the air and forcing the wood to carbonize instead of burning to ash. The whole process took about two days.

Reina found she could uncover a corner of these small pits and remove a few pieces of charcoal. She dug a small hole, dropped the coals in, placed her potatoes on top, and covered the hole with earth, leaving a little hole for smoke and steam to escape. Half an hour later, she dug up the baked potatoes.

As Reina went about her work, she sang a song she had made up herself:

My God, my God, my God,
Come closer to me,
For my soul is in you
And wants to live in you.

That little song said most of what Reina wanted to say to God, and it became her daily heart-cry as she lived and worked and worshiped under the deep blue sky in her beautiful hills. She wasn't alone out there, and she wasn't afraid.

When Reina went to sleep at night, she nestled her body among hillocks of deep, cushy grass. The coyotes howled in the dark of the woods, eerily shrilling and yapping. Hovering overhead, close enough to touch with her fingers, the starry heavens twinkled comfort and presence. Reina wondered how the stars got there. Did Mama know? Did Juan Lopez know? She had no idea, but she never doubted that God was there. "With God I go to sleep," she prayed, and her heart worshiped.

The sheep seemed to feel His presence too as they settled down close around her, chewing their cuds, dozing, and dreaming sheepish dreams.

CHAPTER 7

A Gift and an Attack

Looking like a green plant shoot just beginning to bud, her dress barely reaching her knees, long black braids hanging down her back, Reina slipped out the door of the house and stood watching Chilolo wistfully. He had just come back from growing corn at the coast and was unpacking the load from his horse.

Chilolo turned and noticed her at last. "Reina, how big you've grown! You're nearly as tall as Mama." He hugged her. Smiling mysteriously, he turned and rummaged in his pack, extracted a small package wrapped in brown paper and tied with string, and handed it to Reina. "For you, little sister."

Eyes shining, Reina took the package and sat down by the door, her dusty bare feet crossed under the bench, her fingers trembling. Chilolo had brought a gift just for her! The paper fell open and she gasped. Folded in her lap was the most beautiful fabric she had ever seen, printed with soft brown polka dots scattered over an eggshell-white background. She held it up to her cheek and brushed its softness against her wind-chapped skin. "Thank you! Thank you!" she breathed, looking up at Chilolo with shining eyes.

As Chilolo watched her, the long, steamy days in the coastal lowlands—the planting, the hoeing, the harvesting—seemed a small price to pay to bring this small indulgence into his little sister's life. He knew well the sting of too little, the frustration of never enough.

Glancing down again at her lap, Reina spied two trim brown shoes still resting on the paper wrapping. "Oh, they are beautiful! Beautiful!" she squealed, holding them against her face, inhaling the timeless aroma of new leather, not wanting the magic to end.

She slipped her dusty feet into the shoes. They pinched her big toes a little, but after waiting fourteen years for her first pair of shoes, would she be heard complaining about a little pinch? Not for a minute! As Chilolo turned back to his pack, she took a few cautious steps. She looked down at her feet. The widely-spread toes were gone. How could these elegant feet be her own?

The more Reina looked at her shoes, the more she thought they seemed to angle outward a little oddly. Could it be that each shoe was made to fit only one foot or the other? She slipped her feet out and slid each into the opposite shoe. *Ahhh!* She hadn't known anything could feel like that. The leather cushioned her feet just so, all the way around. Reina laughed. She pranced around the courtyard, glancing behind her again and again to look at the diamond-patterned shoe prints in the fine dust. What funny, delightful footprints they were, without any toe prints at all!

Vicenta, too, was pleased. First thing the next morning, she measured Reina here and there and cut the lovely fabric. Reina found extra ways to help around the place as her mother sat by the hour looping stitch after stitch through the soft calico. Vicenta was a competent seamstress, and the dress took shape quickly.

When the dress was finished, Reina hugged it to her and skipped down the path toward the river. Coming to a pool of water surrounded by a small, thick woods of dense undergrowth, she undressed and washed herself.

Reina slid the dress slowly over her head and thrust her arms into the sleeves, luxuriating in its softness. The soft skirt fell past her knees. She slipped her bare feet into the new shoes, danced, twirled, and laughed out loud. Then, stepping from the shelter of the trees, suppressing her giddiness so no one would notice, she walked demurely toward the kitchen. This was a special occasion; she would serve hot cocoa at supper.

As the family gathered for the evening meal, Reina still felt fuzzy all over. She ladled the steaming cocoa into three clay mugs, using a fourth mug as a dipper. She filled and wiped the fourth mug and handed it to Chilolo. "Thank you, Reina!" His teeth flashed and his eyes twinkled. He made her feel like a princess, dressed up in soft polka dots and new leather shoes.

In the glow of Chilolo's love and approval, Reina lifted the next steaming cup and handed it to Carlos. His eyes narrowed as he took it. A flick of his wrist sent the cocoa streaming down the front of her beautiful dress, burning her skin, puddling brown and sticky over her shoes and the floor.

Reina burst into tears. "You're horrid, just horrid! And I hate you!"

Chilolo slammed his cup onto the table. Grabbing a pallet board from beside the door, he brought it down hard across startled Carlos's back. Carlos hollered and headed out, Chilolo chasing after him, shouting and whacking. Reina's anger turned to terror. What would Chilolo do to Carlos? She had never seen Chilolo so angry. Worse, what might Carlos do to Chilolo?

As Carlos sprinted toward the woods, Chilolo spun around and returned to the house. Flinging the board against the adobe wall, he shouted at his mother, "You have to get that man out of your house! If you don't make him leave, I'm taking Reina out of here." Chilolo sank onto a low stool, dropping his head in his hands.

Vicenta usually had everything under control, but now her hands shook as she twisted the edge of her apron. Tears glistened and trembled under her eyes.

Seething, Reina left the kitchen, walked across the open courtyard to the sleeping room, and replaced the polka-dotted calico for threadbare *manta cantel*. Mama could work the stains out of her dress, but the enchantment was gone.

Several weeks later Chilolo had to return to his work at the coast. Since Carlos did not bother Reina again while Chilolo was there, Vicenta said nothing to Carlos about leaving.

SONG OF THE SHEPHERDESS

One sunny day when Vicenta was gone, Reina was bent over the fire, stirring milk for cheese. The milk was nearly hot enough to add vinegar. She liked stirring in the vinegar, watching stringy curds pull away from clear yellow whey. After that it only needed straining and salting to produce the finished cheese.

A sound outside made her look up. She tensed. Carlos was coming toward the kitchen. Reina kept stirring, stirring, stirring, everything in her willing him to leave. He walked in and stepped behind her. She could hear her blood pulsing in her ears. *What will he find wrong with me now? I don't have the strength for another beating. Please, God!*

Carlos moved closer, and Reina felt his hand against her. She went cold all over. Instinctively she knew this was a greater evil than any he had attempted before. Everything in her cried out to God for His protection.

Reina hardly noticed the heat of the big clay pot as with a single desperate heave she hoisted it off the fire and slung the hot milk over her shoulder.

With a bellow of rage and pain, Carlos bolted out the door.

Reina trembled and crept to the doorway, peering along the trail Carlos had taken. He was already out of sight, headed for the woods. She watched a moment longer until she was sure he was gone. Sinking onto a low wooden box, she felt her strength drain in the wave of relief that followed her deliverance.

Gradually she became aware of a Presence, a great love around her. "Thank you, thank you, my God. You sent your angels to protect me," she breathed. "I love you! I love you!" Sitting alone in the steamy kitchen with milk sloshed across the hard-packed dirt floor and splattered on the adobe wall behind her, she lifted her hands and worshiped. God was still her God, her light after darkness.

Late that night when Vicenta came home, Carlos still had not returned. Reina pulled her mat close to her mother's, whispering the whole story in her mother's sympathetic ear.

The next day Vicenta made Carlos move out.

Still, Reina's life didn't change much. Carlos built a small house on an adjacent property and moved into it, but he spent almost as much time at their house as he had before. The beatings and unjust accusations continued.

Chilolo had sold his sheep, so Reina no longer had an excuse to escape for long afternoons in the mountains. She could not escape to school either, because she had finished the sixth and final grade two years before. Without the walk to school, she rarely saw Yanet, so she could not even tell her about her troubles. Where could a girl feel safe? Would she ever again see a shadow fall across the floor without feeling that awful tightening inside?

CHAPTER 8

Yanet's Escape

Yanet scooped the plate of peaches off the table and winked at Reina. Ducking inside Yanet's bedroom, the girls eased the door closed behind them.

"I'm famished, aren't you? I can't believe our luck! A whole plate of peaches!" Yanet chattered as the girls changed into their night dresses and settled cross-legged on Yanet's sleeping mat with the peaches between them. They bit into the juicy fruit, rolling their eyes. They giggled and whispered, reaching for a second peach and a third. How fine it was to just be sisters for one night!

"*Shhh!* Reina, Grandpa's coming!" A shuffling and thumping approached the bedroom door; then it flew open and Grandpa's face appeared, red and angry. He shuffled toward them, swiping at them with his cane, and the girls collapsed into giggles as he spanked first one and then the other. The more he spanked, the more they giggled and the madder he got. Finally, bellowing at Yanet to put the peaches back where she got them, he shuffled back out the door, and Yanet hurried to return the half-empty plate to the table.

Reina slipped under the blanket, waiting for Yanet to return.

"Why do you put up with it?" she demanded when Yanet was settled in beside her.

SONG OF THE SHEPHERDESS

"Grandpa's not so bad. Sure, he gets mad sometimes, but he's old. You know his spankings don't hurt much. He's kind of mean, but he leaves me alone most of the time."

They lay there for a while, thinking, until Yanet spoke again. "The aunts are the worst, Reina. They can't stand me. They treat me like an animal. They make me do all the heavy stuff: carrying water, grinding corn, scrubbing clothes. It's work, work, work from morning until night. Sometimes I get so tired I think I can't take another step, but they beat me if I slow down. Or if something isn't done exactly right, they beat me for that. And they say awful things to me. Am I ugly, Reina? Am I really uglier than other girls?"

"Of course not, Yanet. You are one of the prettiest girls around. You are way prettier than I am. What makes you ask such a thing?"

"They call me 'toilet face,' and worse." Yanet was crying. "And Mama doesn't care about me either. Why did she let you go to school for six years, but ugly old Yanet could only go for three years? Why do you and Carlos and Mama have real beds? Why did everyone else have shoes by the time they were my age, and I still have to go barefoot?"

"You're barely sixteen," Reina said. "Chilolo didn't have shoes at your age."

"You might be right, but you have shoes now, Reina. I know this isn't your fault, but it isn't fair. Why should I even keep on living just so the fat aunts don't have to do any hard work—just so they can laugh at me?" Yanet buried her face in her mat and cried.

Reina patted her sister's shoulder. "Oh, Yanet, I wish I could do something."

Yanet rolled onto her back, staring at the thatch above her. "I know Carlos beats you awful, but you have Mama. You have one person who really loves you and cares about you. Your very own mama. Sometimes I hurt so bad inside, I think I can't bear it another minute. Reina, you are the only person who cares about me."

Reina put her arms around Yanet and cried, a steely determination building inside her. No one she loved was going to keep on suffering like this—not if Luisa Reynalda Barrios could do anything about it.

"Why don't you just leave, Yanet?"

"Leave? Where in the world would I go?"

"Why not come live with us?"

"You know I can't. Mama could have taken me home when Grandma died. Face it, Reina. Mama doesn't want me."

"I don't think that's true, but if you can't go home, then go to Xela. I have often gone there to the market with Mama. I could go with you."

"You would leave Mama?"

"Of course not. I could never leave Mama. But I would walk with you, and . . . and help you find work. I promise, Yanet, I'll help you get away from here."

Never in her life had it mattered more to Reina to keep her word. The girls lay awake long into the night, plotting Yanet's escape. What did they have to lose?

The day of Yanet's deliverance dawned at last. She had scrunched everything she owned into three rag-wrapped bundles. Reina would arrive any minute.

It had seemed so simple and sensible when they had talked about it a few days ago, but as Yanet stood in her bedroom doorway listening to Tío[1] Lolo pouring milk into jugs, she wavered. She couldn't go without telling Tío Lolo. He was her mother's younger brother, quiet and hard-working—a no-nonsense man. Tío Lolo was the one person in the house whom Yanet respected.

Birdsong sparkled in the air, and sunlight slanted into the courtyard, making the faded flowers glow in their pots as she walked across the courtyard to the kitchen. The uneven places under her feet, the peeling whitewash on the doors, the crack in the biggest flower pot, the vine straggling down into the kitchen doorway—she seemed to see it all for the first time, and suddenly it seemed achingly familiar, even precious. She hated this place, yet it was home. *Will I ever come back? Do I want to come back? Why did Grandma have to die? I need her so badly.* Yanet opened the lower half of the door and stepped into the dim kitchen.

"I'm leaving, Tío Lolo," she said as he looked up. Lolo paused, his milk

---

[1] Uncle.

bucket in midair. Yanet had never noticed the sadness in his big brown eyes, yet now she realized it had always been there. "Reina and I are going to Xela this morning. I'm going to try to find work."

He set the bucket down on the table. "If you don't want to live here anymore, it's okay. I understand." Tears glistened in his eyes. Yanet felt miserable, yet oddly comforted. She knew Tío Lolo understood.

The dog barked outside, and Yanet stepped back out of the kitchen into the sunlight. What would the aunts say when they awoke and no one had gotten water? Reina had gathered Yanet's bundles and was already heading for the gate. Yanet glanced back one last time. Tío Lolo stood watching from the peeling doorway. He was crying.

As the two girls started down the steep lane, the panorama spread before them was almost as breathtaking as the crisp, cold morning air. Dust puffed thick with every step, and the naked landscape exposed the contours of endless hills and craggy trees until both disappeared in the distant haze.

This was supposed to be a joyful occasion, but Yanet didn't feel a bit that way—not with Tío Lolo standing back there crying. Maybe someone besides Reina did care about her.

As they plodded through the miles, nothing seemed worth discussing. When they finally reached the park in the center of Xela, it was past midday—siesta time. Hardly anyone was around, and the girls suddenly felt very alone and a little foolish.

"Now what are we going to do?" Yanet asked. She thought of God. Did He see her standing with her little sister, thirsty and hungry in this deserted marketplace in the middle of this huge city? Did God care that she had known almost nothing but pain all these years since her grandmother died?

Yanet still felt uneasy. For all she knew, the life she was entering could be even worse than the one she was leaving behind, though she hardly knew how.

A woman with a colorful apron strolled across the square toward them, market basket in hand. She greeted them with a friendly "Good afternoon."

It was now or never. Reina plunged in. "Please, señora, do you know anyone who is needing a strong girl to work for them?"

Yanet's Escape

The woman didn't hesitate. "Are you girls looking for work? I've been needing a girl myself."

"She is looking for work," Reina said, pointing eagerly to Yanet.

Yanet didn't feel brave. The lady seemed nice enough, but she was a total stranger. However, Reina felt no hesitation. Hadn't they come to find work? This opportunity was perfect.

The girls followed the woman to her house close by the market. The lady called at a brightly painted door in the wall along the street. It was soon opened by a child who looked clean and cared for, and they entered a courtyard surrounded by flowers that bloomed as if they didn't know it was the dry season.

The lady showed the girls to a little room by the kitchen where Yanet could sleep. Everything was pleasant and homey, and Yanet dared to hope that God had answered her prayers. Reina hugged Yanet and promised to come see her. Then she hurried away, hoping to reach home before dark. It would take four and a half hours to hike back to La Laguna, and this time she would walk it alone.

The sight of the images looking down at her from every arch of the great golden Catholic church spurred Reina across the deserted market square. She was glad Yanet was out of reach of the aunts and their vicious tongues, but already she missed her terribly.

CHAPTER 9

Market Day

As Reina and Vicenta followed the steep footpath toward the main road leading to San Juan, the valley spread wide and green below them. Their route was a series of sloping paths that joined and rejoined the main road. At one place they forded a wide shallow creek fouled by sheep and cows that waded in to drink.

Two and a half hours of walking brought them to the edge of the San Juan market with its inviting jumble of sights and sounds. Here they would spend the day selling their cheeses and needlework, purchasing sugar and coffee, and catching up on local gossip. Reina liked the market, but the best part of the journey was the chance to spend a whole day with Mama, away from Carlos's all-seeing eyes.

As they entered the market, everything was noisy, cluttered, and busy—a kind of controlled chaos. Sagging tarps draped over poles, shading tables of bright wares and sweaty-faced vendors who haggled with prospective buyers and chanted monotonously by turns.

Indian women with tired faces and colorful dresses, too poor for tarps and tables, sat cross-legged on littered streets behind mounds of vegetables, babies on their backs or laps. They chanted the praises of their produce to passersby, cutting small samples from their avocados or pineapples, hoping for a worthwhile day of sales. Young people, lounging in shop doorways behind the street vendors, snacked, laughed, and flirted away the hours. Small, nearly naked children, heedless of the stench and din, darted among the booths. By afternoon, squashed and decaying produce was strewn everywhere.

Reina had gradually come to realize that going to the market as a fifteen-year-old was not the same as going to market as a child. Foolish boys loitered there, more interested in pretty young ladies than in vegetables, housewares, tools, or trinkets. Vicenta had discussed this with Reina on their long monthly walks over the dusty hills to San Juan.

"I don't want you going around with boys who have no respect for girls, Reina. It will only bring you heartache and trouble. Stay near me and they will leave you alone. If a boy doesn't know how to treat a girl with respect, he isn't worthy of you. A boy like that will not make you a good husband."

Young men in her own village and neighborhood had often tried to get Reina's attention, especially at the fiestas where she sometimes went with her friends or siblings. But Reina remembered her mother's warnings. She tried to give them no chance to think she was available to please their youthful lusts. She was dismayed and fearful at the liberties she saw them taking with the girls around her.

One young man had actually asked Reina if she would marry him. "I would give you a good life," Juan had promised, and Reina did not doubt that he would. Juan Lopez wasn't like the other boys she knew. He never partied or flirted. Reina had known his mother as long as she could remember, and she was a good woman. Besides, Juan loved God's Word more than anyone Reina had ever known. But when she asked her mother about him, the answer was a firm *no*. "Juan is nothing but a poor Indian," Vicenta sniffed. "You are too good for him. I will not have my daughter marrying an Indian."

On this fine afternoon in San Juan, however, thoughts like these were far from Reina's mind.

Mama was examining some tomatoes she had plucked off the top of a bright pile. "Two cents," she stated to the gray-haired man behind the tomatoes. She reached into the side seam of her full skirt, feeling for her coins.

"No, no, no! Five cents!" The vendor looked grieved. "These are big ripe tomatoes. See?" He picked one up and patted it affectionately.

As Reina waited for Mama and the seller to agree on a price, she heard the cry of a vendor selling *arroz con leche*[1] not far off. She nudged Mama's elbow. "May I go get some *arroz con leche* and rest in the *kiosko* for a little?"

"Sure, I'll meet you there later."

After buying her rice drink, Reina moved through the crowd and approached the *kiosko*. She liked it here where long stone benches, arranged around a center filled with flowers, provided a place to sit and rest. It was a little removed from the clutter and noise of the market, and a shade of sprawling thatch offered relief from the glaring highland sunshine.

She sank onto a bench, sipping the sweet, thick drink, savoring the sting of cinnamon. A young man entered the *kiosko*. He glanced around the space, then strode toward the side where Reina sat with her empty cup. He sat down on the next bench and sipped his drink. "Where are you from?" he asked a little shyly.

"I'm from Sibilia," she replied.

"What is your name?"

She remembered her mother's warnings. She would be careful. "Luisa Reynalda," she said softly.

"Reynalda!" he exclaimed. She glanced up at him and he was smiling, showing a row of straight white teeth in a handsome face. "How about that! My name is Reynaldo! Reynaldo Monterroso." She smiled back at him. She couldn't help it; he seemed so delighted with the coincidence.

Reina saw her mother approaching the *kiosko*, red tomatoes perched in the top of her filled basket. Reina stood to leave. The young man stood with her and shook her hand. "Glad to meet you, Reynalda." He bowed slightly, with a gentleness that drew her. Despite her reservations, she liked his clear eyes and respectful manner.

---

[1] A sweet, hot rice pudding drink.

SONG OF THE SHEPHERDESS

A week later, Reina squatted on the floor by the fire, shaping balls of soaked masa[2] into tortillas. The corn had been boiled until it was swollen and soft, then painstakingly ground between two stones that formed a crude mortar and pestle. After the corn was thoroughly mashed, enough water had been added to make a soft paste.

Reina reached into the bowl, scooping out just the right amount of the corn paste, whirling it in her cupped hands, slapping the neat sphere of corn first with one hand, then with the other—right, left, right, left—quickly forming a smooth, flat disc between her palms.

"Buenos días!" It was a man's voice, a stranger to these parts, calling as he approached the door. Reina looked up as his shadow fell across the doorway. Her hands paused for a split second. Framed in her doorway and silhouetted against her mountains stood Reynaldo, from the San Juan market. *Pat, pat, pat, pat, pat, pat.* Reina attacked the hapless tortilla. Their house was many kilometers from San Juan, and their nearest neighbor lived a kilometer away on the other side of the canyon. Yet here was this young man, waiting in the doorway.

"Buenos días, Reynalda." He fumbled with the hat in his hand.

"Buenos días," answered Reina and her mother in unison. "Come in," said Vicenta. She smiled at him as he stepped across the threshold and stood by the fire.

Reina dropped a tortilla onto the hot stone and stood up, wiping her hands on her apron. She shook Reynaldo's hand, then turned to Vicenta. "Mama, this is Reynaldo Monterroso. I met him in San Juan last week." She squatted down again and resumed her work.

After the customary small talk, Reynaldo got straight to the point. "I've come because I think we would make a good couple," he said. "I would like to come visit you and get to know you better." Though Reina's hands kept

---

[2] Dough made from ground corn.

60

moving, time stood still. She looked at her mother.

Seeing Reina's hesitation, Reynaldo turned to Vicenta. "Señora, is it okay with you if I come and visit your daughter sometimes?"

Mama looked at Reina's flushed face. "What do you think, Reina? Do you want this man coming to visit you?" Their eyes locked for a second as Reina tried to read her mother's thoughts. But Vicenta's face wasn't revealing her thoughts today. Still, Reina knew her spunky mama. If Mama didn't like Reynaldo, she would have sent him on his way already. *Mama is smitten*, Reina thought. *Tall, handsome, well-mannered, and he's not an Indian—this Reynaldo is just the sort of husband she wants for me.*

Reina felt lightheaded and a little shaky. She continued slapping tortillas, flattening the little balls of soaked corn, dropping them into place, giving the hot discs a quick pat, testing for doneness, lifting and flipping them one by one, deftly, automatically. She paused with an unbaked tortilla limp in her hand and glanced up at Reynaldo. His eyes, widely set and dark, were calm and sincere, with a hint of a twinkle. Despite his direct manner, he was respectful and patient, unlike most boys she knew. She liked him.

Reina looked down, reaching into the bowl, rolling her fingers around a fistful of corn paste, sizing it just right. "It's all right with me if he comes," she said softly. She stole another look at the boy. Their eyes met and his face broke into a wide smile, drawing merry little creases at the corners of his eyes, almost making them dance. She smiled back. Oh, what would Yanet say when she wrote her all about it?

Vicenta poured a cup of coffee for Reynaldo and invited him to sit down.

"Thank you, señora, it is kind of you."

While Reynaldo sipped the coffee, Vicenta refilled the tin can with water and set it on the fire. The boyfriends of her older daughters had brought Vicenta only grief, but Reina, at fifteen, was obedient and upright, a daughter to pin one's hopes on.

"You must always treat my daughter with respect," she told the young suitor. "There will be no touching and no going away alone. You will come here to my house to visit with my daughter, and only when I am at home.

This is the only way you are welcome."

By the time Reynaldo rose to leave, they had agreed he could return in two days.

Twice a week for the next two years, Reynaldo Monterroso walked two and a half hours over the hills through rain and mud or heat and dust from his father's home in La Cumbre to Vicenta's humble house nestled against the slopes of La Laguna. Sometimes he would sit down on a low log, his dusty feet in simple leather sandals planted on the dirt floor. Reina would hand him a cup of sugared coffee, settling herself on a log seat near him, and work her embroidery while they talked.

At other times she would continue her housework, grinding corn, patting tortillas, whatever was at hand to do. Vicenta was always with them, and the three learned to love and trust each other during the long, unhurried visits.

One day as Reina handed Reynaldo his coffee, he took it quietly and remained thoughtful as she sat down beside him. She tried several times to make conversation, but the silences that followed only amplified the background sounds of her life—the crow of a rooster, the bleat of a lamb, the trill of a bird, the small hum of the water can on the fire. Clearly Reynaldo had something on his mind. Reina fell silent, sipped her coffee, and waited.

Reynaldo leaned forward at last, his elbows on his knees, his mug clasped in both hands, and looked at Vicenta. "Vicenta, it is time for Reina and me to marry. I have been coming often for two years, and I think it is good that we marry. May I marry her?"

Without waiting for Vicenta's answer, he turned to Reina. "Reina, I love you." He looked down and paused a long time. When he spoke again, his eyes were misty. "I want you to be the mother of my children."

Warmth flooded Reina's heart. Looking into his eyes, she answered, "Yes, Reynaldo, I will marry you." Everything in her ached to be the best wife and mother any man in these hills had ever known.

Vicenta gave them a few moments to bask in the glow of their promise before calling them to business. "If you are going to marry, then it will be in two weeks. Two weeks is long enough to prepare." This daughter, at least, would go to the marriage altar unsoiled.

They spent the next half hour planning and discussing the few essential details.

When Reynaldo left, Reina followed him out the door. She stood at the corner of the house, gazing at her beloved as he strode past the steep sweep of ripe corn and then disappeared into the woods. Her heart was full. In two weeks she would be his.

The next morning Reina hiked over the hills to the post office in El Edén, a letter to Yanet clutched in her hand. How she missed her sister. They had written regularly, Yanet assuring Reina that she was well, her employer kind, her food sufficient. Yanet even received a small wage, and she was satisfied.

A few times when Mama and Reina had walked to the market in Xela, they had been able to visit Yanet briefly, but Yanet had not been back to La Laguna for three long years. *Surely she will come to my wedding,* Reina told herself. *She must come to my wedding.*

CHAPTER 10

Wedding Day

November 5, 1966, was Reynaldo and Reina's wedding day. The rainy season was spent, and all up and down the hillsides, brown tassels announced the ripening corn.

Reina was dressed in a long, simple gown of silky white. She had combed her hair until it was shiny and sleek, just like the coal-black coat of Princesa, her first cow—the sweetest, gentlest, prettiest cow in these hills, she was sure. Why did all her childhood memories seem so hauntingly sweet and sad this morning?

Had a day ever brought such conflicting feelings? She wanted Reynaldo—wanted to be his wife more than she had ever wanted anything on earth. If only she could ignore the niggling awareness that she had not heard back from Yanet. If only she could ignore the finality of leaving her mother way back on La Laguna by herself. Sure, Carlos still lived in the area, but he hardly talked to Mama anymore, except to complain. Mariano lived nearby, but he was busy with his many children. Mama would be lonely, she was sure.

And she missed Chilolo. His job in the government health department required him to travel long distances, researching malaria, teaching prevention, gathering statistics, and fumigating houses to rid them of mosquitoes.

Her heart was warmed by the thought of her big brother. Today more than ever she realized how much like a papa he had always been to her. Though he had a wife and family of his own, he had sent her a generous gift to buy her bridal clothes, as well as enough for Mama to buy herself a nice dress.

No, it wasn't right, going to her wedding without Chilolo and Yanet, the two people she loved most next to Reynaldo and her mother. *Where is Yanet, anyway?* Three years ago, the escape to Xela had seemed the perfect answer to Yanet's trouble, but now Reina missed her painfully.

She had written Yanet about the wedding three times. Why hadn't Yanet answered? In hindsight that escape plan was looking more and more like a mistake. Reina shrugged. She had done what had to be done. She would not regret it today.

Despite the shadow of Yanet's absence, Vicenta's smile was warm as Reina handed her the lovely wax crown designed to hold her veil in place. The crown was adorned with tiny white wax flowers interspersed with even tinier green paper leaves. Mama fitted the crown over her daughter's veil and stepped back, looking at her tenderly, tilting her head this way and that to better critique the lovely bride.

Reina slipped her feet into her small white slippers, luxuriating in their softness and daintiness, feeling even more like a princess than she had on that day three years before when Chilolo had given her the first shoes and dress fabric she had ever owned.

Reynaldo arrived with his father, Chano, each man riding one borrowed horse and leading another. As they approached, Reynaldo leaned forward as if eager to reach her, his large hands gripping the horse's bridle, his glowing face shining away her shadow and making her heart feel giddy. Her beloved had come for her—had come to make her his.

Reynaldo leaped from his horse's back and hugged Reina. Then, after unfolding a blanket and draping it over the horse, he lifted her up and seated her, laughing, on the horse's broad back. Chano helped Vicenta onto the other horse. Light, happy chatter shortened the journey over the hazy hills to the courthouse in Palestina where the relatives were waiting.

Wedding Day

As they rounded the last curve of the road, Reina suddenly felt shy. In front of the low concrete-block courthouse, the crowd was waiting, craning their necks for a view of the approaching wedding party. Reynaldo grinned and shouted greetings to all as they rode up. Reina smiled. He had a gift for making others feel important—something she had felt the day she first met him at the San Juan market.

Reynaldo sprang from his horse and helped Reina down. The women clustered around, clucking over the bride and congratulating Vicenta, while the men slapped Reynaldo on the back, cupping hard hands over his shoulders. Nervous but happy, Reina clung to Reynaldo's hand. *Reynaldo, I am here—I am yours.* Their eyes met, and his radiant smile wrapped itself around her fluttering heart. No girl had ever loved a man more.

In the evening after the wedding feast, Reina stood in the doorway of her father-in-law's house watching the departing guests. It had been a tiring day, from her home on La Laguna to the courthouse in Palestina, to her father-in-law's house in La Cumbre. Even with her husband's arm around her, Reina felt strangely alone as she watched Vicenta leaving for home. Vicenta, too, though she was surrounded by relatives from El Edén, Sibilia, El Paiz, and La Laguna, looked small and alone. Reina could already picture her mother entering the dark little house at La Laguna without her.

Reynaldo's arm tightened around Reina's waist, his cheek resting lightly against her veil, careful not to crush the little wax crown. She leaned against him, crying, feeling more like a child than a bride.

In some ways, weaving herself into the fabric of her husband's family was easy. Reina was at home harvesting corn, milking cows, and working alongside Reynaldo. Though La Laguna had been beautiful, her father-in-law's farm surpassed it, lying in a gorgeous valley along the side of La Cumbre. Its trees and gardens were watered by a gushing artesian well, producing abundant apples, potatoes, carrots, and other fruits and vegetables. It was a Garden of Eden, cloaked in beauty and bounty, comfort and provision—a garden, she soon discovered, invaded by evil and jealousy, ruled by a tempter and temptress.

Magdalena, Reynaldo's stepmother, had been impossible to ignore on the day of the wedding: tall, lovely, no older than Reynaldo himself, her shining hair cascading to her ankles, her dress trimmed and tucked to advantage. She had seemed to be everywhere, gliding among the guests, laughing into the eyes of the men, attracting many a lingering glance.

Now that they lived in the same house, it seemed to Reina that her presence irritated Magdalena. She grew weary of Magdalena's subtle put-downs and even wearier of her fawning over Reynaldo, as if Chano's wife were more enamored with her stepson than with her husband. Despite Reynaldo's reassurances, Reina chafed at the sight of the tall young woman with the long flowing hair swaggering about the house, barely clothed.

A measure of respite came in the evening when Reina got to sit beside Reynaldo outside the adobe house, shelling corn, watching the shimmering edges of the ragged crimson clouds as the sun sank behind the mountain. They talked as they worked, enjoying each other's presence.

But too often the peace of the evening was blighted by temptation of a different kind.

Reina stiffened as her father-in-law staggered toward them. "Here, son, have a drink," he slurred. Reynaldo tilted the jug and sipped circumspectly. Chano and Magdalena sat down with them, laughing drunkenly and talking too freely. Chano passed the jug to Reynaldo several more times, and each time, Reynaldo took a small sip. The newlyweds were relieved when the other two tottered inside and sprawled across the bed.

"I used to get drunk with him," Reynaldo admitted when Chano and his wife had left. "I felt like I had to. It makes him angry when I refuse, and you definitely don't want to see him angry and drunk. But I'm done with all that now, darling."

A jay screamed in a tree beside the house. "You know what, Reina? I haven't been drunk once since I met you."

Reina was only seventeen. Her trust wrapped his heart with healing. He vowed in his soul that he would always be there to care for her and for their children. Who knew better than he the excruciating price *cusha* demanded?

Wedding Day

Aware of the daily tensions with Magdalena, Reynaldo decided to move back to Vicenta's house on La Laguna. The relief of escape soon wore off, however, as life brought new pressures to their growing family. When Conrado, the child they had dreamed of, came screaming into their lives and howled day and night for most of his first five months; when Dionel was born one year after Conrado, and Eliza two years later; when Conrado grew into a strong-willed toddler, and Reynaldo's attempts to discipline him sparked heated arguments with Reina and Vicenta; when the income Reynaldo could make by raising wheat, sawing lumber, and helping on building projects was never quite sufficient to support his growing family; when the quiet days and tender words of their early marriage gave way to chronic strife and turmoil; when the flame of hope Reynaldo cherished for his home was barely flickering—that was when someone mentioned the abandoned still on the mountainside.

CHAPTER 11

The Still and the Strife

Reynaldo dropped his *azadón* in the corn row and sprinted toward the house, his hat flying off as he ran. The neighbor boy who had brought him the message was already skittering back down the hill toward the cover of the trees.

Bursting into the house, Reynaldo hissed, "Quick! Get the *cusha* to the woods. The police are coming!"

Seven-year-old Dionel snatched the blanket off the cache in the corner. Grabbing a jug in each hand, he fled out the door, across the lane, and up the narrow wooded trail, where he turned and plunged into dense underbrush. Five-year-old Eliza scampered behind him, followed by three-year-old Aide, her mournful little face pinched with worry. What if they took Papa to jail? What was jail, anyway? She was sure it was bad.

Nine-year-old Conrado came last, carrying more than all the little ones together, having practiced this operation many times. Bitterness stung his mind. So what if Papa went to jail? Then he couldn't get drunk anymore. Still, Conrado didn't intend to give the police that satisfaction if he could help it.

Reynaldo was back in the field, his hat on his head, his body bending to the steady chop and crunch, chop and crunch. Swinging high, drawing down, steady, steady, his face glistening, his *azadón* slowly churning the hillside into a hundred mini-steps that wrapped like bleachers around the base of the mountain.

He looked as innocent as the fresh-turned earth, as if the mountain behind him knew nothing of midnight gatherings around the still, of *cusha* flowing golden from the copper pipe, of shameful things that happened there after his family went home and only his wife's cousin stayed behind to help him. No one must know *that*. It would crush Reina, he thought—but what did she expect? She had become such a shrew, harping at him for his drinking, arguing with him over Conrado's sassiness, and complaining when the money didn't reach around. Maybe she *did* know about her cousin. He wished he didn't care.

I wonder what the police want this time. There isn't any money to give them today. That means they'll probably take the cusha *if they can find it. They probably won't bother to arrest me—there is more profit for them in the* cusha, he thought bitterly.

It's good there are enough stills to keep them riding the circuit for a couple of months before they come back to pounce on me again. Why don't they get to work themselves instead of robbing a poor man trying to make a living?

As he hoed, Reynaldo kept one eye on the house. The police paraded into the courtyard, reining in their horses. Reina, with baby Sonia on her back, was greeting them—arguing with them, from the look of it. Vicenta strode up the hill from the river, a basket of clean laundry on her head, bearing down on the scene like a cow toward a threatened calf. She planted herself beside Reina, waving her arms, commanding the men to be on their way.

When two of the police dismounted, handing their reins to a third, and shoved past the women into the kitchen, Reynaldo's bitterness turned to fear. The children had probably saved all the bottles from the sala, but there was too much sugar in the kitchen. How had he forgotten to take it up the mountain last night?

Later that evening the children sat silent on their log stools, clutching cold tamales and staring at the coals that quivered red between blackened fieldstones. Vicenta ladled steaming greens into their bowls—greens Eliza had gathered that morning when everything was okay. Papa's empty place screamed mutely. Fear and guilt throbbed in the silent dusk of the house. *Maybe if we hadn't run so fast, maybe if we had left a couple of jugs behind so the police had something to take instead of Papa . . .*

Word of the arrest had spread, and two local ladies were in the house talking seriously with Reina. "Reina, it's time to stop talking about it and really make a change. *Cusha* is destroying your family."

"I've never wanted to do it," Reina explained. She remembered the terror she had felt many years before when the police had taken Mama Vicenta to jail. She remembered her futile childish pleading with them and her desolation when her mother had walked up the trail between two policemen. This afternoon, her children had experienced the same thing.

She thought of Reynaldo's determination to break the curse of *cusha*. How had their lives come to this? When had the trusting little shepherdess who sang her heart out to God on the mountain become this frustrated, unhappy woman? "What else can we do?" Reina said. "We have many children."

"You and Reynaldo need Jesus," her neighbor said firmly.

Reina leaned forward, her heart a sponge. "What do you think we should do?"

"You need to find a good church. It isn't God's will for you to be making *cusha*. Reynaldo is ruining himself with drinking. He needs to be born again. He needs to stay home with you and the children and keep away from María."

Reina's heart went cold. So the neighbors knew about that too.

"Come with us to the Prince of Peace church," her neighbor said. "It is different from the Presbyterian church."

Reina thought about the proposition. Religion seemed to make no real difference in the lives of most Presbyterians she knew. Juan Lopez and Benigno Calderón were sincere, but for most of them, church seemed to be a social event. They would leave thinking and talking and acting just like their faithless neighbors, no matter how much the preacher read from the Holy Scriptures on Sundays. Maybe this Prince of Peace church would have real answers. How she longed for peace.

Vicenta moved about the kitchen as the younger women talked, wrapping leftover tamales in a cloth and draping another cloth over the unfinished skillet of greens. Her shoulders were a little straighter than usual, her step firmer, her nose tipped upward, and her lips almost amused. This talk was all nonsense. A man had to do something to feed his family. Where did the young people get these scruples anyway? On the other hand, there was little profit in making *cusha* if you drank so much you could hardly do your work, all your profits were confiscated, and you kept ending up in jail.

"I'm going to the jail tomorrow to have a good talk with Reynaldo, and I think we could help a little with the bail money," the friend offered generously before she went out the door. "A man can't provide for his family if he's sitting in jail."

She kissed Reina on both cheeks, patted the heads of the older children, and squeezed baby Sonia's little leg; then both visitors disappeared down the dark path, leaving a palpable hope in their wake.

CHAPTER 12

Prince of Peace

The following Sunday, as Reina wrapped a shawl around baby Sonia, she felt almost young again. How she had missed the preaching, the singing, the reading of the Holy Scriptures!

"Are you ready, Eliza? There now, button Aide's jacket," she instructed.

It's been more than ten years, she mused. *I just never had the heart to go to church after Yanet left.*

Oh, where is Yanet? Did she keep seeking you, God? Were you there when she needed you? The familiar throb of pain felt too heavy to entertain this morning. Some questions could never have answers, she guessed.

Reina wrapped Sonia against her chest, marveling again at the softness and sweetness of the tiny girl whose big, expressive eyes looked trustingly out of her perfect round face. Reina laid her cheek against the soft mop of baby hair. *She needs you, God. All my children need you. Without you, what hope is there for any of us?*

Reina stepped into the fragrant freshness of a morning bursting with birdsong. Reynaldo was waiting in the yard with the older boys, his thick hair parted, wetted, and combed. All were freshly scrubbed and dressed in their best clothes, which weren't much.

SONG OF THE SHEPHERDESS

Vicenta thought the whole idea of going to this church was a dangerous whim. The evangelicals were big-mouthed and empty. But with her usual goodwill, she had washed and mended clothes for hours yesterday. If they were determined to go, they may as well look respectable.

Even Conrado seemed to be in good spirits this morning. Dionel and Eliza, the conscientious, serious-minded siblings, dared to hope this might be the beginning of better days for the family.

Later they all sat quietly in the meeting, listening intently to the preaching. Reina drank in every word of the Holy Scriptures. She tried to ignore her uneasiness about the immodesty of the church women and her disapproval of their leading roles in the meeting. It didn't seem to fit with what Juan had read from the Bible years ago. Still, it was good to be in church again, and better yet, this time Reynaldo and all her dear children were with her.

Reina's neighbor had kept her promise to visit Reynaldo in jail. She had found him broken and sorrowful, grieving over the pain and trouble he had brought to his wife and family. He had been ready to listen to her earnest appeal. Disgusted with himself, humbled and embarrassed to learn that his midnight meetings with his wife's cousin were known, Reynaldo had agreed that they would all attend the Prince of Peace church the following Sunday.

So began many Sundays of walking three miles over the hills to the Prince of Peace church house. Each Sunday Reina's thirsty soul drank again of the river of life—and joy of joys, Reynaldo followed through with his commitment to quit making *cusha*. Even better, he quit his drinking.

Thieves made off with the still, leaving the rock bare, washed by the clear spring water. The wind whispered hope among the eucalyptus trees of Panorama.

Vicenta remained skeptical. She refused to go with the family to church, refused to go near the clapping and hoopla, refused to be shouted at by the preacher. But even she could see that Reynaldo was doing better, staying sober and keeping up with the field work. She would try not to interfere.

"Welcome, friend!" Juan Lopez called from inside his house one day as Reynaldo shouted a greeting from the courtyard. Juan gestured toward the stool by the fire. "Let me get you a cup of coffee."

Sitting on well-worn ends of small sections of tree trunk, sipping their coffee from red clay mugs, the two men began talking of religion. "The men and boys at the Presbyterian church have formed soccer teams," Juan said. "They are scheduling games to compete with teams from other churches." His black eyes flashed, and not just from the reflection of the glowing coals.

"The pastor is the captain of the team. He cuts the sermons short so he can make it to the soccer competitions in the afternoons. I have talked to the pastor. I told him, 'If we want to play soccer, then let us play it like the Bible teaches, just a little for bodily exercise.' But the preacher doesn't want to change anything.

"I guess they all like their sports more than they want to obey the Scriptures. I know young men like to play and compete, but a Christian must value what Jesus Christ values. Christ was not motivated by fun and competition like this world is. He did His Father's business."

Juan sounded sad as he finished, "We are not going to church there anymore, and Benigno and Valeriana have quit going too."

"Juan," Reynaldo said, "you and Amalia should come to the Prince of Peace church. They preach the Bible there. Maybe you won't agree with everything there, but the preacher is serious, and they don't have soccer games. I think you would like it."

The next day Reynaldo told Reina about the conversation as they planted corn together. Reina thought back to the youthful Juan who had come to their house each week and read to her and her mother from the Holy Scriptures. She remembered the many nights he had come by their house to walk with her and Yanet to the Presbyterian church. How she hoped Juan and Amalia would find the truth they sought.

As she mused, Reina heard the unmistakable low of a cow tending a new calf. Reina smiled as she dropped seeds into the furrow, feeling a moment's tender connection with that cow as her precious, growing baby pushed against her own ribs. She was thankful for the twins the cow had just birthed. How would they have gotten along all these years without Chilolo's cows?

SONG OF THE SHEPHERDESS

He had left two cows with them when he began to work for the state health department, and those two had multiplied to a herd of fourteen. Through all the family's hard times, the cows had been a continual blessing. Though most cows gave birth to single calf, these usually had twins. Chilolo's cows provided milk for the little ones and cheese to sell at the market for cash.

Reina straightened and stretched, pressing her hand into the small of her back and wincing.

The sky, arching clear and high above her, the slight smoky scent in the downdraft of the cooking fire, the rhythmic crunching chop of Reynaldo's *azadón,* the cry of a jay from a distant tree, the gorgeous vista of her beloved hills—all these things drew her senses and her heart, calling her to the heart of an eternal Love, a Love which she had known but which she felt mostly eluded her now.

Reina watched Vicenta bending over the next row. Her dear face was weathered and leathery, but her long braid still shone thickly. Her bare feet were calloused and crusted as she followed Reynaldo down the row. Her dirty apron was twisted around her left hand, forming a pouch for the corn kernels, which she dropped into newly punched holes in the earth.

A bus paused on the road high above them, and a lone figure stepped out. The bus growled on its way, leaving a plume of black against the sky. Puzzled, Reina squinted at the small figure picking her way down the steep trail toward them.

CHAPTER 13

A Guest from the City

Reina stared at the high trail, brushing her hands on her apron. She lifted one hand to shade her eyes, knowing she should be minding her business, but she couldn't pull her gaze away from the stranger approaching in the distance. The woman was clearly not a local, for she was dressed in the tasteful and sophisticated style of the city.

What was most perplexing was that this trail was not a through road. The stranger must be coming to visit them. She continued down the steep trail, then struck out across the field toward them with the confidence of one sure of the footing and the place. Only when she was near enough to see Vicenta and Reina's ragged, dirty clothes, their weathered faces, and their earth-stained hands did the visitor hesitate, a thoughtful sadness crossing her face.

Their eyes met then, and Reina caught her breath. She wanted to shout, to laugh, to run toward the visitor. Instead, she stood rooted to the tilled earth. *What do I say to her? It's been ten years. I thought she was dead!*

The next moment the two sisters were in each other's arms, shoulders shaking with sobs, tears forming clear streams down the cheeks of the one and muddy streaks on the cheeks of the other. "Yanet! Yanet!"

Vicenta waited shyly to one side, her face wet.

When finally Yanet released Reina, she turned toward her mother. In that moment the resentment she felt as a child gave place to an unexpected wave of tenderness, sympathy, and sadness for this impoverished woman in a dirty, tattered dress, planting corn on the rugged slopes of La Laguna—this woman who was her mother. Painfully, as if for the first time, Yanet truly saw Vicenta, and her heart went out to her.

"Come inside," Vicenta urged. The three women made their way up the hill and into the small, dim kitchen, where Vicenta stirred the fire and began heating water for coffee.

"Oh, Yanet," Reina exclaimed, "you can't know how Mama and I have cried for you, wondering whether you were safe or even alive! Wherever have you been?"

Yanet looked down at her lap, then lifted eyes filled with sadness to gaze at the wall.

"I'm so sorry. I know I should have written. It was selfish of me. Somehow I just couldn't write anymore after I heard you were getting married, Reina." Her voice quavered.

"But where were you, Yanet? Mama and I couldn't find out anything about you. The lady you lived with in Xela couldn't tell us anything, either."

"Okay, I'll try to start at the beginning." Yanet looked directly at Reina. "As you know, that lady was fair and treated me well. Once I was away from Grandpa's house, I started really thinking about what I wanted to do with my life. Then, when I heard that you were getting married, I realized we'd never be . . . Oh, I don't know. I guess I just didn't see any reason to stay in touch anymore. I just tried to forget who I had been." She dropped her eyes, lost in thought.

"I moved to Guatemala City and threw myself into studying, starting with the three years of grade school I had missed. I worked hard and got where I wanted to go. I became a nurse. When I was twenty-four, I married a nice man—I want you to meet him sometime—and we have two beautiful children.

"But I didn't have peace. I couldn't bear the thought that my children

A Guest from the City

might grow up without God in their lives. My husband didn't understand my desire for God, and he didn't want to go to church. So I took my little children and began to go to church alone. God touched my heart, and I returned to Him."

Vicenta sat a little straighter and gazed out the door toward the hills, small vertical frown lines forming between her eyes.

"Eventually I knew I had to come back to see you, to tell you how sorry I am that I didn't communicate with you for so many years, and to let you know that I am okay. We live in Xela now. We are not wealthy, but we have enough." As the distant *chop-chop* of Reynaldo's *azadón* carried into the room, Yanet became thoughtful. "I guess I had almost forgotten how it is out here."

At lunchtime the children all trooped into the smoky little kitchen and met their aunt Yanet for the first time. She spoke sweetly to them, admiring them, handing out candies and fruits from her large basket, and they quickly fell in love with her.

Reina was overjoyed. Yanet—dear, kind Yanet—had stepped back into her life again, more refined, more educated, but as precious as ever. For the first time in years, Reina felt glad for her part in helping Yanet escape the mountains.

That afternoon, Yanet climbed the trail to board the bus that would take her away from these hills again, away from this hard, meager life, away to her home in Xela.

As the bus rattled away over the hills, Reina stood at the bottom of the hill watching, remembering two barefoot girls with three rag bundles walking half a day over dusty trails, trying to forget the last ten long, lonely years.

Eliza, with baby Sonia on her hip, stood beside her mother as the other children clustered around, watching the bus grow smaller and smaller. To think that Aunt Yanet lived in the city. What a fine, beautiful woman she was! Deep in the children's hearts, a seed had been sown, a seed of hope—and deception.

CHAPTER 14

The Demon Returns

Eleven-year-old Conrado burst out of the woods, wild-eyed with terror, heedless of the sheep he had left behind on the mountain. He raced to the house and flung himself across the bed, drawing long, ragged breaths and stammering incoherently. Reina put her hand on his forehead. It was hot, and he looked at her glassy-eyed. In a moment he jumped up and tore out of the house and down the hill, crying, "It's following me! It's following me!"

"Dionel, go bring in the sheep," Reina said. "Conrado is very sick."

When Dionel returned an hour later with the sheep, Conrado still had not come back to the house. When the family gathered for supper, the little ones said, "We saw him go across the river. He was going up the mountain."

Reynaldo's face was haggard. "Come, son," he said to Dionel. "We need to find him."

As they trudged together down the long, lonely trail, through the cornfield, across the river, and up the mountain of Panorama, Reynaldo was silent, inhaling long drags on his cigarette, lost in his own childhood memories of darkness and evil. From far up the mountain, a tortured scream sliced the air.

"Conrado! Conrado!" they called, but the only response was the distant screaming. As they climbed the last steep stretch to the spring, they heard sobs between the screams. Conrado lay sprawled, shaking, on the grass by the great rock. No one there knew that Conrado lay exactly where the witch doctor had stood thirty years before, the night death claimed Conrado's grandfather Bacilio.

"Conrado, come. It is too cold out here. Come home with us." Reynaldo bent over his son and pulled him to his feet. Calming down a little, Conrado allowed his father and brother to lead him back down the mountain, among giant ferns, beneath the soaring canopies of trees, through clearings with breathtaking glimpses of the valley below, golden in the sunset.

When they arrived at the house, Conrado collapsed onto his wheat straw mat. Dionel, too, went to bed, haunted by Conrado's strange struggle and longing to know what it all meant.

Early the next morning the crowing of a rooster rang through the dark. Conrado bolted upright in terror. Reina was already awake, watching with a sinking heart as he sprang from the bed, screaming, "He is after me! Can't you see? He is coming after me!"

Again Conrado sprinted out the door and down the hill, past the cornfield, across the river, away to the mountain of Panorama, as far as he could flee from La Laguna where he had encountered the awful presence that haunted him.

Seeing Dionel was also awake, Reina called to him. "Dionel, come with me. Conrado has gone again. He is burning with fever, and it's cold out there."

An hour later Reina and Dionel returned with Conrado, still wild-faced and glassy-eyed, between them. Once Conrado was settled on his mat, Reina sat down on the rumpled bed across the room from her suffering son. Cuddled next to her heart, little Juana's breath was warm and sweet. Sonia, tousled black hair framing her round face, was still asleep on the mat against the opposite wall.

What will happen to my family? Reina cried inwardly. *God, where are you?*

Conrado lay sick and confused for three long, trying weeks. At last his fever broke, and he led Reynaldo up the mountain to show him where he had seen a creature crouching, perched on the tip of a branch hanging low overhead. The creature was greenish-gray and hazy, he said, and when he had tried to run, it leaped onto his head.

When Reina heard the story, she remembered another day twenty years before—a green haze lurking over a mountain trail and a terrifying blindness. Who would deliver them from the evil stalking their family?

One evening several months later, Reina watched uneasily as the children crowded around the window, their eyes fixed on the road that crawled along the hill above them. *What could be keeping Reynaldo?* she wondered. *He should have been home hours ago.*

"I hope he brings a pineapple," Dionel said.

"I hope he brings mangoes," Eliza said. Her eyes shone.

"We sold lots of wheat. He'll bring pineapples and mangoes and bananas and grapefruit and . . ." Conrado expanded the possibilities.

Papa had gone to San Juan to collect the money for the sale of their harvest. This day was the highlight of the year for the children, and a blessed relief for the adults—the single day of each year when there was plenty of cash to buy what they needed, as well as a few special treats.

Five-year-old Aide lounged on the bed, leaning against Reina, who sat nursing baby Juana. "I want Papa to come home. Why isn't he home, Mama?"

"I don't know, honey. Maybe he will come soon. There is still one more bus tonight."

The sheep were brought in, the cow was milked, the chickens were fed, supper was eaten and cleared away; then there was nothing left to do but wait. Reina tried to pray. For the children's sake, she tried to be strong and act natural. When the last bus crept along the crest of the mountain, six sets of black eyes strained to follow its progress in the fading daylight, willing it to stop and let Papa out. The bus crawled heartlessly past the top of the trail.

Reina tried not to think. What good would it do? Why should she imagine the worst, anyway? Maybe Reynaldo had just finished his work in town late and was spending the night with his father.

It was getting dark. Reina watched the children turn from the window and settle down in their beds, disappointment shouting from their silence.

The crowing of the roosters woke Reina the next morning. What was this shadow that oppressed her mind? Awareness returned like a thunderbolt—Reynaldo had not returned. If only she could stay asleep. Or wake up and find that it had all been a dream, that Reynaldo was waking up next to her as on other mornings. Instead, she rose to face the day, waiting, as she moved mechanically from task to task, for the bad news she was sure would come.

A neighbor stopped by mid-morning to report that he had seen Reynaldo lying beside the road, drunk. Someone was bringing him home.

Reina's dread surrendered to cold knowledge. *Cusha*. The demon was back. What would happen to them all?

When the children came in from milking, Vicenta had tamales ready for breakfast, warm on the stones alongside a small pot of beans and a scanty pan of scrambled eggs. She divided the food among their plates as they perched on their stools in a ring around the fire. Reina looked into their trusting faces, wishing she could flee or rewrite reality.

From deep within her memory, a picture unfolded of four-year-old Eliza running barefoot, hair flying behind her, desperately clinging to a rope attached to a small black pig. As the little girl struggled for control of the pig, it careened into the edge of the cornfield, mowing down several plants with the rope. Catching sight of the accident, Reynaldo lunged at the little girl with his machete, beating her mercilessly with the flat side of the blade as she screamed in terror. Sobbing, she had fled the house and did not return home until the next morning. It had been the longest night Reina had ever known.

The past two years had been so different from those days. Reina had dared to hope that horror was behind them for good.

The children were chattering again. Surely Papa would come today.

"Children." Reina shrank from the sound of her own voice. "Your father didn't come home last night because he was drinking."

Conrado's face hardened, and tears glistened in the eyes of the younger children. Reina wondered why they didn't say something. If they would talk, she could answer and maybe soothe the awful disappointment and resignation in their eyes.

Juana's wail broke the silence, and Reina turned wearily to quiet her. What could she say to the children anyway when her own heart was wrenched, feeling in one moment like a cold lump of lead and in the next like a smoking volcano.

Even the children understood that the undelivered fruit was the least of their family's problems.

When Reina considered the load Reynaldo carried, struggling to provide for their growing family, she felt vaguely guilty about the chronic tension and fighting that had invaded their relationship.

She sighed. What could she do? She had been so hopeful that the Prince of Peace church would be the answer to their family's needs. But the long walks on Sunday mornings had proven to be anything but peaceful for Reina.

Another family had walked to church regularly with them—a family about their age, with the same number of children. It had soon become clear that Reynaldo was enjoying the company of the other woman more than that of his own family. Eventually he refused to walk with Reina at all, and for a while he walked to church alone. In the end they gave up attending altogether, and the other woman's husband moved with his wife and family to a distant town.

The strife that had flared between them during that time had only continued and intensified since. Conrado's rebellion and disrespect were a constant source of tension. But there remained in both Reynaldo and Reina a burning desire to know peace with God. Both knew the life they were pursuing was a dead end. Somewhere, surely, there must be more.

CHAPTER 15

The Mennonites

While the farmers around El Edén and Sibilia worked their hillside fields with wide *azadones,* planting corn for a fall harvest, another harvest was already ripening in those hills. On Saturday afternoon, February 15, 1980, Reina slipped into the semi-darkness of Benigno Calderón's sala and settled herself and baby Juana on sagging bedsprings. She leaned her shoulder against the adobe wall, feeling detached, weary, and mostly hopeless, glad for this quiet place at the end of the room where she could just watch the bustle and conversation—and think.

The gringo visitors introduced themselves to everyone, smiled, and jostled their babies. Reina noticed the quiet modesty of the ladies' long dresses, and she wondered at the absence of the lace, ruffles, and fancy stitches the Guatemalan people loved so much. The ladies wore their long hair pulled back into buns, covered with pleated white caps; curious, yet attractive. The men, their short hair combed crisply, wore dull-colored, long-sleeved shirts under dark suit coats. Weren't all foreigners wealthy? These people's dress was certainly fine enough, but also simple, and they wore no jewelry.

A round-faced young mother with a baby in her arms sat down on the bed opposite Reina. The smile she flashed at Reina radiated peace and joy.

"Good afternoon. I am Esther, Leland's wife. You sure have a sweet little girl there." Esther smiled at Juana on Reina's lap.

Mennonites, Amalia had called them. They had built a meetinghouse and a schoolhouse out at La Cumbre, not far from Reynaldo's father's house. They were spreading some radical teaching about following Jesus. They taught that the Scriptures were meant to be lived, and that God wants us to be holy—and Amalia's aunt declared that they actually lived what they taught.

Reina had been glad when Juan and Amalia had invited her to this meeting at Benigno and Valeriana's house. The invitation had felt like a lifeline at the time, but now that she was here, it seemed the world of these gringos had little to do with hers.

Leland Seibel, scarcely more than a boy and just as lively, stepped into the open doorway facing the room. Sunlight glinted off his thinning blond hair. He opened his hymnbook.

Benigno, small, dark, leathery, and much older, stood beside him. "Everyone, please be seated," Benigno said, "and Brother Leland will lead us in singing."

The rub of chair legs on hard earth, the creak of bedsprings, and the squawk of a hen tossed through the doorway by a boy's bare foot blended into a general shuffling and jostling. Rough boards supported by short sections of log filled out the seating for the little crowd.

A tall, confident young woman with dark hair settled next to Reina, extending her hand. "Hi, I'm Nancy. May I sit beside you?"

Reina smiled timidly at Nancy. "You are welcome to. I'm pleased to meet you."

Benigno sat down. Leland burst into the opening line of song, and voices from all over the room joined in. Reina closed her eyes and listened. The purity and simplicity of the four-part harmony, the majesty of the music-soaked message pulsing between the adobe walls of the crowded sala—it almost hurt as it bathed her tired spirit. She wished they would never stop.

After the singing, another man read a passage from the Bible. Then a third stood and preached. Frank Martin explained that these Holy Scriptures reveal

The Mennonites

Christ to us. He said they show the way Christians should glorify God in their work, recreation, dress, speech, and relationships.

Reina missed the next part as Esther, the young mother across from her, lifted her cute baby girl, revealing an unhandy golden spot on the blanket on her lap. Esther glanced around the room, and Reina saw her dilemma. If Esther could high-jump over the maze of makeshift benches, she would still need to crowd past Frank, whose frame filled the doorway as he preached.

The baby girl was crying. The young mother glanced at the open window above her, then whispered to the one called Nancy, handing her the baby. With a twinkle in her eye, Esther scrambled onto the bed and hoisted herself through the window, her pretty skirt dusting the sill as she disappeared. Nancy thrust the baby out into Esther's uplifted hands.

Smiling with the other women, Reina turned her attention back to Frank.

Some of the teaching they heard that day was familiar to these devout evangelicals. They were already convinced that the Bible teaches a woman to dress like a woman and a man like a man. They agreed that Christians should not be consumed with competitive sports. Some of the teaching, however, was brand new.

At the end of the meeting, Benigno Calderón, Juan Lopez, and Juan's brother-in-law, Rigoberto Ochoa, gathered around the men from La Cumbre. They pored over the Scriptures while Frank Martin and Leland Seibel, their Bibles open on their laps, patiently discussed the answers to their many questions.

After setting Juana down to play with the other little ones under the supervision of the older girls, Reina joined the women. She served *atole*[1] to the men, keeping one ear open to the conversation surging among the emptying glasses.

Reina heard many new things that day, most emphasizing one awesome truth: God requires holy lives of His people. The men explained that when a person's mind is renewed in Christ, he will not love or value the things the

---

[1] A sweet drink made of ground corn or rice with milk and cinnamon.

world loves and values. They explained that Christians love not only their neighbors, but also their enemies; that Christians bless those who curse them, and that because of this higher law, Christians never use force against others, not even in war or self-defense.

The apostle John, Leland explained, had written that those who say they love God but don't obey what He says are liars. Hearing these plain teachings from the Scriptures, some of the listeners wondered whether they had ever truly been followers of Christ at all. They all believed in Jesus for salvation, but these gringos insisted that God requires much more than mere belief.

When it was time to leave, the visitors promised to return in two weeks to teach them more.

Reina's heart thirsted like the deer for streams of water. She knew too well what physical hunger and thirst felt like, but this hunger was more consuming than any physical hunger she had known.

Reynaldo, too, was thirsty for truth and hope. Reina wished he could have been with her to hear these life-giving words, but he was spending a few days helping his father prepare for planting, and doing whatever else he and his father did together. Was there yet hope for their torn little family?

Vicenta was at home with the rest of the children. She thought Reina was crazy for going to listen to the teachings of these strangers. Vicenta still could not understand why her daughter was not satisfied with Catholicism.

Somewhere deep inside, Reina still sang her prayer song: "My God, my God, come closer to me." The prayer of the little shepherdess on the mountain had become the yearning cry of the brokenhearted wife.

CHAPTER 16

The Decision

The La Cumbre meetinghouse was packed that Sunday morning. The heat of the crowd assisted the wood stove in warming the room against the cold wind rattling the corrugated metal siding.

Reina snugged her shawl around her shoulders, looking through the window across the bleak March landscape. Her father-in-law's house was down in that mist-shrouded valley, a house of darkness, candles, images, and incantation—the house where Reynaldo had stayed last night. She shuddered. What a contrast to the hope, warmth, and harmony surging around her in this place!

Reynaldo had promised to be at church this morning. How she hoped he would get here soon!

The young man leading the singing sat down, and a man she had never seen rose and stood behind the pulpit. She thought he must be Carl Sensenig, a preacher and mission board member from Pennsylvania. Yesterday at their bi-weekly cottage meeting in El Edén, Frank and Leland had announced that he would be here, and they had encouraged everyone to come out to La Cumbre this morning.

Now Carl began speaking in English, and Frank Martin listened intently, translating everything into Spanish: "There are seven things every man will do sometime in his life," Frank translated. "If you choose to do them now, you will receive the gift of salvation. If you wait, you will indeed do these seven things, but you will be brought under condemnation."

"Jesus calls today," Brother Carl said. " 'Come unto me, all ye that labour and are heavy laden, and I will give you rest.' "[1]

Rest. Everything in Reina ached for it. Rest from the confusion, contention, and condemnation. Laboring and heavy laden—that described her and Reynaldo.

"If you refuse this tender call of Jesus now," Carl continued, " 'the hour is coming, and now is, when the dead shall hear the voice of the Son of God.'[2] That call is the solemn call to the judgment seat of God. That call is no longer a call to rest; it is a call to judgment. Dear friends, someday you will answer Jesus' call. Why not answer today?"

Just down the bench from Reina, a baby stiffened on its mother's lap, letting out a loud wail. Patiently the mother bent its small body back into a sitting position and whispered in the little ear. The baby relaxed.

"Secondly, sooner or later you will call on God for mercy. 'Seek ye the Lord while he may be found, call ye upon him while he is near.'[3] This is God's call to you today. God is listening, alert to your call for mercy; ready and longing to respond and pour out that mercy on you; ready to forgive and save. But the time is coming when men will call for mercy, and God will turn away from their call. 'Because I have called, and ye refused,' God says, 'I have stretched out my hand, and no man regarded . . . . Then shall they call upon me, but I will not answer; they shall seek me early, but they shall not find me.'[4] Dear friends, sooner or later you *will* call on God for mercy. Do it now."

Lord Jesus, have mercy on me and my family, Reina cried in her soul, ignoring

---

[1] Matthew 11:28
[2] John 5:25
[3] Isaiah 55:6
[4] Proverbs 1:24, 28

the fussy baby down the bench.

"Third, someday every man will confess that Jesus Christ is Lord. If you confess with your mouth today that He is Lord and believe in your heart that God raised Him from the dead, you will be saved."

Saved. Saved from sin. Reina knew too much of the slavery of sin. Oh, to be saved from sin—from the emptiness and futility of the life she and Reynaldo were living.

"The Scriptures declare that someday even those who reject Jesus now will bow their knees, and every tongue will declare that Jesus Christ is Lord." Brother Carl leaned forward, his eyes seeming to pierce right through Reina. "Confess that He is Lord today—and be saved."

Jesus, I know that you are Lord. I guess I have always known it. I just didn't understand what it meant to let you really be the Lord of my whole life. Her thoughts blended into the fourth of the seven points, as Brother Carl explained that sooner or later all men will forsake their sin. That was the part she and Reynaldo had never really understood until these people came. These Christians not only told them what it meant to forsake sin—they demonstrated it.

What would it be to truly have Jesus as Lord, to have sin no longer reigning in one's life? Reina couldn't help noticing the parallel between her own life and the fretting of that willful baby.

"The fifth thing that will happen someday is that your sins will be brought to judgment. If you confess and forsake your sins now, there is mercy and forgiveness. If you wait, you only store up 'wrath against the day of wrath';[5] against the day when God's righteous judgments will be revealed, the day of eternal separation from God for those whose sins are unforgiven. Confess and repent, and let your sins go before you now to be judged at the mercy seat."

Reina adjusted her position to allow the young mother with the fretful baby to exit the bench, steering a reluctant toddler toward her husband on the men's side. The husband smiled up at her and lifted the diverted toddler

---

[5] Romans 2:5

to the bench beside him as the mother and baby continued to the back of the room. Out of the corner of her eye, Reina saw Reynaldo in the back, leaning against the wall. Good!

"Jesus says, 'If any man will come after me, let him deny himself, and take up his cross, and follow me. For whosoever will save his life shall lose it: and whosoever will lose his life for my sake shall find it. For what is a man profited, if he shall gain the whole world, and lose his own soul? Or what shall a man give in exchange for his soul?'[6]

"There is no question of keeping the things we try to hold onto in life: friends, possessions, ungodly entertainment, lusts of the flesh. This is the sixth thing you will certainly do: you will give up these carnal things. Either give them up voluntarily now, follow Jesus, and know His peace and wholeness, or they will be taken from you in the end anyway, at a terrible price."

What would this mean for Reina, Reynaldo, and their family? She could hardly wait until she had a chance to talk with him about it. She managed another quick look back; he seemed to be absorbed in the message.

Reina wished Vicenta could hear the message, but she could not be persuaded to come. Besides, who would have stayed with the children? Reina had walked two and a half hours with the others from El Edén to get out here this morning.

The preacher was moving on to his seventh point.

"Finally, although we don't like to think about it, we all must suffer. The apostle Paul writes, 'All that will live godly in Christ Jesus shall suffer persecution.'[7] No Christian can wholly escape persecution from the people of this world. Jesus was rejected and persecuted while He was on earth, and He said that if this world hated Him, it would hate His followers. The disciple is not greater than his Master.

"Jesus promises that 'if we suffer, we shall also reign with him.'[8] However,

---

[6] Matthew 16:24–26

[7] 2 Timothy 3:12

[8] 2 Timothy 2:12

The Decision

if we try to avoid this temporary suffering, the Scriptures say we will someday suffer 'the vengeance of eternal fire.'[9] Will you suffer ridicule, misunderstandings, even persecution at the hands of the world now, or will you suffer under the judgment of Almighty God later? It will be one or the other.

" 'I have set before you life and death, blessing and cursing: therefore choose life, that both thou and thy seed may live.' "[10]

Brother Carl called for a song. "If you want to say yes to Jesus, yes to eternal life, stand to your feet as we sing. If you are ready to answer Jesus' call; ready to forsake your sin; ready to deny yourself, take up your cross, and follow Him; ready to send your sins ahead to the mercy seat rather than wait until you no longer have the choice, you may stand. Someone will pray with you afterward."

The congregation began to sing softly, a song of invitation to follow Jesus. Toward the back on the men's side of the meetinghouse, Benigno rose to his feet, and Valeriana quickly stood beside him. Near her, Amalia's sister-in-law Julia stood too. It occurred to Reina that she wouldn't know if Reynaldo stood, for he was already standing in the back.

She didn't want to stand alone, but nothing had ever drawn her like this before. This church was what her family needed, she was sure, but she wanted this decision to be something she and Reynaldo chose together.

Her heart thumping in her chest, Reina stood, slipping down the side aisle to the back and approaching Reynaldo, who stood with his head bowed. She touched his arm and he looked at her. She saw in his eyes that he wanted to respond to the call. But Reynaldo was not an impulsive man. He needed more time to think it through. He didn't want to make a commitment in a moment of emotion.

When instruction classes began at Rigoberto's house in early April, Reynaldo and Reina were there. *It is exactly as it ought to be,* Reina thought, looking around the room at the small group of neighbors and relatives

---

[9] Jude 1:7
[10] Deuteronomy 30:19

Juan and Amalia Lopez with daughter Roselinda in 2013.

gathered there with their children. Dionel and Eliza were there too, their young faces eager to learn.

Leland stood in the doorway, his Bible open. In the courtyard behind him, a huge bougainvillea bloomed in a riot of purple, and chickens scratched and strutted.

"How many of you have Bibles to follow along as we read?" he asked.

Juan Lopez held up his Bible. Its cover was missing, and its pages were brown and dog-eared. In memory Reina saw that same Bible, much newer, resting on his lap as he sat on a block of wood at their house, reading to her and her mother.

On the chair beside Leland, towering tall and tantalizing, Reina saw a stack of brand new Bibles. She tried not to hope prematurely. Besides the New Testament given to her as a child in the Presbyterian church, Juan's Bible was the only one that had ever been in her house. Now, as Leland laid his own Bible on the table and turned to pick up the stack of new ones, everyone's eyes lit with anticipation.

"Here. Each of you take one. They are yours to keep." There were nine

Bibles, one for each person in the instruction class. Reina fought to keep from crying as she took the precious book from Brother Leland. Could it be true? She saw Reynaldo reach out eagerly, a look of reverent wonder in his eyes.

The rest of that April meeting was charged with hope, joy, and anticipation for what God was doing in these hills and all it could mean for their families.

After the Bible study, as the women bustled about ensuring that everyone was fed well, Frank waved the flies from the chicken sauce on his plate and looked around. "There are many children in your families. We will want to have a school ready for them to attend, maybe by October." Frank said it as if it were all in a day's work, building schools or shooing flies. It had to be done, so they would do it.

That afternoon as they walked home carrying their precious Bibles and discussing all they had heard, Reynaldo and Reina cherished the closeness they felt to each other and to their children. Conrado, Dionel, and Eliza were excited about the hope of going to school. It was all they could talk about on that long walk home. They had attended the government school on top of the hill intermittently, but none of them read well. The parents listened to their happy chatter and smiled. In their wildest dreams, they had never imagined having a Christian school for their children to attend.

"I heard the men say they will be looking for land for a church and a school," Reynaldo said to Reina. "Shall we give them some of ours? Your mother already gave us your share of land. What do you think?"

"Oh, Reynaldo, there is nothing I would rather do. Imagine having a church and a school right next door." Reina had already been thinking the same thing, and her eyes filled with tears to think God had put the same dream in each of their hearts. "I would love to give something real to God, after all the time and energy we've wasted on ourselves," she said.

Thunderheads were piling up in the west, sunlight gleaming gold along their ruffled edges. Two sheep left their grazing, skittering from the roadside in a blur of spindly legs. Reina felt the unfamiliar weight in the woven bag slung from her shoulder and caressed the hard outline of the Bible inside—hers. Just now, she didn't trust herself to say more.

CHAPTER 17

The Baptism

The sun was low above the mountains the next day when Reina found a chance to sit down alone with her Bible. Settling down on the bench outside her door, she opened it carefully, smiling at the crackle of new pages parting. She skimmed the introductory pages until she came to Genesis, where she began reading: "In the beginning God created the heaven and the earth."[1]

Really, God?

In the majesty of that simple declaration, a lifetime of fog lifted from her heart and cleared from her eyes. She raised her eyes far up to the darkening blue above the mountain, where sunset-tinted clouds thickened near the horizon. *God made the heavens!*

Her eyes swept down across the trees, so thick and soft in the distance that she imagined she could walk barefoot over their crowns.

God made the earth!

Reina read on. God had made everything. Everything! He just spoke, and it was. She paused. Scrubby yucca bristled at one corner of the house, sharp

---

[1] Genesis 1:1

shafts tipped with brown. Yucca was God's idea. Every shrub, every tree, every blade of grass—everywhere she looked, La Laguna was filled with His thoughts, His provision, His power. A jay shrilled at the edge of the woods, and a cow lowed. A large hairy spider lifted dainty legs, marching across the hard dirt at her feet. Reina laughed. God had made it all! What would Mama say when she told her?

Reina read until the words blurred in the dark, then closed the book with a sigh. Yes, God had made everything that moved or grew—everything that existed. She could hardly wait to read more tomorrow.

Living and moving for the first time in the wonder of knowing God made her, Reina found everything took on new meaning. The God of light was her own Creator. The Scriptures became her daily bread, and she feasted whenever she found a spare minute. As she read, she understood more and more of His holiness and His will for His people. For the first time, she understood that she sinned against Him every time her temper flared, every time she yelled at Reynaldo or the children, every time she entertained a hateful thought about Carlos.

Reynaldo also read and grew. Peace such as they had never known filled the little house against the mountain.

A few weeks after the distribution of the Bibles, everyone gathered again in Rigoberto's sala. Ben Eshbach, an overseer from Pennsylvania, was here this morning. He stood against the wall, where sunlight streamed through a small window.

A small brown pet monkey crept through the open doorway and picked his way along the wall, approaching the preacher respectfully. He wrapped his thin arms around Ben's leg and peered up at him solemnly with round black eyes. The children giggled. Ben continued his sermon, seeming not to notice the interruption, but only the monkey was listening now. Grins split every face in the crowd as the hilarious visitor toyed with Ben's pants and shoelaces.

As Ben preached on, unruffled, the monkey grew bored and settled down for a nap on the soft leather Bible cover on the floor at the preacher's feet.

The Baptism

Only then did the human congregants turn their attention back to the well-planned sermon.

"Marriage is a lifelong covenant between one man and one woman, and God himself witnesses that covenant," Ben Eshbach explained as he finished reading Malachi 2:14–16.

When the meeting was over, Chabela, Rigoberto's wife, directed the women in the kitchen as they prepared the meal. The children skipped into the courtyard to play with the neighbor's monkey, and the men launched into a lively discussion about what they had heard.

Sitting quietly at one side of the circle of chairs, Benigno adjusted his glasses and went over and over the passages Ben had read, following the lines with his finger. For a while the other men's discussion and the children's background laughter swirled around him unnoticed. Finally he looked up. "I never married my wife. We never made a covenant with each other. We have no legal document either."

His neighbors sat around the room, stunned at the implication of what he was saying. They all knew Benigno Calderón as a godly man. Benigno and Valeriana had begun living together when they were young. Together they were raising a family of rambunctious boys and one saucy-eyed little girl. Yet they had made no covenant. Were they living in fornication?

"Do you have another wife living?" Brother Ben asked.

"No, there's never been anyone but Valeriana," Benigno said.

"And was she ever married to another man?"

"No, no, it was always just us."

"Do you love Valeriana?" Ben asked next.

"Oh, yes," Benigno replied, glancing fondly toward the kitchen, then dropping his eyes to the floor in confusion.

Brother Ben's eyes twinkled. "Is there anything to keep you from making the covenant today?"

Benigno's face relaxed into a broad smile. "Could we?"

The preachers consulted for a moment and then sent one of the children to call Valeriana from the kitchen.

SONG OF THE SHEPHERDESS

"What have I done now?" Valeriana laughed, putting down her stirring spoon and wiping her hands on her apron.

After talking awhile to Benigno and Valeriana, the preachers sent a child to call the rest of the women to the wedding.

Benigno and Valeriana stood beaming before a brilliant backdrop of Chabela's orange geraniums. Valeriana smoothed her apron—she was a bride, after all, though the thought made her giggle a bit—as Brother Ben pulled a slender black book from the back of his zippered Bible cover and opened it to the marriage vows. "Do you, Benigno, take Valeriana, this sister by your side, to be your wife . . . ?"

The humor of the scene gave place to a holy hush, interrupted only by the droning of Brother Ben's voice and the crunch of a hen snatching a cricket from the crusty earth. All the couples had time to ponder the promises, considering their own commitments.

"I have decided to follow Jesus." The courtyard rang with the voices of men, women, and children. Reina looked lovingly at her little ones, then at Reynaldo, and knew that there would be no turning back for her family. They would do whatever it took to be real followers of Jesus—to do whatever He said.

It was another mile marker for the little band of believers.

Later in the afternoon, over bowls of chicken, rice, and tomato sauce, the men discussed the need for more teaching and oversight. Benigno, Juan, Rigoberto, and Reynaldo all felt they needed more than just one meeting every two weeks.

"Maybe we should come in here and haul you all out to La Cumbre each Sunday," Leland said. "That may require fewer people and less time than conducting a separate meeting here each Sunday."

"We're stretched pretty thin right now," Frank added, "but God will provide what we need. We'll figure out some way to help."

After some discussion, everyone concluded that La Cumbre was too far to walk regularly for church meetings. They wanted a church right in El Edén or at La Laguna.

The Baptism

Reynaldo said, "We have land, brothers, and we want to give it to God for a meetinghouse and a school." Over the laughter of the children—the neighbor's monkey was springing from shoulder to shoulder—Reina strained to hear what the men would say about Reynaldo's offer.

"God bless you, brother," Leland said, smiling at Reynaldo.

"Your land would be well located for Benigno's family, and just around the corner from Juan's," someone observed.

"But the road! There is really no way to drive in there."

"In the rainy season it would be impossible."

"The shortest way in is too steep even for a horse."

"It might be better to stay out here closer to El Edén and Palestina, where more people are."

"Well, brothers," said Leland, "we all need to pray about it. Reynaldo has offered his land. It may not be the best suited for the need, but we will consider it."

The discussion concluded with a compromise for now: the four couples from El Edén and La Laguna would continue walking the two and a half hours to La Cumbre on Sunday mornings, and then one of the preachers from La Cumbre or La Victoria would come each Sunday afternoon to hold Sunday school in the Ochoa home in El Edén.

In May, Chabela directed the Ochoa boys in moving the beds out of their sala into a little outbuilding. The sala became a meeting room for the new church. The first Sunday meeting there was on May 15, 1980.

For the next few months, a group from El Edén gathered in the dark each Sunday morning to walk the two and a half hours to La Cumbre. The group included the families of Juan and Amalia, Benigno and Valeriana, Reynaldo and Reynalda, and Rigoberto and Chabela.

Chabela had to get her brood up much earlier than the rest to do the chores and clean and prepare for the local afternoon meeting, since there would be no time when they returned from La Cumbre.

Older family members took turns staying with the children too little to walk all the way to La Cumbre. For the oldest children and the parents,

Rigoberto and Chabelo Ochoa in 2013, standing in the courtyard where the early church services were held.

those long walks were times of glorious oneness and shared hope in Christ.

When the morning meeting was over, they all gathered behind Larry Weaver's house. There they ate their noon meal in a hurry before piling into a couple of the mission vehicles. Two or more of the families from La Cumbre and San Juan would drive them back to El Edén for the four o'clock meeting in Rigoberto's sala.

In September of 1980, in Rigoberto's courtyard, Reynaldo and Reina were baptized into Christ, along with the others at El Edén who had committed themselves to follow Jesus.

After much discussion, the fledgling church decided that Reynaldo's land at La Laguna was too remote and inaccessible for regular meetings. They purchased land near El Edén, not far from Rigoberto's home. The newly purchased land already had a couple of small buildings that could be used for schoolrooms.

The Baptism

The Mennonite congregation at El Edén in 1981.

On the hill above the planned school, men and boys fought rain and mud to finish a house for the teacher. The house was finished in January 1981, and Carl Martin and his family moved into it just before school began in February. That same February, the church began regular Sunday morning meetings in the schoolrooms in El Edén, and the long Sunday walks were over.

CHAPTER 18

Reynaldo Goes Missing

Guatemala's most valuable natural resource is its fertile farmland, vast tracts of which are held, not by Guatemalans, but by American fruit corporations. In the 1970s and 80s, leftist guerrilla forces were engaged in a fierce civil war with a series of corrupt and brutal military dictatorships. Their goal was to return more control of the government and land to the impoverished and often landless indigenous people of Guatemala.

In January 1981, the same month the teacher's house was completed at El Edén, Ronald Reagan took office as President of the United States. Within the next couple of years, President Reagan would reverse President Carter's ban on support to Guatemala's brutally repressive military government, and would supply the death squads of General Rios Montt with combat training and millions of dollars' worth of jeeps, trucks, and helicopter parts.[1]

A guerrilla offensive in early 1981 was repulsed by a fierce Guatemalan army counteroffensive, forcing the guerrillas into mountain camps where they ran short on supplies. At night the guerrillas ventured into mountain

---

[1] Bernard Gwertzman, "U.S. Lifts Embargo on Military Sales to Guatemalans," *The New York Times*, January 8, 1983, <http://www.nytimes.com/1983/01/08/world/us-lifts-embargo-on-military-sales-to-guatemalans.html>, accessed on January 23, 2017.

villages to beg for food. If villagers resisted, fearing reprisals from the army, the guerrillas often took what they needed at gunpoint. Frequently, when word of such an encounter did reach the army, they would raid the village the next day. Anyone the army believed to have assisted the guerrillas, voluntarily or otherwise, would be shot without trial.

While Reina and her family rejoiced in a new church and school, rumors of kidnappings and killings seeped in from the mountains around. One day an army helicopter full of soldiers landed between the church house and schoolhouse in La Victoria. While some of the soldiers blocked the roads out of the area, others went from house to house, assembling the entire La Victoria community on the main road. Then the soldiers ushered three masked men from the helicopter. These masked men went silently through the crowd, pointing to individuals whom the soldiers then arrested.

About a year earlier, after the land for the church house was purchased, a group of locals had requested a couple of meetings with the local missionaries to share their concerns that the gringos were paying prices far above the local rate, causing land prices to climb out of reach for local farmers. The locals had presented a contract, which the missionaries signed, agreeing not to purchase any more land in the area for ten years.

When the helicopter arrived in La Victoria, many of those arrested were people who had been involved in those earlier land meetings. It seemed these peaceful neighbors had been representatives of a guerrilla faction, now betrayed by fellow townsmen whom the army had previously arrested for guerrilla involvement. Most of the men the army took that day were never heard from again.

It was a long, lonely walk from La Laguna to La Cumbre, where Reynaldo had gone to collect cash for his wheat crop. Reina expected him back on Wednesday, but Thursday and Friday passed with no word of him. On

Reynaldo Goes Missing

Saturday afternoon, she and Vicenta hiked over the hills to discuss the matter with Carl Martin.

Reina thought she had never felt as close to her mother as she did today. She thought back to the evening a few months before when Leland and Esther had visited for a long time with Vicenta. As they shared with Vicenta the Biblical picture of a life in the Spirit, she had acknowledged that it did not match the fruit of her life. She was living for Vicenta, not for Jesus. Vicenta had humbly repented and surrendered her life to Jesus' lordship.

"I'm so glad you are with me, Mama," Reina said.

Despite her concern over Reynaldo, Vicenta's eyes shone when she looked at Reina. "Only one week until my baptism. Oh, Reina, for so long I did not understand. But God has forgiven me. I am truly a new creation in Christ."

They walked up the lane and knocked on the school teacher's door.

Carl's forehead creased. "You say you were expecting him home Wednesday already?"

"That's right. We didn't worry at first. Sometimes he doesn't come back from his father's place until the next day," Reina explained. "But with so many people disappearing—we just never know."

"Yes, I understand your concern," Carl said.

Reina heard the radio crackling to life in Carl's office. "I'm sure it's Larry," Carl said. "I was expecting the call. I'll tell him about this." He disappeared through the doorway.

Reina felt hope. Larry lived just up the hill from Reynaldo's father's house. Maybe Larry knew something.

While the men chatted on the radio, Carl's wife Irene invited the two women into her cool, spacious kitchen for sweet coffee. The setting was pleasant, but the minutes ticked by slowly for Reina.

Carl soon returned. "I told Larry about Reynaldo. He's going down to Chano's house this afternoon to see if he can find out anything. If we hear any news, we'll send someone to your house right away. In the meantime, let's pray."

A measure of peace entered Reina as Carl led them in prayer: "Father, you know exactly where Reynaldo is and what he is facing. Be right there with him, and let him know that you are there. Protect him, and let us soon hear a good report about him."

Irene hugged Vicenta and Reina before they headed back down the steep lane. Fog hung in the valleys. Behind the mountains to the northwest, the Tajumulco volcano rose startlingly sharp and clear, its outline an indefinable comfort.

" 'I will lift up mine eyes unto the hills,' " Vicenta murmured.

Reina knew God's power to handle this crisis was infinitely greater than the power that ripped open the earth untold ages ago—the heat and pressure that set Tajumulco in place. But everything felt shaky inside and around her.

When Vicenta and Reina finally broke out of the woods into their own high canyon, the first thing they saw was Reynaldo, working his way along a terrace as he chopped the earth in preparation for planting. Behind him swarmed a troop of children, poking holes in the newly prepared earth and dropping in seeds, while behind them, Dionel raked the rich black earth back into the holes.

Reina felt a flood of relief, then a flash of anger. Where had he been?

Forget it. The children will be hungry.

Reina stepped over two hens who followed her into the kitchen. She blew the fire to life, added a few more sticks of wood, and shoved a pot of beans over the flame. It had been three weeks since they had last eaten meat. She dug into a burlap bag on the floor near the door and tossed the hens a couple handfuls of cracked corn. The chickens attacked the corn with a chorus of bickering.

Settling herself on a low stool where she could keep an eye on the beans, Reina picked up Juana and held her, resting a hot cheek against Juana's fuzzy hair. Reynaldo would soon be in. Then she would find out where he had been. Did she want to know? A familiar sickness that had nothing to do with her advanced pregnancy kept grabbing at her insides, making her feel breathless and weak. *God, I don't want to mistrust him. I just wish I didn't have to know.*

Reina's mother came in with a jar of water on her head, followed by Eliza

Reynaldo Goes Missing

carrying a pail of foaming milk. Both of them, the seventy-year-old grandmother and the nine-year-old granddaughter, straight and supple, walked with quick, sure steps. Despite the weariness of her body and soul, Reina felt a surge of affection for these strong women who shared her life. Why did she feel so deeply tired tonight?

When Reynaldo came in, he smiled at the children and hugged Aide. He tossed four-year-old Sonia into the air and caught her again before landing her on her little stool by the fire.

Surely Reina had been imagining things; everything was fine. But she didn't feel any better. Was he avoiding her eyes?

"Where have you been?" Reina blurted. It must have sounded harsh. She knew it was no way to make his heart warm toward her, but she was so tired, so afraid.

"I'll tell you the whole story after we pray," he said.

Grandma dished the last spoonful of beans into the last tin plate and sat down on the only empty stool in the little circle. They bowed their heads over their bowls of beans, and Reynaldo prayed a short blessing.

Reina knew she couldn't eat until he told his story. She couldn't shake the conviction that his merry mood seemed contrived. The children dug into their beans.

"I was coming home Wednesday afternoon," Reynaldo said at last, "and I had fifty quetzales[2] in my pocket from the lumber I sold and for a little work I did for my dad. I was planning to stop at the market in Palestina and pick up a bag of corn and other things we needed."

Clucking hens and scraping spoons filled the awkward pause. Then Reynaldo went on. "I was only a little ways out of La Cumbre when two men jumped out from behind some bushes and grabbed me. I don't think I had ever seen the men before, but they had rags tied over their faces, so I couldn't be sure." He balanced his plate on his knees and brought his forefingers together between his eyes, drawing them away from each other

---

[2] Basic unit of currency in Guatemala.

across the tops of his cheeks. "Just their eyes were peeking out." The little ones looked up at him, their faces serious.

Reina strained to see Reynaldo's eyes through the smoke haze in the kitchen. Maybe if she could see his eyes, she would know.

Vicenta seemed taken with his story. Oh, how Reina wanted to believe him.

"Did they hurt you? Is that why you didn't come home?" It was one of the little ones who asked, and it was just as well; Reina knew she couldn't have asked so trustingly.

"I wasn't really hurt, just shaken up pretty good. I started walking toward home, but I just couldn't do it. I kept looking around, all tensed up. I was scared they'd come back. I had just passed my cousin's house, so I finally gave up and went back. I thought by today it would be safe to come home."

Part of Reina felt relieved; the story could be true. Whether or not it was true, it was what he said happened. It would give her something to say when the church people asked tomorrow.

An uneasy tension charged the air all evening. It wore at Reina. Maybe nobody else felt it, but Reina figured that Conrado and Dionel, at least, suspected they weren't being told everything.

Vicenta was at peace, but she would believe a skunk didn't stink if it looked innocent. It wasn't that she wasn't smart; she was smarter than most. But since she had become a believer, she didn't seem to have room in her heart for suspicion or condemnation.

On Sunday morning Reina's head hurt. She hadn't slept well the past several nights while Reynaldo was gone, and having him home hadn't helped much. Her emotions felt like a cork bobbing on the end of a snagged fishing line, swept helplessly from warm tenderness to angry suspicion to cold denial and back. There seemed to be no safe, steady way to think about it all.

As Vicenta and the children finished the chores and prepared to leave for church, Reynaldo announced that he was staying home. "I don't feel like going," he said. "I guess I'm scared to face everyone."

Reina stayed behind with him. When the children's chatter faded into the woods, leaving only the sounds of wind and sheep and birds, Reina asked him, "Is that really what happened, Reynaldo?"

He didn't answer—didn't even look at her—but headed out, leaving her alone to pray and think and cry.

In the schoolhouse across the mountain, the congregation stood for the benediction. Brother Leland prayed, " 'Now unto him that is able to keep you from falling, and to present you faultless before the presence of his glory with exceeding joy, to the only wise God our Saviour, be glory and majesty, dominion and power, both now and ever. Amen.' "[3]

As soon as the prayer was finished, Irene turned to Vicenta. "Have you heard anything from Reynaldo?"

"Oh, yes, he was home when we returned last evening. Two men jumped him and took his money when he was coming home on Wednesday. He was afraid to come the rest of the way, so he stayed at his cousin's house for a couple of days."

"Oh, I'm so sorry about the robbery, but I'm relieved that he is safe. Carl will be wanting to know." Irene moved toward the men's side of the meetinghouse, where Carl was already making his way toward her. "He's home," Irene explained. "He was robbed and stayed out there a couple of days because he was afraid to come home right away."

One of the men standing nearby raised his eyebrows. "If it is Reynaldo you are talking about, my brother saw him at the fiesta in Palestina, drunk."

The light in Dionel and Eliza's eyes went out. Irene looked on in motherly concern. Vicenta's brow puckered as the men launched into a lively discussion of who had seen Reynaldo, and when, and where.

Leland interrupted, "Men, you are speaking about our own brother. We have only the second-hand testimony of one supposed witness. We should be slow even to *believe* such a report, and even slower to repeat it." His voice was pleading. "If you love your brother, pray for him. If you think this story is true, go see him. Love him enough to ask him about it. If it turns out to be true, encourage and admonish him in the Lord."

---

[3] Jude 1:24–25

SONG OF THE SHEPHERDESS

That afternoon when Carl and Leland reigned their horses to a stop in the front yard of Reynaldo's house, he walked slowly in from the field to meet them. If Reina had harbored any faith in her husband's story before, it evaporated as Reynaldo sat down with the brothers. He looked like a tired little boy. Her heart went out to him.

Small talk seemed too small, and Leland wasted no time getting to the point. "Brother," he said gently, "there has been an evil report of you. I refuse to believe it. I have come to hear from you whether it is true. Someone said they saw you at the fiesta in Palestina last week. They said you were drunk."

Pain and shame etched Reynaldo's face. Staring at his lap, he muttered, "It is true. Yes, I was drinking." He sat quiet for a while. "I am sorry, so sorry. I know I sinned against God, against the church, and against my family."

"Do you want to tell us what happened? Did you make up the story about the robbery?" Leland asked.

"No. The robbery really happened," Reynaldo said. "That happened first. Then when I was at my cousin's house, he gave me *cusha* to drink. I didn't have any money left."

Reina picked up Juana from the floor and moved into the kitchen, out of earshot of the men. She had felt compassion for Reynaldo—he had looked so beaten and sad—but now she wondered. Was he still lying? Was she being unfair to mistrust him? He had admitted to the drinking, but what about that robbery? Would she ever be able to trust him completely again?

The next Sunday, Vicenta was baptized. Reina had prayed and dreamed of this day for years, and her mother was overjoyed, but for Reina the day was clouded by the heavy shadow of Reynaldo's failure and her own worries about their growing debt. After his fall into drunkenness, Reynaldo was removed from the church fellowship until he would prove himself faithful.

Over the next four months, Reynaldo stuck to his work, sometimes at his dad's place, sometimes at home, but still there was never enough money. Leland regularly rode his horse over the steep trails to Reynaldo's home, bringing food, school clothes, and encouragement. The loving and generous spirits of Carl Martin and Leland Seibel and their wives felt like Reina's only safe place during those hard days, and she often told others of her gratitude toward these families.

As time passed, Reina felt increasing tension in her conversations with other Guatemalan women, whether she met them at church or around the neighborhood. She suspected it had something to do with the gringos' gifts, but how could she hide them, especially the clothes? Worn or on the line, they were their own herald.

CHAPTER 19

Attack at the Mill

After Reynaldo's fall into drunkenness in March, things were never again the same with the other church families. Despite all their odd ways, Reina found the gringo Christians more forgiving and merciful than her own countrymen. Was it that they had more experience in walking in love and forgiveness? Would she and her people ever get it right?

Rumors still circulated frequently about Reynaldo. Reina was afraid they were true. Once, she knew she smelled alcohol on his breath. It was unmistakable, revolting, and crushing, all at once.

"Don't you dare tell anyone," he threatened, his face dark. She stayed quiet.

Sometimes Reina asked herself why she refused to tell anyone what was going on. Was it loyalty to Reynaldo that kept her quiet about his sin? Maybe—she hoped she was loyal. Was it pride? The church at El Edén was growing rapidly, but their family had been one of the first to join, and one of the most prominent. This sin was embarrassing and shameful.

Was it fear? Reina remembered the ominous sound of Reynaldo's voice when he told her to be quiet about his drinking, and she knew that even if she could master her pride, she would tell no one. She had seen how unreasonable he could be, especially when he was drunk. She didn't want to find out what he would do to her if he thought she had squealed on him.

One pleasant morning in July, Reina set out for the mill with a large basket of corn balanced on her head. She felt deep thankfulness for God's provision through the missionary families. This corn was like a hug from her heavenly Father. What would she do without the help of God's family?

The mill was in sight now, just up the hill ahead. Susana, one of the ladies from church, approached from that direction carrying a small basket of freshly ground corn on her head.

"Good morning," Reina greeted her, smiling.

Susana, however, saw nothing to smile about and seemed to find the morning anything but good. Certainly she saw nothing good about Reina, smiling from beneath her basket of donated corn.

A few moments later Reina was staring dazedly at the blood dripping on her skirt, spreading ugly stains among the printed flowers. She dragged the shawl from her basket and clamped it over her nose. How had it come to this?

Her face throbbed. She removed the shawl and lifted her fingers to her nose, touching it gingerly. Then, crying, she squatted on the road and began scooping handfuls of gravelly corn kernels into her basket. Marixa, warm and sweaty against her back, wailed loudly, and Reina bounced and jiggled to hush her. She picked several hairpins off the road and put them in her pocket.

When Reina stood at last, her knees wobbled. She was in no shape to be seen. Hurting all over, more weary than angry, she staggered over the hill to Carl and Irene's house, where she called at the door.

"Whatever happened, sister?" Irene exclaimed, her eyes taking in the bloody rag, the torn and dirty dress, and the blood on Reina's veil. "Come in! Sit down. Are you okay?"

Reina poured out her story. "She pulled off my veil and yanked my hair down and beat me up."

"But why? I don't understand!"

"I don't know why. I met her on the path near the mill. It all happened so fast."

"Here." Irene took Marixa from Reina's arms. "Let me see your nose."

Attack at the Mill

Reina removed the rag from her face, and Irene gasped. "Your nose is all black and blue. It must surely be broken. And your lip is all puffed up. Let's get you cleaned up." Irene hurried to the bedroom and came out with an armload of clean clothes.

Reina went into the bathroom and closed the door. On the counter lay a soft blue towel and a blue washcloth with a pure white bar of soap nestled on top. She indulged her bruised body in the soothing sensations of the warm shower as long as she dared; then, knowing she had already been away from home longer than expected, she turned the handle down and stepped out. Irene's dress was a little baggy on Reina, but it was clean and all in one piece.

"I'd like to bathe the baby before you go," Irene offered when Reina appeared in the kitchen a few minutes later.

"Thank you, but I really need to get home. They weren't expecting me to be gone so long," Reina answered.

With a dismayed glance at the dirty baby, Irene handed Marixa to her mother. Nancy came in just then. When they told her what had happened, she offered to walk home with Reina. She thought the sight of Reina in Irene's clothes, with her hair and covering in order, might be enough to set off another attack.

Nancy stuffed Reina's clothes, dirty and torn, into a plastic bag, and together they started across the mountain.

The next day Susana appeared at the Martin home, eager to pour out her version of her encounter with Reina.

"What you have done is very wrong, no matter what Reina has done against you," Carl told her. "Jesus never acted like that, not even to His enemies. We must follow His example."

Susana burst into tears. "I know. I know it was terrible. I have never done a thing like that before to anyone. I was just so angry."

Carl and Irene leaned closer, straining to understand Susana's broken recital of all the wrongs she had endured from Reina in the past months. "Seeing her smiling so smugly under that huge basket of corn—it was just too much. The rest of us have to work for what we eat! But I know it was wrong," she sobbed, "and now everyone will find out what I have done. I am ashamed to face the rest of the church. What will everyone think of me?"

"What really matters is what God thinks," Carl said. "You didn't handle this God's way. Jesus says that if our brothers or sisters sin against us, we are to go alone and tell them what we feel they have done against us. If they don't repent, we take someone with us to help us determine where the problem really lies. Finally, if that doesn't resolve the issue, it must be taken to the church so all the brothers and sisters can help bring understanding to the situation.

"Instead, you let the envy and resentment grow bigger and bigger inside you until you were so angry you took it into your own hands. You sinned against your sister. Now you must go to her and repent and ask her forgiveness."

Susana looked up in horror. "I can't! Not until this anger passes." She shook her head. "There is no way I can ask her for forgiveness now."

No amount of persuasion could change Susana's mind. She left an hour later, no closer to repentance but willing to talk with one of the ministers about it the next day, a Sunday.

Reina had no heart for going to church that Sunday morning. She longed to be with Reynaldo and to tell him all about it, but Reynaldo had gone to his father's place in La Cumbre. She decided to go find him.

After Vicenta and the older children left for church, Reina pushed ashes over the coals, shooed the chickens out of the kitchen, and then followed them out, closing the door behind her. With Marixa tied snugly against her back, she set out on the long walk to Chano's house to find Reynaldo.

Dust puffed around her shoes as she walked. The leaves on the trees wilted in the heat. "Oh, Father, I'm thirsty too, and tired—so tired." She reached up and gently felt the tenderness of her swollen nose.

Though she wanted to deny it, Reina knew the animosity between her and Susana had been growing steadily over the past year. They both had felt it, yet neither had taken responsibility to reach out in love and blessing.

Would there be no end to the strife, misunderstandings, and accusations? There seemed no answer, except for the great silhouette of Tajumulco beyond the distant mountains, blue against a hazy sky—a constant reminder that there is a God in heaven who sees and understands all and judges justly. This God holds the world in His hands, and Reina knew that even now He held her in His heart of love.

By the time Reina walked past the church house just outside La Cumbre, the morning meeting there had ended. Marixa slept. Trail dust gritted between Reina's teeth as she plodded down the mountain, coming at last to the beautiful valley where Chano reigned.

Reynaldo, who was preparing to eat lunch, listened to her story with concern. The next step seemed clear. After the meal, they walked together up the mountain and called at Leland's door.

Meanwhile, back in El Edén, Susana and her husband were having a long talk with Frank and Carl and their wives. By the time the afternoon was over, each woman—one in La Cumbre and one in El Edén—had acknowledged her part in the tension that had come between them. Each was ready to talk to the other, to repent and forgive.

When Reina and Reynaldo left the mission house that afternoon, they felt a freedom they hadn't felt in a long time. More than that, they felt deeply thankful for the kindness and honesty of their church leaders. How different this church was from anything they had known before! The Christian way was a way of peace and rest and blessing. Surely everything would come out right.

CHAPTER 20

The Making of a Man

The simmering civil violence struck the North American missionaries in September 1981 when John Troyer, a missionary from another Mennonite mission and well-known to the people of El Edén, was shot and killed by gunmen who attacked his home at night. Six weeks later, a threatening note was found on one of the mission vehicles at La Victoria.

Out of caution, Carl Martin, Leland Seibel, Larry Weaver, and other Americans returned with their families to the United States. Frank and Marilyn Martin and their family stayed and continued coming to El Edén for Sunday meetings, Frank preaching for them.

In February of 1982, Leland Seibel's family returned and moved from La Cumbre to El Edén. Carl Martin's family also returned, just in time for another school term.

Dionel was glad Carl was back, though some of the students grumbled that he was too strict.

One day Carl called Dionel out of the schoolroom. Dionel followed, sensing he was in trouble. Juan Calderón, his best friend, had just reentered the schoolroom looking sober and tearful.

"I hear you boys were playing on the way home from school again," Carl said to Dionel when they were alone under the shade of an apple tree outside.

"But, Brother Carlos, I didn't go off the road." Dionel looked up into Carl Martin's serious face.

"Did you go directly home, son, or were you with them?" Carl asked, sweeping a giant hand toward the schoolhouse where the other boys sat distracted at their desks.

"I was with them," Dionel admitted.

"Do you remember what I told you yesterday?"

"You said we should go directly home and not play around or go off the road. You said the neighbors had complained. But I didn't go into the field, Brother Carlos. Honestly, I didn't."

"Dionel, you were with them. I told you to go straight home without loitering, and you did not obey." Dionel could hardly look away from Brother Carl's face. No anger was there, only a strange mix of grief and concern.

"Son, I know you didn't intend to disobey. You thought it was okay to stand on the road if you didn't go into the field. But God tells us to flee temptation, to avoid even the appearance of sin. He tells us not to keep company with those who are doing wrong.

"The man has complained again that his oats were trampled." Brother Carl paused and leaned closer. "But even if no oats had been harmed, you disobeyed, Dionel. Your character is much more valuable than those oats. I want you to become what God wants you to become—an obedient man of God."

Dionel dropped his eyes to Brother Carl's big leather shoes, then to the cracks in his own plastic ones. *I really didn't obey,* he admitted to himself. *It isn't enough to do better than the others.*

Brother Carl wasn't done. "This may seem like a small thing, but small sins lead to bigger sins. I am going to spank you, Dionel, because you did not follow my directions." Carl reached for the stick leaning against the trunk of the apple tree.

Afterward, the two sat on the ground together, Carl's arm around Dionel's thin shoulders. "Determine now, in your youth, to fear God, to obey Him, and to love Him. At your age, that means obeying the authorities He has put in your life, your parents and your teachers. Love the Lord your God with all your heart, with all your soul, and with all your strength, and you will be a son of God, a man He can use. God has great plans for you, Dionel."

Dionel could have stayed all day in the grip of that fatherly arm. A deep resolve to live righteously took root in him.

That evening the three oldest Monterroso children privately processed the day's happenings; Dionel, penitent and purposeful; Eliza, understanding and sympathetic toward both Carl and her brothers; and Conrado, bitter and boiling.

When thirteen-year-old Conrado had realized he was about to be spanked, he had bolted from his teacher. Conrado had made a resolution of his own: no teacher would lay hands on him, ever!

The next morning the four oldest Monterroso children started down the hill toward school together, but when they were far enough from home that they were concealed by the trees and the hill, Conrado split for the mountain trail. He did the same thing the next day. His parents soon found out, of course, but no amount of pleading or insisting could change his mind. Conrado refused to return to school.

In the little adobe house on the slopes of La Laguna, the storms of strife that had twisted their home for years raged with new fury. Conrado, who despised his father's weakness, grew ever more headstrong and wicked, disregarding his parents, lashing out in anger at his younger siblings, and stealing from the neighbors. Vicenta remained Conrado's loyal ally, even when he refused to obey her. If his mother tried to get Conrado to do something, his grandmother objected. If Reynaldo was at home and tried to discipline Conrado's defiance, both Vicenta and Reina argued with Reynaldo.

Those were hard months for Dionel. His family had become a spectacle, and it was embarrassing to face everybody at church. The Monterrosos were the poor ones, the dirty ones, the needy ones, the ones whose father was found drunk along the road. Dionel knew his shame arose partly from an ungodly pride, but he didn't know how to escape it.

SONG OF THE SHEPHERDESS

Reina and her family: Reina and Vicenta in the back; Conrado, left, and Dionel, right; the girls, from oldest to youngest: Eliza, Aide, Sonia, Juana, and Marixa.

When Reynaldo asked Dionel one summer day to return a borrowed horse to Benigno's house, Dionel was glad to go. Papa had used the horse to haul corn home from Sibilia, since their own corn wouldn't be ready for several more lean weeks.

As Dionel rode toward Benigno's house, dust puffed from the horse's heavy hooves. A cool breeze flowed down the mountain, and the evening rang with birdsong. As he neared Benigno's house, Dionel heard a whoop of welcome from the yard and raised his eyes to see Juan waving at him, grinning from ear to ear.

Benigno and Valeriana's house was a happy place, full of big friendly boys—Baldomero, Isabel, and Juan—and one grinning little sister, Milagro. Dionel liked it here. He respected the godly Benigno. Valeriana, his mother's cousin, always made Dionel feel like one of her own, and Juan was like a brother to him.

Baldomero took the horse and led him around to the back of the house. Yelling for Dionel to come along, Isabel and Juan headed for the ravine, where their new swing hung fearsomely high in a tree. It was nearly dark before the boys tired of taking turns swinging out over the chasm and back again. Then, laughing and talking, they trooped into the house.

There Dionel lost himself in chatter, warmth, and friendship until the last glimmer of sunlight disappeared behind the mountain.

"I need to go," he said at last, looking uneasily out the window. He reached for his jacket, shrugging his shoulders into it. It was *really* dark out there.

"Just sleep here tonight, my son," said Valeriana. "You can go home tomorrow."

"No, Mama would worry, and I'd be in big trouble." Peering out the door at the inky darkness, Dionel recoiled, but he had no choice.

"Good night," he said, "It was nice to be here. Thank you for letting us use the horse."

And then it was just him, the dark, and the path toward the woods. As he entered the shelter of the woods, he shivered, and not from cold. An owl hooted; then all was quiet. Something rustled behind him. Glancing over his shoulder, Dionel thought he saw a rat-sized form a little way back. Oddly, it seemed to be following him.

Dionel quickened his steps, and so did the creature. Dionel broke into a run, and the next time he peered over his shoulder, the thing was running too. Worse, it was bigger each time he looked at it.

A dead branch hung over the trail. Dionel wrenched it loose and pivoted to face the thing that followed. The monster, as big as a bear now, rushed at him. Screaming, he swung his club frantically at it. Finally, seeing an opening, he flung the club aside, darted around the creature, and fled back toward Benigno's house, screaming all the way.

Above the strangled sound of his own screaming, Dionel could hear Baldomero's voice calling him through the night: "Dionel, what's wrong?"

Dionel stumbled into the yard, then into the stream of lamplight coming from the open door. As the family clustered around him, all asking questions at once, he shoved past them into the house. Everyone followed him in, and Milagro slammed the door. Gasping and drawing short, ragged breaths, Dionel grabbed at his throat and beat his chest. He pointed through the door toward the woods.

"Poor boy, he's out of his wits with fear," said Valeriana. Pulling a bottle off a high shelf, she removed some sort of soothing pill, handed it to him kindly, and found him a stool to sit down on. They had no trouble now in convincing him to stay for the night.

At the table next morning, his hands clutching a mug of hot coffee, Dionel told the family the whole story. Listening, their eyes grew wide. "Let me go with you," Baldomero said. "I want to see where it happened."

When Dionel was ready to go home, all the children followed him. At the place where the creature had caught up to Dionel, the underbrush was trampled in a large circle by something far larger than a rat. The children gaped at the battlefield, then at Dionel; how had he escaped alive?

As they parted and Dionel continued home, he wanted to thank God for protecting him. But would God hear him? Was it really God who had protected him last night? He thought so. Why else didn't the evil thing, whatever it was, finish him off?

There was so much to think about, and it was so dark and heavy. He wished he could talk to Brother Carl, but he had gone back to the States. He would go talk with Brother Leland. Maybe Leland could help him sort it out.

CHAPTER 21

Benjamín

Reina stroked the tiny, silky cheek lying on the bed beside her. Maybe life would be better for *this* little boy.

Just last month, March 1983, the church leaders had talked with the congregation about taking Reynaldo back into fellowship. The Guatemalan believers had not been willing; in the last few days someone had spread a fresh report of having seen Reynaldo lying in a ditch.

Reynaldo claimed he had merely fainted on the way home from town.

Reina wished she could believe her husband's story as Brother Leland seemed to, but she couldn't help but wonder. Meanwhile, the local women at church were accusing her of lying and covering for her husband. Sometimes she wasn't sure herself if she was being truthful.

Reynaldo entered the room and stood quietly looking down at the two of them for a moment. "He's beautiful," Reynaldo said, but his eyes said more. Reina allowed herself to rest for a moment in the openness and tenderness she saw in his dark eyes. This was the Reynaldo she had married, and more. This Reynaldo was committed to following Jesus and leading his family in righteousness. Dare she hope that this time it would last? Oh, how she needed him.

SONG OF THE SHEPHERDESS

"I'm so tired," she said.

He squeezed her shoulder. "Rest then. I'll watch the girls."

The door closed behind him, and soon Reina heard the whoops and laughter of four little girls racing around the yard, each pretending to try to stay out of Papa's reach yet hoping he would catch her.

Reina smiled a little. This pregnancy had been hard. She had been sick more than she had been well, and the drugs the doctors had prescribed were too strong for an expectant mother. For weeks she had been unable to manage the long walk to church.

Now the weary pregnancy was over. Now she would enjoy the baby, a son again after five daughters. She put her finger in his tiny palm and drank in the sweetness of his perfect round face. They had decided to call him Benjamín.

"Buenos días!" Norma González's voice floated over the courtyard. Reina heard Vicenta inviting her in. With Norma were several other ladies from church, including the new schoolteacher's wife, Gwen; Gwendolina, the children called her.

Two weeks later, word came from La Victoria of the tragic drowning of Percy Stauffer, a young man who had served at the mission station there. Reynaldo and Dionel walked out to La Victoria to find out what had happened. They learned that nineteen-year-old Percy, swimming at the coast with Herbert Ebersole's family, had been caught in a rip current and swept away from shore, despite Herbert's best attempts to rescue him. His body had been found and retrieved hours later by the coast guard. The death of this sincere and energetic young man, a friend to all the boys, made a sobering impression on Dionel.

As the mission was immersed in preparations for Percy's funeral, Reina was fighting for her baby's life in the little house on La Laguna—fighting and losing. Less than three weeks old, her darling Benjamín was growing weaker

Benjamín

by the day. Fever raged in his tiny body, and though he nursed, he seemed to digest nothing. His bones protruded beneath his thin skin. Reina's every interaction with him had become a prayer for help.

Saturday night when Reina opened Benjamín's diaper to change him for bed, her heart sank and desperation clawed at her mind. There had been traces of blood in his diaper for a couple of days, but now it was all blood. Her baby was dying.

She wrapped the little one snugly, held him against her body, and prayed. She slept only in snatches that night, yearning for morning. Little Benjamín was almost too weak to cry.

When the family woke up at last, Reina told them her fears. "Benjamín is very sick. We need to find somebody at church to take him to the doctor in Xela. Conrado, will you go with me? Papa will be away at Percy's funeral in La Victoria this afternoon, and I want someone to walk home with me after we've seen the doctor."

Although Conrado had not been to church for months, he readily agreed to walk out to the church house with the family and accompany his mother to the city. He felt protective of her, and he was worried about the baby too.

Reynaldo wrapped the baby against his chest and started out on the long, dusty trail with his family. He was lost in troubled thoughts, both about this ailing child and about the corn in his fields, shriveling up for lack of the rain it had needed weeks ago.

That morning portended an unusually warm day. The air was hazy, the earth thick with dust. When Reina and Reynaldo approached Leland with the sick baby, he took things in hand immediately. The new schoolteacher, Henry Hertzler, was just entering the churchyard with his wife, Gwen, and their baby. Brother Leland hurried to meet them.

"Hey, would you be willing to drive Reina to the doctor in Xela this morning?" he asked. "Her baby needs to be seen right away."

"Sure, we can take her," came Henry's ready response.

Conrado and Reina followed the young couple back to their house next door and climbed into the mission jeep parked there, while Henry and

Gwen dashed inside to prepare for the journey. They would have to hurry to be back in time to drive people out to the funeral at 1:30 in the afternoon.

In a few minutes they were on their way to town, Henry driving and making small talk, getting acquainted with Reina and Conrado, who sat in the back seat. Gwen, who spoke little Spanish, held Benjamín. The towheaded Hertzler baby sat between his parents, plump and healthy. The Jeep bucked and whined, and the dust that filtered in gritted everyone's teeth.

When they arrived at the doctor's office, Reina and Conrado took Benjamín inside while the others waited.

Reina was dismayed at the doctor's verdict. "Your milk is making your baby sick," he said. "The medication you have been taking is much too strong for a baby. It is irritating his stomach. You must feed him baby formula."

Later, as they rode back out of town, Reina told Henry what the doctor had said. *It is ridiculous,* she thought. *How am I going to buy formula? Formula is for rich people.* Benjamín began to fuss, and Reina pulled him close and nursed him.

When they returned, Gwen invited them inside and fed them a meal she had prepared that morning. There was a little conversation with Henry, but with Gwen there was only the companionable frustration first experienced at the tower of Babel.

CHAPTER 22

Suffering and Triumph

A few weeks passed. It was late May 1983. The glowering sky threatened afternoon rain. During the previous two days, parched fields had drunk deeply of the laughing rivulets of rain that ran down their sides to the streams. The long dry spell had broken at last.

The rain chased the specter of starvation from Reynaldo's family for this season, at least, and washed some of the worry lines from his face. The corn would make ears and the wheat heads would fill out; there would be a crop. Sloshing down the lane on their way to school this morning, the children had been in high spirits.

Reina, on the other hand, felt little relief. Baby Benjamín, too thin already, had coughed all night. She leaned against the *pila* now, watching without seeing as Vicenta rubbed her sponge against the bright orange ball of soap in the little dish beside the dishpan before attacking another bowl from yesterday's pile of dishes.

"Mama, he's not getting better. We can't let him die." Reina's body screamed to sleep, to cry, to quit. She thought she couldn't bear to hear another of the hoarse little barking sounds she was powerless to stop. But she wouldn't quit. She would get help for this baby if she had to drag herself to the ends

SONG OF THE SHEPHERDESS

Henry Hertzler with his class in 1983. Eliza is second from left in the front, and Dionel stands directly behind her.

of the earth. The problem was, she didn't know where to go.

Vicenta looked up from the shallow pan of water, her hands still moving—sponge on the soap, sponge on the bowl, rinse and invert the bowl, reach and repeat. "I wish we had some honey," Vicenta said. "Honey is just the thing for a nagging cough, but we don't have any, and Esther doesn't either."

"Maybe Gwendolina would have honey," Reina suggested.

Vicenta didn't hesitate. "I'll go find out," she said. Her face showed her concern, not just for the baby, but for Reina too. "While I'm gone, you try to rest. The rain has these dishes nearly washed anyway. Maybe the next one will finish them up." She squeezed out the sponge and plopped it onto the orange soap ball.

"Sonia! Juana!" Vicenta called. "Bring Marixa and come play here by the house until Eliza gets home from school." As Vicenta headed down the trail, she glanced at the sky and tugged her shawl a little closer around her shoulders. It was twenty minutes to the house where the new teacher and his wife lived on the hill above the church house. She probably wouldn't beat the rain.

It was pouring when Vicenta reached the teacher's house. She knocked and called.

Henry listened with concern as she explained, "The baby is still very sick. Do you have honey? Honey is good for a cough."

Henry explained Vicenta's request to his young wife, who shook her head. But she rummaged around and soon produced a bag with a little medicine and curdled milk—*yogurt,* she called it—that she thought would help Benjamín.

Carrying the bag of remedies from Gwen, Vicenta slogged back over the soggy trails to the little house against the mountain. When she walked in the door, Reina looked up, relieved, from where she was wrapping Benjamín in a blanket. "Brother Leland agreed to take us to the doctor in Xela," Reina said.

Dionel took the baby from his mother, and together they started out, slipping and sliding down the trail to the road where Leland would meet them. With the footpaths this bad, the roads would be all but impassable. It would be a long drive out to Xela.

Hours later, the doctor held his stethoscope against Benjamín's swollen tummy. The baby's thin legs and arms flailed weakly as he coughed. A nurse hovered nearby, concern shadowing her face. Straightening up, the doctor probed the baby's tummy with his thick fingers, frowning and rolling his eyes toward the fly-specked ceiling. Then he flexed the tiny legs and arms.

Bending down again, the doctor peered past his penlight into Benjamín's eyes, into his tiny nose, into his mouth.

He thrust the light into his pocket, turning his piercing eyes on Reina. "This child has all the signs of malnutrition," he said. "There are three stages of starvation, and this baby is in the second. He is metabolizing his body fat and the fatty tissues in his organs. Without proper nutrition he will die. On the other hand, with an adequate diet, I have good hopes his issues will resolve." He scribbled some instructions for the nurse and walked out of the room.

SONG OF THE SHEPHERDESS

Reina bottle-feeds baby Benjamín.
Would he become strong and healthy?

Reina felt like the doctor had punched her in the stomach. She picked up her baby boy, wrapped her shawl about him, and held him close.

The nurse glanced at the departing doctor, then down at the note in her hand. "So what have you been feeding your baby?" she asked.

"I have powdered milk for him. I hardly nurse him at all because the doctor said my milk was making him sick."

"Powdered milk! If the baby cannot nurse, he needs infant formula. Can't you see your baby is starving? Surely the doctor told you to feed him infant formula. Powdered milk is *not* infant formula. Do you care about your baby, or don't you?"

The nurse's words were like knives in Reina's heart. She was glad she had not mentioned that she sometimes used coffee or herb teas in the baby's bottle to save the powdered milk. Embarrassed, she glanced into Esther's eyes, but to her relief, there was only kindness there.

Suffering and Triumph

"We'll stop and get some formula for him on the way home," Esther promised.

About a week later, the Monterroso family was just finishing supper when they heard a shout in the yard. It was Leland Seibel's voice. Ben Eshbach and Isaac Sensenig were with him. The family rushed out the door to greet the visitors as they swung down from their horses. The drizzle of the May afternoon didn't dampen the smiles, handshakes, and greetings.

"Could we talk with you and your wife?" Leland asked Reynaldo. Noting the joy on Leland's face, Reina felt a surge of hope. She took the baby from Eliza—he was putting on a little weight, she noticed—and followed Reynaldo and the church leaders into the house.

After asking a few preliminary questions, Leland announced, "Your brothers in the church are ready to welcome you back into fellowship, Brother Reynaldo. In our evening meeting this coming Wednesday, we want to publicly welcome you back as one of the family, a disciple of Jesus."

Reynaldo and Reina exchanged a quick look of joy; then Reynaldo looked down at his hands. Reina wanted to cry—whether from happiness, from sympathy for her husband's embarrassment, or from her own confusion and pain, it was impossible to tell.

"Satan has tried you sorely, brother, but you have stood strong," Leland said. "We trust God to finish the work He has begun in you."

Reina brushed her lips against baby Benjamín's hair. His cough was nearly gone, and he was alert and peaceful.

Thank you! Thank you, God!

The following Wednesday afternoon, shimmering sunlight broke through the clouds, casting a faint rainbow above the mountain. Reina smiled as she watched Reynaldo and Dionel strolling up the path from the spring, deep in discussion. This evening Dionel would be baptized and Reynaldo would be restored to fellowship.

As the two reached the house, their talk dropped away, but it seemed that light lingered on their faces. Reina found herself humming the song of the young shepherdess: "My God, my God, come closer to me; for my soul is in you, and wants to live in you."

"Only now, God," she whispered, "I want my whole family to be in you. Thank you, Father, for what you have done in Reynaldo and for what you are doing in Dionel. But please, Father, don't forget Conrado."

Reina bowed her head, feeling the ache that always accompanied her thoughts of Conrado these days. She wondered where he was just then. Times like these made her long for heaven, where rainbows and sunbeams and praises would never be shot through with pain.

When the locals gathered outside the galvanized metal meetinghouse that evening, mud was everywhere. Someone yelled that Leland's Blazer was coming, and the crowd shifted toward the road, watching for the mission vehicle to round the bend, listening with a mix of dismay and amusement as the engine whined, idled, shifted gears, and whined again, accompanied by the sound of spinning wheels.

Several of the men and boys ran down the road to see if they could help. The men took up positions behind the Blazer, prepared to push, while the little boys threw small branches and rocks in front of the tires. Leland backed up and got a run for the hill, but spun out again, spraying mud all over the pushing men.

After several attempts, the gringos gave up on driving the rest of the way. In pressed suits and polished shoes, the Pennsylvania preachers joined their spattered Guatemalan brothers and slogged through the mud, up the hill, and into the churchyard.

As the congregation sat on the benches and sang, rain pelted the metal roof of the meetinghouse and drowned out the singing for a stanza and a half, but no rainstorm could drown out the song that rose from their hearts.

CHAPTER 23

Night Patrol

The August morning was damp and cold. As Reina followed Vicenta and the girls into the meetinghouse, mud squished around her bare feet inside her cracked plastic shoes. Someone had been here early to light a fire in the stove. The warmth was good, and the family was pleased to have finally arrived on time.

Most of the Guatemalan families were in their places already. A hum of conversation buzzed around the room as everyone tried to figure out why none of the gringos were at church. It must be that time change again!

Though some of the gathered families had heard about the time change, none had remembered it this morning. Sure enough, the clock in the back of the church showed 9:15, while the sun said it was after 10:00. How could a person turn the hands on a clock and insist the time had changed? They couldn't change the time the sun came up.[1]

Despite the skewed clock and the slippery journey to church, Reina felt thankful this morning. There had been no major incidents since Reynaldo's

---

[1] For two months in 1983, Guatemala unsuccessfully tried for the second time to implement DST. The first time had been a decade before, from November to February. Since then, the country has attempted it twice more, in 1991 and in 2006.

SONG OF THE SHEPHERDESS

The Monterrosa family, with Vicenta, on Sunday, August 21, 1983. Reina is holding baby Benjamín. The three oldest—Conrado, Dionel, and Eliza—are not pictured.

membership was restored two months ago, they were getting plenty of rain again, and the family was together and at church—everyone but Conrado.

Reina squeezed Benjamín against her. How could it have been only three months ago that the doctor had poked and prodded Benjamín's bony little body and said—what had the doctor said? He was in the second stage of starvation? Well, he was in the second stage of fat and cute now, Reina guessed as she nuzzled the soft place in the side of his neck. Benjamín giggled.

The hum in the church house subsided. The clock crept to 9:55.

Leland and Esther and their two children walked in, their shoes looking fairly decent; the Blazer had made it through the mud this morning.

The congregation sang, and one of the men read a passage of Scripture. Brother Leland walked to the front, adjusting the damper on the stove as he passed. Reina never could understand why it mattered—that little trail of smoke escaping from the joint in the metal pipe.

"Turn with me to 1 Corinthians 13," Leland said after his usual cheerful preliminaries. Bible pages rustled like wind in dry leaves.

" 'Though I bestow all my goods to feed the poor, and though I give my body to be burned, and have not charity, it profiteth me nothing.' "[2]

Reina thought of her cousin, Carlos. The years hadn't erased the animosity between them, and living near each other provided many occasions for tension and trouble. She had given the matter to God over and over, she thought. Still, sometimes she feared she didn't really love him. Sometimes she still wished to see him suffer a little of what he had made her suffer.

Brother Leland continued explaining, and Reina listened, hoping to understand how she could know for sure if she loved Carlos. "Love is patient and kind." And a little later, "Love does not seek its own."

God, help me to truly love, she prayed. Tears sprang to her eyes at the thought of the small baby Carlos and his wife had recently buried. They had buried several other babies before this one. *Help me be willing to bless him.*

Then there was Reynaldo. Walking with God as she and Reynaldo were now, their relationship was more peaceful than it had been since their early marriage. As Reina thought of her husband, she was thankful for the grace God was giving them.

"Love is not glad to hear evil about another. When we truly love, we believe the best about our brothers and sisters," Leland continued. "This passage says that love thinks no evil."

Reina's eyes clouded. Would the brothers and sisters here ever be able to think no evil of her and Reynaldo? True, Reynaldo had been accepted back into fellowship, but the rumblings of mistrust continued. It seemed that some were glad to trade any nugget of gossip about Reynaldo's family.

Leland had often encouraged Reynaldo and Reina to live such upright lives, and to give so much love to their brothers and sisters, that accusations and suspicions would not stick to them.

God, help us, Reina prayed. *Give me true love for my brothers and sisters. Give me true love for you.*

---

[2] 1 Corinthians 13:3

SONG OF THE SHEPHERDESS

After the sermon, the little congregation once again filled the meetinghouse with song.

What tho' the way be lonely
And dark the shadows fall;
I know where'er it leadeth,
My Father planned it all.

Reina's eyes filled with tears, and the room seemed hallowed.

He guides my falt'ring footsteps
Along the weary way,
For well He knows the pathway
Will lead to endless day.

<u>Chorus</u>
I sing thru the shade and the sunshine,
I'll trust Him whatever befall;
I sing for I cannot be silent,
My Father planned it all.[3]

Two days later, a shout outside the door announced the arrival of the police. It was early Tuesday morning, August 23, 1983.

Each man in the neighborhood had to take his turn patrolling the roads through the night in a government effort to deter guerrillas. It was Reynaldo's turn, and he had not showed up.

Reina watched as Reynaldo opened the door and stood silhouetted in

---

[3] Public domain.

Night Patrol

the doorway, the pale morning light just beginning to brighten the green cornstalks in the fields beyond him. "I can't do it," he said calmly to the two officers who confronted him.

"Can't do it?" the officer in front exploded. "What is that supposed to mean?"

"I cannot take a club and walk the roads to keep intruders out. I am a Christian. I will not use force against another person."

"You're a coward!" The officer spit out the words. "What kind of wimp leaves his family and neighbors at the mercy of the enemy because he's too chicken to fight?"

Reynaldo took a deep breath and looked into the accusing eyes of the policemen. "Jesus said His people are to love their enemies and do good to those who try to harm them. I am a disciple of Jesus. I will never carry a club to harm someone else, even if he intends harm to me. Jesus' way is love—returning good for evil."

"So you think you can sleep in your bed with your wife and family while other people stay out all night and risk their lives for you? No, if you won't do your duty, you can sit in jail while some real man protects your family."

Reynaldo winced inwardly. He had caused his family plenty of harm, he knew. Still, was walking the roads with a club the way to prove his love for them? That would only add another sin to those he had already committed, he thought. It felt so good to be clean and strong, a papa his children could be proud of. Conrado might scorn him for this decision, but the rest of his family would stand with him, he knew.

"Do what you need to do. I am a disciple of Jesus Christ, and Jesus said we are to love our enemies. He said those who use the sword will die by the sword.[4] He said His kingdom is not of this world; if it were of this world, His servants would fight.[5]

"I am not trusting other men to care for my family; I trust the God of

---

[4] Matthew 26:52
[5] John 18:36

heaven and earth. We are in His hands. You know we are willing to do other public service. Our church has offered many times to help our neighbors in peaceful ways."

Swearing under his breath, the officer reached into his saddle bag. A set of handcuffs clanked as he jerked them out.

The children watched wide-eyed—the little ones afraid, the older ones impressed. It wasn't the first time the older ones had seen Papa marched up the hill between policemen. But this time, though they felt frightened, they felt no shame. Had not Jesus said that those who suffer for His sake are blessed?

The officers ordered Reynaldo onto a horse, wheeled around, and started back across the field. "Where are you taking him?" Reina asked. Her question dangled in the air unanswered, and tears blurred her eyes as she watched them move up the corn-flanked trail until they were swallowed by the mist.

Her man was standing strong. She could hold up her head among her brothers and sisters at church. The police probably wouldn't keep him in jail long, but no matter how long it was, she was proud of Reynaldo, with a good, grateful pride. *Thank you, Jesus! Please keep him from harm.*

Dionel stood beside her. "Shall I go tell Brother Leland?" he asked.

"Yes, go right away."

Almost before the words were out of her mouth, Dionel was running in long leaps down the hill toward the river. Brother Leland would know what to do.

CHAPTER 24

Jailed

Dionel called as he neared the door. Then, after a pause, he rapped his knuckles against the wood of the door the way the gringos did. It seemed rude and insistent, but the gringos didn't think so, and this morning all that mattered was that the door was answered as soon as possible.

Dionel was still panting from his run when Leland opened the door. "They took Papa—they took him away—they handcuffed him, but they wouldn't tell us where they were going."

Leland looked confused for only a second. "Ah, yes, he was scheduled to serve on the night watch. Come on in, son. Esther, can you get Dionel a drink of water? Sit down here a minute while we think."

Dionel sat down, feeling suddenly self-conscious as he noticed that Leland's family had visitors. Everyone was dressed for a trip, with shoes on and jackets buttoned. The little ones stood waiting near the door while Esther packed sandwiches into a box in the kitchen. He must have interrupted an outing.

Leland spoke in English to his visitors, and they nodded, looking at Dionel with concern and interest. Esther finished packing sandwiches and handed Dionel a tall glass of water. "I'm glad you got here when you did; you almost missed us. We were just ready to leave for the lake, but don't worry, we're not going anywhere until we find out where your father is."

More English chatter followed as the families hustled the little ones outside and everyone crowded into Leland's Blazer. "You come with us," Leland said to Dionel. "We'll check first at the jail in Sibilia. That's probably where they took him."

As they wound up the highway to Sibilia, they passed the top of the steep trail leading down to Reynaldo's home. Leland stopped and Esther got out. "I'll stay with your mother," she said to Dionel.

Dionel could hardly wait to get to the jail. From the road, he had often seen the long, low building, vastly blue, wrapped with pillars and porches and partly obscured by a giant spreading tree. This was where people came who were caught making *cusha,* or who got in a nasty machete fight, or who stole a cow. Was it as beautiful inside as it was outside?

When they arrived, Dionel followed Leland across the hard-packed courtyard and under the big tree. The bottom section of the tree trunk was painted white to match a white strip that ran around the bottom of the jail wall.

If Papa was in here, Dionel thought, it was for Jesus' sake. Papa had become another in a long line of men who were hated and persecuted because of their faithfulness to God. Abel had been the first. His brother Cain had killed him, not for anything wrong that Abel had done, but because God was happy with Abel's sacrifice and not Cain's. Sometimes the teachers read stories in school about Christians who were imprisoned and even died because their enemies did not want to know about Jesus' kingdom of love.

As Dionel walked across the porch, he saw that the jail looked crumbled and tired—not half as grand as it appeared from the street. As he stepped through the doorway and his eyes adjusted to the dim light, the first person Dionel saw was Frank Martin.

Frank turned from the desk as they entered. His eyes, framed by thick plastic glasses under heavy dark eyebrows, softened and smiled at Dionel. It was enough to make a young man feel like crying to find that someone was there—ahead of you even—who cared about you and could fix things up. How in the world had Frank gotten here so fast all the way from San Juan?

Jailed

"Is Reynaldo here?" Leland asked.

Frank nodded. "I haven't been able to see him yet."

After asking around for the proper official, Frank and Leland finally secured permission to see Reynaldo. Together they followed a guard down a cold, dark hall. Dionel tried not to stare into the cells at the blank faces of the men sitting on the floor.

The guard stopped in front of a grim, gridded door just like the others. He nodded at them, then strode away down the hall, around a crumbling concrete corner, and out of sight. A chill crept into Dionel's heart as he peered into the dim interior of his father's cell. A draft seeped along the stone floor. Everything was clammy and dim and bare.

Then he saw Papa, straight, strong, and steady, emerging from the gray shadows. Dionel felt love and admiration swell up in him, and he was glad no one could see the tears that stung his eyes.

There was no bed in the cell, no chair to sit on, not even one little window to look through. The only break in the damp stone was this barred door. When Dionel's eyes adjusted more fully to the low light, he noticed a couple of boards on the floor in the corner. It was a lot easier to read about the martyrs than to be one, he decided.

Reynaldo was talking softly to Leland and Frank. "I am willing to suffer for Jesus," Dionel heard him say, and the chill in Dionel's heart was replaced by the warm knowledge that his father was standing strong. His father was at peace.

"They said I'll be here for twenty days—the amount of time I was assigned to night patrol. However, they said I could be released if I pay a fine of one dollar per day of the sentence," Reynaldo explained.

"We'll take care of the fine," Leland said.

Reynaldo protested. "Really, I am okay. I can stay here. If they know they can get twenty dollars out of it, they'll try it again next time one of the brothers' turns comes around." Though Dionel wanted his father back home now, his spirit agreed with what Reynaldo was saying.

Through an opening in the middle of the door, Frank stuffed a blanket, then some bread and cheese. "Thank you," Reynaldo said, reaching for it gratefully. Dionel felt a little better. At least now Papa wouldn't be quite so cold and hungry.

After Esther had been dropped off at the trailhead above Reynaldo's house, she had walked down to meet Reina, who joined her for the long walk to the jail. With every step, Reina savored the blessed contrast between this suffering for righteousness' sake and the old suffering that had been the consequence of sin.

When they finally passed the visitors' playground outside the jail, Reina saw the Seibel's guests pushing some of their children on the swings and helping others down the slide. Several chickens scratched about the steps of the big porch, and a small black pig skittered out of the way as Reina and Esther approached.

With a warm sense of belonging to a big, wonderful family, Reina stepped through the front doors of the jail and came face to face with Leland and Frank. They explained to her what was happening.

"It's okay," Reina said. "We are glad to suffer for Jesus. Nobody needs to pay the fine."

The men smiled. "God bless you, sister. That is exactly what your husband said."

The knowledge that she and Reynaldo were unified in this made Reina want to cry for joy. She felt strong and anchored. *Oh, God, may it always be so.*

Following the men's directions, Reina headed down the dark hall to see Reynaldo while the others waited.

"Nothing needs attention in the fields right now," Reynaldo assured her, "and the children can take care of the animals. Do you think you'll be all right?"

"Don't worry about anything," Reina said. "It is only twenty days. We'll be fine." She reached through the opening in the middle of the door, resting her arm against the cold metal as he squeezed her hand.

In the front office a little later, Reina learned that Frank and Leland had decided to pay the fine and let Reynaldo return to his work and family. After tracking down the appropriate officials and filling out reams of paperwork, they finally walked back down the hall, where a guard unlocked the cell and handed Reynaldo his release.

Leland, Esther, and their guests left for the lake, and Reynaldo, Reina, and Dionel started for home. An hour later, as they crested the final hill, the rest of the children ran shouting from the house to meet them. Long after dark they sat together indoors in the candlelight and wished the night could go on forever.

CHAPTER 25

More Church Problems

In October, six weeks after Reynaldo's release from jail, Reina sat in her usual place near the back of the women's side in the little church house. Her head was down, and her cheeks burned. This might be a normal Sunday to everyone else, but not to her.

When Carl Sensenig and Leland had come last week to tell her that her church membership would be terminated, they had been kind. She knew the church leaders were responsible to guide and keep order in the flock, and she respected them for doing what they felt God required. Still, this seemed very unfair.

Apparently, malicious neighbors had been telling some church members that Reynaldo and Reina were in the church only because of the gifts the gringos gave them. "They are no different from the rest of us," the neighbors complained. "They just keep up a good front with the gringos so they will keep helping them." Through the gossip channels of the close-knit mountain community, other rumors rippled, accusing one or another member of the family of unfaithfulness, ungodly attitudes, or caustic words.

Reina had denied that the rumors were true, but one or two ladies from church had insisted she was lying.

The church leaders were caught in the middle. Could a brother and sister be expelled from the church based on evil reports without solid proof?

Reina suspected that Reynaldo had been drinking a couple of times, but why should she confide her suspicions to the preachers? Then everyone who had brought false accusations would feel vindicated. She knew that Reynaldo wanted to do right and that she loved God with all her heart. If only they could find someone who would understand enough about what was going on in their family to show them the way through. The leaders had tried to sort it out, but people's trust in Reynaldo and Reina had fallen so low that anything they said served only to fuel more rumors.

As Carl Sensenig, the bishop, walked to the front of the room, Reina's mind seemed to run in circles, and she turned her hot face toward the window. Brother Carl coughed a postponing cough before beginning to read.

"To the congregation at El Edén: As a ministry we have discussed the problem of numerous complaints that have been coming from members as well as from the unconverted about Reynaldo and Reina. Some complaints are that Reina doesn't always tell the truth and that Reynaldo doesn't manifest a Christ-like attitude at times. We are not sure if all the complaints are true, but we are concerned that so many concerns come."

The written statement explained that until there was a better testimony in the community around El Edén and better reports of the times when Reynaldo worked at the coast, Reynaldo and Reina would be restricted from church membership, and Reynaldo would not be allowed to do any teaching in the assembly.

"May you as members at El Edén be careful not to gossip, but rather pray that this matter would be cleared and that our brother and sister would again find their way in fellowship with Christ and His Church." Tears stood in Leland's eyes as Carl folded the paper slowly, tucking it inside his Bible cover, each crackle of the paper amplified in the tomb-like quiet.

Eliza and Aide were looking at their laps. Reina felt shaky inside, her hands clammy and cold. Were some in the church glad this was happening? She shut her eyes.

More Church Problems

Everyone bowed their heads as Leland prayed aloud. Reina fought tears as she prayed silently: *My God, my God, come closer to me.*

Child, I am with you. I know everything you are going through. I know the truth about you. Trust me to deal with those who slander you. No matter what happens, I love you and believe in you, and I will use this to mature and purify you. Be still.

Oh, God, let that be enough for me.

In the following weeks, more accusations bombarded Reina until she felt they would bury her alive. Even people who had once had confidence in Reina and Reynaldo began to doubt them now.

One of Reina's accusers, a church lady named Elena, was advised by the leaders to bring her concerns directly to Reina. The two women met with the church leaders and their wives at the church house. Elena's list of accusations was long and pointed.

When she was done, Reina protested. "None of those things ever happened!"

"Elena, do you have any other witnesses to the things you are saying?" Leland asked.

Elena jumped up from her bench. "She is lying, lying, lying, and you are believing her!" she screamed. Running out of the church house, she tore the veil from her head and threw it on the ground.

After this outburst, Elena was also put under the discipline of the church.

Several weeks later Elena stood in the Sunday meeting and apologized for her anger. She came to Reina afterward and told her she was sorry. Reina wanted to forgive, but a certain tension within her would not ease. Did Elena feel differently toward her, she wondered, or was she only apologizing to take the pressure off herself?

Sometimes Reina thought she had forgiven Elena. But if she had, why did she sometimes feel a smugness at the way Elena had been humiliated recently? She prayed for Elena, for herself, for her home, and for the church. *Oh, Lord, what happened to the oneness we once knew as we all walked together to La Cumbre on Sunday mornings?*

None of the reports against Reynaldo could be proven either, and in December, two months later, he was received back into full fellowship at his request. Reina, however, was excommunicated for "lying and showing an un-Christ-like attitude."

"Pray for her repentance and restoration," the visiting bishop told the congregation when the decision was announced. Reina did not observe the gentleness in his voice or the sadness in his eyes, because she was not there. Humiliated and desperate, she had stayed home that morning, cuddling Benjamín and crying. Feeling guilty on only a few small counts, innocent on most, and helpless on all, she feared the coldness settling into her heart. There was no point in trying to explain anything.

There may have been a chance to clear things up, she thought, if Reynaldo had been willing to speak in her defense, but a strange darkness seemed to have entered her husband that shut her out. He would hardly speak to her or acknowledge her presence. Whenever possible, he avoided even walking with her. Yet he was pleasant and even-tempered with others. No, even if she tried to explain, she was sure no one would believe her. No one would understand.

In Sibilia, it was customary for a mayor approaching the end of his term to appoint his successor. In January of 1984, Reynaldo was chosen to serve as the next village mayor. His term was set to begin in May.

Because of Jesus' teaching that his followers should not be entangled in the affairs of earthly governments, Reynaldo determined not to take the position. Together he and Brother Leland appealed to the authorities for an exemption. By this time, four months after Reynaldo's release from jail, the church had worked out an arrangement with the local authorities to exempt their members from serving on the night watch and in civil government in exchange for helping with road and bridge construction.

More Church Problems

Benjamín's first birthday party. Not many one-year-olds receive land as their first birthday gift!

While Reynaldo waited for the summons, he worked side by side with his children, teaching them the centuries-old principles of planting and cultivating crops: corn, wheat, carrots, cabbages, fava beans, potatoes, and other vegetables. Occasionally he led them all in Bible reading and prayer as they sat around their sala.

In April, Benjamín, the apple of his father's eye, was one year old. "We're having a party," Reynaldo announced. Vicenta and Reina prepared tamales and *atole* to serve the neighbors and church families who gathered to celebrate with them. Reynaldo bought a little more than an acre of land from Vicenta and gave it to Benjamín as a birthday gift.

In May, when Reynaldo declined to appear for duty as mayor, the authorities chose to overlook it.

Reina prayed and tried to hope. Reynaldo appeared to be walking strong again, but she knew something was wrong in his life that she was powerless to explain. Besides this, there were still fights about Conrado. Things remained tense in their relationship. Furthermore, Reina's relationship with the church was not restored.

CHAPTER 26

Crumbling Hopes

Reina dragged her gaze away from the rigid carcass of their only milk cow, bloated and useless against the coarse grass. *God, we needed that cow. Benjamín is only eighteen months old, and you know another baby will be here soon. Why couldn't we keep the cow?*

Reina was crying. It wasn't really about the cow, she knew.

Reynaldo had not come in the night before, and in the morning, the last shards of Reina's restless sleep had been shattered by the dog's incessant barking. Fifteen-year-old Dionel knew well what that barking meant. The disappointment and resignation on his face as he paused in the doorway in the pale orange dawn, waiting for Eliza to join him, made Reina feel shaky and hollow. The two youth knew the routine well. The little dog would show them where to go.

Reina had wanted to go back to sleep and never wake up.

The dog had quieted down as soon as he saw the children coming, but by then little Benjamín had already woken and was wailing. Reina had dragged herself to her feet and lifted Benjamín from Eliza's bed, then watched numbly as Dionel and Eliza headed down the trail behind the faithful dog, who bounced and gyrated with pleasure at having mustered help for his master.

SONG OF THE SHEPHERDESS

That dog would follow Reynaldo to the ends of the earth.

Reina had felt that kind of loyalty once, but it had been a long time ago.

As the children and the dog passed out of sight, Reina had pressed her forehead against Benjamín's little shoulder and burst into tears, dissolving in the torrent of pain and disappointment, her hopeless wailing punctuated by heaving sobs. Vicenta had come and lifted Benjamín from her arms.

Now Reina turned from the dead cow and plunged up the trail toward the woods. She leaned against a mountain alder, pressing her hot forehead against the cool, rough bark. Weeping on the unsympathetic tree, Reina felt like her world was collapsing. Last week she had found a cache of new shoes in a hole under a tree. One of the children told her Conrado had stolen them in town and hidden them there. Not knowing what else to do, Reina had taken them to Leland. She felt a crushing pain at her helplessness to stop Conrado's downward course.

She thought back to July, three months before, when she had been restored to church membership, but the memory carried a murky mix of joy and shame. How was she to sort out her thoughts when part of her mind was still picturing her two faithful children following the worried dog to the father they loved, collapsed by the road in his own vomit?

As her weeping spent itself, Reina slumped into a patch of ferns. The reason this hurt so much, she thought, was that she had dared to hope again. Back when he was drunk every week, she had toughened to it; but this time Reynaldo had stayed out of *cusha's* clutches for two years—until a few weeks ago, when a new report had oozed back from the coast that he had been drinking again. As soon as Leland heard about it, he had driven all the way down there to talk with Reynaldo.

The report had been true, and Reynaldo had been broken and repentant. Though the news had wrenched her heart, Reina had felt sure he would never go back to drinking the way he had before. He had been faithful for so long, and though she had never been certain that Reynaldo was completely free, she had never known him happier. He had fallen only because he was far from home and in bad company.

Crumbling Hopes

Sitting among the ferns, Reina admitted that it hurt less to expect nothing, to stay numb, to keep aloof from what Reynaldo did or might do. She would still pray for him, but hope was too dangerous.

How did her mother do so well? She went calmly about her work, finding things to be thankful for in any old day, making the children smile whether they felt like it or not. Vicenta possessed a deep-down peace, like the peace the apostle Paul wrote about to the Philippian church, and it really did surpass Reina's understanding.

Once, Reina had been sure she could solve any problem they faced. Not anymore. She still believed God had the power to deliver them from this hell, but how to claim that power, she didn't know. *Cusha* was a raging lion, straining toward their door on a flimsy leash, breaking loose and devouring without warning.

Well, she didn't intend to tell anyone at church about what happened the night before. Maybe it was just a one-time fall. Incidents like this usually scared Reynaldo enough to keep him sober for a few months. As long as he kept getting up and trying again, why did anyone need to know every single time he got drunk?

Work was waiting at home. Reina started down the trail. How could the sun keep moving steadily up the sky, unperturbed while their world fell apart? As she passed the dead cow again, Reina thought bitterly that God had some explaining to do. Tears welled up again. *Forgive me, Lord. I know you are good no matter what happens. Please help me to never doubt that.*

A week or two later, Leland and the deacon, Gabino, came to see how they could help with Reynaldo's material needs. The church paid to replace the dead cow. But all their kindness could not stop the specter of *cusha* that haunted Reina's family. She was glad that at least Reynaldo stayed sober most of the time, and the littlest children remained happily oblivious to the family's problems.

Reina ached to be honest with someone about her pain and fear, but each time she mustered the courage to confide in someone, her resolve was swamped by waves of confusion, fear, and pride—confusion about whether a godly wife should expose her husband's failings, fear of what Reynaldo would do if she exposed him, and pride that feared what everyone would think if they knew.

Oh, God, she groaned, *if I defied his orders and talked to someone about it, would I be a disobedient wife? If he forbids me to tell the truth, do you hold me responsible for lying?*

Another fear plagued her. If she did tell, would anyone know what to do? Drinking was only part of the conflict in their relationship. Around others, Reynaldo was easygoing, pleasant, and humble. Would anyone unacquainted with his dark side believe what she had suffered with him?

She tried to pray, but praying was getting harder. She felt numb, as if her sins and her questions had separated her from God. Where was the God of light who had heard her and opened her blind eyes so many years before?

You are greater than this darkness, Father. You can take the evil away. Oh, God, what will happen to me and my family? What will happen to this innocent baby?

As her baby's time drew near, Reina grew weak and sick. Sensitive to her needs, Reynaldo tried be kind and strong for her and the children. That at least was a comfort.

On the last Sunday afternoon of the year, Leland brought Reina communion at home. The symbols of Christ's death and suffering touched her deeply. He had died because He loved her and all the other messy, broken people in this world. He had died to bring healing to the broken-hearted and freedom to the captives—but right now that healing and freedom seemed out of reach for her and Reynaldo.

CHAPTER 27

Joel

The Christmas season was here again. For nine days before Christmas, processions moved through the streets. People passed images of Joseph and Mary and the Holy Child from house to house. They feasted and prepared gifts. Reina was confined to her home this year, so she didn't see the parades and displays, but she went to bed each night listening to drums and firecrackers.

The neighbors and relatives knew Reynaldo's home was no longer open to the posada procession, the ritual search for a home for Joseph and Mary. And Vicenta had quit the midnight Mass three years ago, the same time she had taken the candle off the corner shelf. In their new commitment to Jesus, there did not seem to be room for Christmas. Reina was grateful to be free of that wasteful idolatry and to experience worshiping Jesus in spirit and in truth. If only all their old habits were so easy to release.

After the deafening explosion of Christmas Eve fireworks and before the noise and commotion of New Year's Day, Reina felt the first pains of childbirth. She sent Eliza over the hill to Leland and Esther's house to ask for a ride to the hospital. She filled a bag with a few personal items, a neatly folded blue baby shawl, and a tiny shirt and diaper. Then she shuffled out the trail to meet Leland's Blazer at the road.

December 29, 1984, found Reina recovering in bed at Frank and Marilyn Martin's house in San Juan. She had come here to rest for a few days before braving the rough road and the foot trails of La Laguna. Joel's breath made warm puffs against Reina's cheek. She smiled into the tiny, perfect face. Surely everything would turn out all right for her family.

Reynaldo came into the room and stood looking down at her. He put his finger into the little hand flung open against the sheet, and a row of minute fingers closed over his. Though Reynaldo said nothing, the softness and longing on his face as he looked down at his newborn son filled Reina with an aching cry for healing for them all.

Until October, the past year and a half had been good for their family. Benjamín had been born in an interval of peace, and Reynaldo had shared the joy of his babyhood in a way he had never done with the others. Would Reynaldo stay strong for this little one?

Leland and Esther arrived that evening with the Blazer to take Reina back to La Laguna. She climbed into the back seat and Reynaldo handed her Joel, asleep in his snug blue shawl; then he crowded into the seat next to her. His strength and gentleness next to Reina filled her heart with tenderness toward him. If only this moment could last forever.

When the Blazer stopped at the foot of their trail, Reina drew the shawl over the baby's face and handed him to Reynaldo. They stepped from the warmth of the Blazer into the crisp cold and climbed through the dusk to the house.

As soon as they opened the door, the children crowded around.

Three-year-old Marixa's eyes widened. She stretched out a hand, touching the soft blue blanket, tugging back a fringe covering the baby's tiny cheek.

"What is his name?" Juana and Sonia breathed with one voice.

"His name is Joel," Reynaldo said, smiling down at them. He tipped the baby down a bit, giving Benjamín a better look. Then he handed him to Eliza, who was waiting with shining eyes beside her older brothers. She clutched the baby against her while the others watched, smiling, a circle of

Joel

family love, knit together by this miracle.

Vicenta leaned close and gazed into the baby's face. "He's got a nose just like his papa's. You're looking good, Reina, but lie down and get your rest. If the baby fusses tonight, Eliza or I can get up with him."

It was bedtime, but no one wanted to go. No one wanted this evening to end.

Joel was two weeks old. The children had been asleep for hours, but Reina was still up, waiting, praying, listening for the bark of the dog, longing for the sound of Reynaldo's footsteps outside, yet dreading it.

At last she heard him. He came in and closed the door softly. Relieved, she approached him in the darkness. The revolting smell of alcohol hit her like a wall.

"Reynaldo, you've been drinking again!"

He leaned toward her, and she shrank from his breath.

"What is it to you? Get out of my life!" In the sleeping house, his words were quiet, for her ears only, but measured, deliberate, and forceful. "It's. My. Life. I'll do what I want with it."

There was nothing to say. She would choke if she tried to speak. Pain clutched her heart, as if her life were being sucked out in a soundless scream. She stumbled back to her bed and lay frozen, longing to sleep, to wake in the morning, to find it was all a bad dream.

Reina fogged awake to the barking of the dog. The sun was barely up. Leland's voice was calling in the courtyard. Vicenta, already starting the day's work, answered him, and Leland asked for Reynaldo.

Reina shook Reynaldo's shoulder to wake him. When he understood that Leland was there to see him, he went out. The men spoke in low voices, but Reina caught most of the conversation.

"Brother, we are sorry to come so early," Leland said, "but I need to go to the city today, and I didn't want to wait another day to talk to you. We've come to find out if all is well with you."

In the heavy silence that followed, a rooster crowed somewhere.

"Reynaldo, someone said they saw you drunk last night. I refuse to believe it unless I hear it from you."

There was more quiet discussion, and then she heard Reynaldo's voice clearly. He was crying. "I just don't have the strength to keep trying. I stayed free of it for almost two years. I thought I'd never go back to drinking. So why did I start giving in again? What good is it to keep fighting?"

The rooster crowed again, a wail in the foggy morning.

"It's too hard. I'm a failure at everything I ever wanted to be."

"Oh, brother, repent and press on. God has said His strength is made perfect in our weakness. He says He will never leave you or forsake you. You have a beautiful family who loves you and needs you. You have a new little son, brother. You have so many reasons to try again, so many reasons to be faithful!"

"They would all be better off without me," Reynaldo said. "My wife doesn't want me. I'm no good to anybody. All I do is hurt and disappoint the children. You don't understand how it is."

Reina was crying now. If only there were someone to talk to who *would* understand. Maybe she could talk to Esther—but what could Esther understand of the wrenching hopelessness Reina was feeling? Her mind traveled in a circle, as if calling at the door of one friend's house after another, seeking a safe place to pour out her heart, a person who could clear the darkness of her mind and make everything right again. But always she returned to the lonely knowledge that no one on earth could make her life right. No one.

Oh, Lord, you are my only hope, and I don't know how to pray. Lord, you know I want to love my husband, and you know how I pity him. Still, right now I feel mostly resentment. I feel too empty and weak to hope anymore. Oh, God, sometimes I think I hate him.

Reina brushed her lips against Joel's silky black hair, then crushed the baby to her breast. Tears scalded her cheeks.

Joel

As days turned to weeks, Reynaldo and Reina moved through their days like two tomcats, keeping their distance from each other, attacking if the other passed too close. There seemed nothing left to talk about—nothing they agreed on anyway. Sometimes Reina tried to intervene when he lashed out at one of the children, but it only made things worse; he would turn on her or stalk away to drink. She hated when he sent one of the girls up to the little store on the mountain to buy his *cusha*.

When he was drunk, the children tried to stay out of his way. It hurt them to see their papa inflamed with *cusha*. It tore at their hearts to run from the papa they loved when he staggered after them with a machete.

It hurt them too to see Mama arguing with Papa, both when he was drunk and when he was sober. Couldn't she give him a little space? Couldn't she see he felt bad enough already?

Reynaldo was sober less and less often. Once again fear and hunger haunted the little house against the mountain. Aware that Reynaldo was no longer providing for the family, Leland came to talk with Vicenta and Reina about the family's needs.

"The children are embarrassed to go to school," Reina admitted. "Their clothes are worn out or too small, but I have no way to buy them clothes. If they have anything nice, Reynaldo disappears with it. If we harvest anything, we have to eat it right away, or he sells it to buy *cusha*."

"We had a nice kettle we used for cooking the corn and heating water," Vicenta said. "Yesterday when I got back from washing clothes at the river, it was gone."

"We will do what we can to help" Leland said. True to his word, every two weeks, and sometimes oftener, he rode his horse down the steep trail, bringing corn or beans or rice or school clothes. The neighbors looked up from chopping wood or scrubbing clothes and nodded knowingly at each other.

"Reina is milking them for all she can get."

"That's all she wants with that church."

"She takes clothes from those foreigners and then turns around and sells them. I saw the clothes myself, hanging from Evelina's clothesline."

As the rumors erupted again, casting more shame and suspicion on her family, something wound tighter and tighter inside Reina. *What good does it do to keep trying? People will think what they want to think.* She laid her Bible on a high shelf and refused to open it.

CHAPTER 28

Homeless

The pasture was dry and meager, and the cow looked hungry. Reina headed toward the cow shed to throw her an armload of the hay piled just outside. Reynaldo was standing near the shed, she noticed, his eyes bloodshot and his hand gripping a machete. She hated to go near him when he was this drunk, and she kept him in the corner of her eye as she hurriedly stooped for an armload of hay.

He raised his machete, and Reina dropped the hay and ran. Her foot caught on a root, and she sprawled onto the ground. Searing pain shot through her back, ripped down her legs, and popped in her head as the flat of his machete caught her where she lay across the scattered hay, begging God to spare her life.

Reynaldo hit her only once and then walked away. She could hear him crying.

Reina staggered to her feet, surprised that she could stand. Her nose was bleeding. She lifted her apron to wipe away the blood, then looked at it in horror. It wasn't just blood, but a transparent, blood-tinged fluid.

Lying across her bed that afternoon, Reina cried as she pondered the shape of her life. She still went to church on Sundays when no one was sick, but her heart was not in it anymore. She didn't belong there; there were too many misunderstandings. She didn't feel safe anywhere.

Who would help her and her Reynaldo?

One day not much later, Reynaldo sharpened his machete and asked Reina to follow him up the mountain. Afraid to go and afraid to refuse, she went with him.

They trudged up the mountain trail in silence until they were far from any houses, way up where Reina had known freedom and joy as a girl, gathering berries and baking potatoes and embroidering tablecloths—where God used to live. How could this be the same mountain, the same girl? A numb terror pushed at her pores. *Where is he taking me?*

Deep in the woods, Reynaldo sat down on a log. His elbows stuck through holes in his shirt sleeves where he propped them on his knees. Gripping his sharpened machete with one calloused hand, he dropped his head into the other and sobbed.

Reina waited. She reached her hand toward him just a little, then drew it back. Her hand looked so small beside his. She had always admired his hands, but they made her feel confused now, and full of a deep, helpless longing.

She looked up through trees to the sunlit sky. Leaves fluttered and flashed like a canopy of dancing green lace. She looked down at her husband sobbing into his hands. It was hard to breathe. The machete lay in deep grass between his feet.

She reached out again. This time she softly laid her hand on his shoulder. "Reynaldo?" Her voice was strained.

He didn't look up.

"Reynaldo, what's wrong? Why are you crying?"

No answer.

She stood still a long time, listening to the crying. Any new move might be the wrong one. Funny how little it mattered. What was there to live for anymore anyway? Still she felt clammy—breathless one moment, breathing too hard the next. Pain flowed like acid through her veins—pain for both of them and for all their dear children.

Homeless

Reynaldo stood up as if she wasn't there and started back down the path. She followed his slumped back and unsteady steps at a safe distance all the way home.

Reynaldo's violence escalated as his drunkenness increased. Several more times he made Reina go with him when he headed up the mountain with a freshly sharpened machete. Each time he sat up there and cried, until finally he picked up his machete and went home. He worked less and less, and he drank the little money he made. Without Leland's help, they might have had to live on wild plants. Reina felt desperate. How long could they go on like this?

In May 1985, Dionel and Eliza contracted measles. Already in their mid-teens, they got sicker than any of the family had ever seen them. They lay day after day, limp and miserable and feverish beyond belief. Vicenta wiped their faces with cool cloths, and Reina worried. *Oh, God, I'm afraid they will die. How could I live without those two?*

While the family suffered and waited, Reynaldo was out drinking again.

One evening Vicenta set glasses of fresh water beside Dionel and Eliza as the others wearily went to bed. Soon the house was quiet except for an occasional moan from one of the sick ones.

Suddenly the door flew open. They burst awake as Reynaldo charged into the house, hollering, "Get out of my house, all of you!" He was swinging his machete.

"Be reasonable, Reynaldo," Reina pleaded. "You're waking all the children, and Dionel and Eliza are sick. Besides, where would we go?"

"I don't care where you go. Just get out!" he shouted. "All I get is bickering and criticism, and I'm sick and tired of it. It's time a man has a little respect in his own house."

"Please, it's the middle of the night. This is ridiculous."

"I said get out!" Reynaldo lunged toward her and waved his machete in her face. The children watched wide-eyed from their beds.

Reina picked up Joel. He was wailing, but there was no time to feed him or even to bounce him quiet. She tried to hush him with a hand over his mouth.

Vicenta began helping the little ones up and out the door. "Here, get your coats or put your blankets around you."

Eliza groaned, a pitiful little sound, as she got up and tried to pull her coat on. Dionel's eyes were glassy, his face sad. They were too sick to be out of bed, but there was no choice.

Together Vicenta, Reina, and the children slipped and slogged in the dark over the muddy trails toward Leland and Esther's house. They hated to wake the Seibels, but it was too cold to keep the little ones outside all night.

The next day, Leland rode his horse to La Laguna and tried to talk with Reynaldo. Reynaldo was still angry and unreasonable. "I'm done with this," he said. "I don't want them in my house."

Leland helped the family move to an empty house high on the hill along the road to Sibilia. The house belonged to one of Reina's relatives. With floors of concrete and walls that kept out the cold, it felt like a mansion to the children from La Laguna.

Reina paced the floor of the house on the hill, crying. *This house isn't my home. We can't live forever on the mission's charity. If we can't go back home, we'll have to pay rent, and we can't pay rent without money.*

Eliza and Dionel lay on blankets on the floor, coughing, their skin a scaly mass of cracks and rash, their eyes gunky and seeping, their breathing painful. Reina felt like crying every time she looked at them. Vicenta was doing everything that could be done, but that wasn't much. She had just had one of the girls borrow a pail of water and a cup from the neighbors, and she was urging the sick ones to drink.

Reina paced the floor with Joel. She sat down and thought. She watched the children moan and toss and cough and scratch. She stood again and paced.

She loved the children, but how could they know it? It was all she could do to stay sane from morning to evening. One day recently, before they had left home—one day when she had borne more than she could handle— Reina had told Reynaldo she was done with it all. She had grabbed a rope and headed up the trail toward the woods. Sonia, Juana, and Marixa had all run after her, scampering, stumbling, and crying, "Mama, don't! Don't die, Mama! Come back!"

Somehow she had shaken them off. But up in the woods alone, she had gotten hold of herself and had returned. She still cringed at the memory of her children's tear-streaked faces and fear-filled eyes as they followed her that day. She loved all these precious children who depended on her... but she was so tired.

Conrado, consumed by a new hatred for his father, disappeared for four days after Reynaldo chased them out. Leland went looking for him without success. Dionel and Eliza were still seriously sick. The darkness threatened to engulf Reina.

Leland returned to La Laguna to get a few things Reina needed. He had another talk with Reynaldo, but Reynaldo didn't budge. Laden with a skillet, a kettle, a few spoons and plates, some ragged blankets, soap, and the latest decree from Reynaldo, Leland stopped by Reina's temporary shelter. The household items helped, but they wouldn't make this place home. The whole family longed to go back to La Laguna.

In that fine house that was not hers, a plan slowly unfolded in Reina's mind. *Love finds a solution,* she thought, and there was no one else to do it. She borrowed a little money and caught a bus to Guatemala City, where she poured out her problems to Yanet over cups of sweet coffee. Yanet listened with sympathy and concern, and together they discussed Reina's options.

When Reina returned to the borrowed house outside Sibilia, Leland came to talk things over again. "Reina, have you considered putting at least some of your children into other homes that might be better equipped to care for them for now? I am sure there are families in the church who would be willing to help."

Reina shrugged slightly, her lips compressed into a tight line. Juana's round face appeared in the doorway, laughing. Sonia grabbed her from behind, and both girls ran off, giggling. Juana's new shoes flashed in the sunlight, a cherished reward from her first-grade teacher for good work in school. *Why shouldn't all my children have new shoes? Maybe they could... Maybe I will show everyone that I, Reina, can buy them new shoes.*

Until her plans bore fruit, however, something else would have to be done. But giving away her children? She hated the idea. Still, if she couldn't be with them anyway . . . "Let me think about it," she told Leland.

Norma came and took Dionel and Eliza to the doctor. Slowly they began to improve. At least here in the borrowed house, they could get the rest they so desperately needed. It wasn't home, but it was safe. Between spring downpours, the men from the church came and leveled a building site on Vicenta's land, a bit farther up the canyon and even tighter against the mountain than Reynaldo's house.

Months would pass and the dust would blow again before Vicenta would move into her new wooden house with a metal roof, standing strong and solid on its block foundation. But before Vicenta's house was finished, Reina had left for the city.

CHAPTER 29

A New Normal

Reina found a job that suited her, cleaning offices and keeping house for a wealthy lawyer in Guatemala City. Because a doctor had told her Aide was suffering from malnutrition, she kept Aide with her in the city. During the day, Aide stayed with the family of Reina's boss. At fifteen, she helped the lawyer's wife around the house and cared for the children too.

On weekends, Reina and Aide attended the Mennonite Air Missions church in Guatemala City. The meetinghouse was only a short walk from her job, and Reina liked the church. The people were kind and accepting, and she was free of the baggage of suspicions and rumors that weighed her down in the little church in El Edén.

At home, Reynaldo was miserable. Reina! His hopes and dreams had been built on her. She was the key to his dream: a cozy home, with sons and daughters growing up in a mother's love. A mother who touched them, sang to them, listened to their childish hopes and fears, taught them right from wrong. Now she was gone. He could hardly bear to look at three-year-old Benjamín and six-month-old Joel.

He knew he had made her life miserable, but didn't anyone care that he was miserable too?

Living alone in a house he had built for his family, lonely, hopeless, angry with himself and with Reina, he fled for comfort into the arms of the very vice that had robbed what was most precious from his own boyhood, the same vice that had now stolen from him and his sons what he most wanted to give them. Oblivion was easier than this crushing depression.

Reynaldo had let go of Jesus, the Healer. Now he was alone to fight the clawing cravings, and to bear the knowledge that by his own choice, *cusha* had sunk its fangs into his family and torn his children from their mama. *How have I fallen so low?* he thought. *I make my own little girls go over the mountain to get* cusha *for me . . . I must be out of my mind . . . It's all Reina's fault . . . If only Reina . . . What a miserable father I am! I'm nothing but a failure.*

After Vicenta's house was finished, she and the children always slept there, although they once again began spending their days at Reynaldo's house, where Vicenta would cook and care for everyone.

Joel's first birthday was torture for Reynaldo, with its barrage of memories—memories of Benjamín's first birthday, of hope, happiness, friends, and family. *Why did I ever think it would last?* Looking into Joel's innocent little face while Vicenta cleaned up supper that evening, Reynaldo experienced a jolt of clarity. *Oh, God, what have I done to my family!*

When Carl Sensenig and deacon Gabino came to see him a week later, Reynaldo wept in grief and repentance. He would try again. This time he would be strong. That night Reynaldo held Joel until the baby fell asleep, his dark hair tousled and sweaty against his father's arm. *Oh, Lord, surely this time I'll be true. I want you, and I want my family.* Peace crept into his soul.

Reynaldo returned to his work with determination. Maybe it was not too late to bring the family together again. A few weeks later he was walking on government land when he came upon a massive dead eucalyptus tree. Pushing his hat back and gazing upward, he made some quick calculations and smiled. This tree would yield a lot of good lumber. It was like a gift right from God's generous hand.

According to the law, a special permit was required to cut down any tree, even on one's own land—unless it was already dead. Anyone found working up a tree with signs of recent life faced a fine. A dead tree on public land was a treasure.

Reynaldo found a lumber buyer who would pay in advance. Dionel was glad to help out with the sawing; he liked working with his father. Reynaldo was a patient teacher. A few times when Dionel was younger, he had gone with Reynaldo to farm at the coast. Reynaldo had shown him how to cut the hairy green sesame stalks and stack them together in shocks to dry. When they were dry, he had taught Dionel to shake the stalks over a cloth to save every seed in the fragile, fuzzy pods.

At the end of the season, when all the corn and sesame seed had been sold, Papa had handed Dionel a share of the money. "Here, son, you worked hard, and you earned this. Be careful with it." Then he had smiled encouragingly and added, "I want to see how you'll spend it."

To Dionel it had felt like a sacred trust. He would see to it that his father never regretted giving him this money.

That had been a long time ago. Now, standing beneath the sawmill he had helped Reynaldo erect over a deep gully, Dionel tipped his head back and squinted into the top half of the glistening face above him. His father's dark eyes looked down past the bulbous toe pads that held him steady on the edge of a heavy hand-hewn support timber.

The log they were sawing rested on two parallel timbers, between which ran the blade of the rip saw, pulled up and down by a man on each end, one standing on top of the log, one beneath. Since the underside of the log was the easier end of the saw, but also the most dangerous, they took turns—sometimes up and sometimes down. It was hard work, but the long, grating strokes, one after another against the grain of the conquered tree, the alternate up-and-down pull, the body above in perfect coordination with the one below, slowly sliced board after board from what had once been a round log.

A neighbor walked by. "Found yourself some lumber, huh? I know a guy in town who is looking to buy some."

"Well, send him out. Maybe we can make a deal," Reynaldo answered.

Once the neighbor was out of earshot, Dionel asked Reynaldo, "Isn't this lumber already sold?"

"Yeah, I sold it already, but the buyer doesn't care where the lumber comes from, and he doesn't want it for a few months yet. I'll find another tree before then."

Dionel thought of the chicken compost his father had bought on credit from a farmer in San Juan months ago. Reynaldo had assured the chicken farmer that he would pay for the compost when his wheat sold, and Dionel had thought no more of it until a letter came from the farmer asking where his money was. By then the wheat had been harvested and the money spent.

Dionel felt embarrassed for his father. He knew where much of the wheat money had gone. He missed the Papa who had pressed the sesame seed money into his hand and trusted him to spend it wisely. Still, he knew Papa was trying. He would do all he could to help.

Reynaldo sold and delivered the lumber to the second buyer. When it was time to deliver the lumber to the original buyer, Reynaldo still hadn't found another tree to cut. The buyer was enraged. "I was counting on that. I paid for it. You're nothing but a no-good thief!" He threatened to get his cash back, no matter what it took.

Since Reina had gone to the city, there was less fighting in the family, but every couple of months, she came home for a week or so. Sometimes she would sleep at home and sometimes at Vicenta's house. Conrado lived at home too, and he and Reynaldo were in constant conflict. Even during good times, there had always seemed to be arguments, yelling, and chaos around Conrado.

The burden of trying to provide for them all, the strife in the family, and the guilt of his dishonesty placed tremendous pressure on Reynaldo—and always in the background he could hear the call of *cusha*.

On one of Reina's visits home, she and Reynaldo had a long talk. Despite her city job, unpaid bills were stacking up. Something had to be done. The cheated lumber buyer would need to be satisfied. Furthermore, their supply of corn was almost used up, just as the market price was soaring.

A New Normal

"We could sell the spring," Reina suggested. Clear cold water was the one resource they had in abundance.

They sold the spring.

On another desperate occasion when they could not meet their obligations, one of them suggested offering to sell some land to Leland. Vicenta had already divided most of her land among her children, and Reynaldo and Reina sold Leland a piece of Reina's share. As long as they had land, they were not completely destitute.[1]

The sale of the spring and the land enabled them to pay off some, but not all, of their debt and buy corn to feed the children and the cow until the next harvest. As the two of them pulled together to make things work, Reina began to hope. *If Reynaldo stays sober, maybe I can return home.*

In early February, at corn-planting time, Leland came to look over the piece of land they had sold him. It was steep, but clear and tillable. Leland walked down to the lower field to talk to Reynaldo. "Go ahead and plant this for your family as you have always done," Leland told him.

When Reynaldo opened his mouth to answer, Leland's heart sank; Reynaldo had been drinking again.

As Reynaldo gradually returned to drinking, Reina gave up her hope of returning home. Philip and Karen Ebersole, who had replaced Henry and Gwen Hertzler in the house above the schoolhouse, had once offered to take Sonia into their home. Should Reina let her go? The thought of Sonia in the care of that godly young family comforted Reina's heart, and it would be one fewer mouth to feed.

So it was arranged, and in June of 1986, exactly a year after Reina went to work in the city, ten-year-old Sonia left her family to live with Philip and Karen Ebersole. Sonia would still see her siblings every day at school, and the Ebersoles' two little boys helped fill her time, but she still missed her own little brothers.

---

[1] Guatemalan soil is rich and deep, the most important natural resource in the country. Because of that soil, Guatemala—despite the depth of its poverty—is more prosperous than its neighbors.

SONG OF THE SHEPHERDESS

A few weeks later, Carl Sensenig, who was visiting from Pennsylvania, and Gabino, the deacon, came to see Reynaldo at his request.

"I had a dream." Reynaldo could barely compose himself to tell his story. "I was in hell. It was an awful place. The suffering, the darkness, the oppression, the hate—there is no way to describe how terrible it was. No one cared about anyone there; they were totally bound up in their own agony. If you had seen and heard what I did, let me tell you, you would do whatever it takes to keep from going there."

After a long pause, Reynaldo continued, "Brothers, I need help. Twice already I have had uncontrollable tremors. They say that can only happen to you two times. If it happens a third time, you die." His voice was low and desperate. "If I keep drinking, I know it will happen again. If it does, I'll die, and I'll be in that horrible place!"

Carl reached out and grasped Reynaldo's trembling hands, his heart weeping with his brother.

"It isn't too late, Reynaldo," Carl said gently. "You are still here. God hasn't given up on you. His arms are open to receive you back."

"I am afraid it is too late for my family. I'd give anything to have us all together again, but my family is torn apart. My wife is in Guatemala City, and when she is here, all we do is fight." More tears streamed down Reynaldo's weathered cheeks. "I couldn't take it. *Cusha* was the only way I could get away from the frustration. And of course that only made it worse."

As Carl prayed for him, Reynaldo dropped his face into his hands and wept. "Whatever happens, I have to quit drinking," he said, looking up at last. "I must be done with it forever. I'm sick of it. I just want to know peace with God and have my family together again. My children need me, and I want to be ready to meet God when I die. I know God sent that dream as a warning. You can't imagine how awful it was."

Bowing his head, Reynaldo poured out his heart to his heavenly Father in repentance, pleading with Him for His mercy and for strength to be faithful.

Carl and Gabino encouraged Reynaldo in his renewed commitment and promised to stay in touch. Reynaldo's story tore at Carl's heart. How little he himself had known of this level of addiction, grief, and depression, but Jesus was no stranger to this, and Carl felt His compassion for this troubled brother.

In August the Ebersoles prepared to return to their home in the United States. They had learned to love ten-year old Sonia, and she was content and happy in their home. Vicenta came to talk about Sonia's future.

"Sonia, do you want to stay with the Ebersoles?" Grandma asked, sadness showing in her eyes despite her calm demeanor. "They would like to adopt you and keep you for their own little girl."

Sonia thought about it. Not once in the two months she lived here had she been truly hungry. It seemed another meal was on the table every time she turned around, but the food wasn't nearly as good as Grandma's. Her bed here was always soft and clean and warm, but there were no sisters to share it with. Her hair was always clean and combed, and Brother Philip was kind, but he wasn't Papa.

Sonia felt ashamed when she thought of the night Brother Philip had found Papa lying drunk beside the road. Brother Philip had brought him into his own house and given him food, clean clothes, and a bed. Sonia was glad Brother Philip had found Papa and that he was snug and safe in bed. But in the morning when they all had woken up, Papa was gone—with Brother Philip's nice clothes on, his own pile of rags left on the floor by the bed.

Sonia knew Papa would never do something like that if he wasn't drinking. Drinking turned Papa into a different man. But now Papa had repented and quit drinking. At school, Juana had told her that Papa was planting again and cutting wood.

Her mother was away in the city, so Sonia wouldn't see her much either way, but Papa was at home and Grandma was at home. Sonia knew when she looked into Grandma's face that Grandma wanted her very much. Grandma didn't want her to be the Ebersoles' little girl and go far away to the United States where she might never see her again—where even if Grandma did see her again, she would be Sonia Ebersole, not Sonia Monterroso.

Sonia Ebersole would always have everything she needed—everything but her own dear brothers and sisters, her own Papa and Mama, and her own sweet Grandma.

Sonia Monterroso would be hungry and cold. She would have to work hard, and her clothes would be torn and dirty. But Sonia Monterroso would be with her own family.

Sonia knew what she wanted.

Sonia walked home with Grandma that day. They left right after lunch to beat the rain. All the way home, Grandma held her hand, as though she was afraid Sonia Monterroso would disappear.

The year of 1986 was tough. Even in good years, many highland families run out of corn, their chief staple, a month or two before November's harvest, forcing them to buy enough to carry them over. This year buying corn was a nightmare, with prices at an unheard-of seven dollars per hundred pounds. Reynaldo didn't have that kind of money, and he shrank from borrowing, as lenders were charging interest rates of ten percent a month. Besides, he was still carrying debt from previous years.

Sometimes Reynaldo felt the financial pressure would crush him like a corn kernel between the two giant stones at the mill. He craved alcohol. Yielding to the voice in his head that screamed at him to escape the anguish and pressure, he began drinking again. After a drinking spree, the guilt and hopelessness of failure added to the cravings clawing at his mind—until he numbed them again.

CHAPTER 30

Churchyard Showdown

"I can't go back to Conrado's house!" Lidia's eyes filled with tears as she sat next to her parents and looked across their kitchen table at Leland and Esther.

Lidia had married Conrado a year before and happily moved from her parent's home in El Edén to Vicenta's house on La Laguna. Her joy had been short-lived as she came to know her husband's selfishness and cruelty. However, she loved and respected Conrado's mother, grandmother, and sisters.

Vicenta had invited Lidia to come along to church, and in that place of love and acceptance, Lidia had heard the message of Christ's sacrifice for her, and of His forgiveness and healing. She had believed the good news and repented. On a rainy day in October 1986, Lidia had stood beside Aide, her thirteen-year-old sister-in-law, as both of them were baptized into Christ.

The love of her heavenly Father became a source of deep comfort to Lidia as Conrado grew increasingly abusive. After a particularly brutal beating, her parents had insisted that she return to their home. "Next thing you know he'll do something that will kill the baby, if he doesn't kill you first," they said.

Now Leland and Esther listened to her story with sympathy. "Conrado didn't mind at first," she said. "Lots of girls go home to have their babies. But now he is angry that I won't come back." Lidia looked up trustingly at her father.

"We have forbidden her to go back to him," Lidia's father explained. "It isn't safe."

"We understand," Leland said. "But we have missed you at church, Lidia. It is important for you to come to church."

Lidia's glance darted about the room. "I would love to be with you all at the meetings, but I am scared. I can't go there anymore," she said.

"Has something happened to make you so afraid?" Brother Leland asked.

Lidia pressed her cheek against her baby's mop of curly black hair, and her eyes filled with pain. "It's Conrado. Last Sunday I met him on the road. He grabbed baby Alberto and ran off with him. He yelled at me that I would never see my baby again." A sob shook her shoulders. "Just then a neighbor came around a bend in the road, and Conrado got scared and slowed down. I ran to him and reached for Alberto, and he handed him back to me. Then I hurried home as fast as I could. I haven't gone out alone since then."

"I understand your concern," Leland said. "How about if I come and get you with my car?" He looked at her father. "I will take responsibility for her safety and bring her back here when the meeting is over."

The older couple looked doubtful.

"It is important to spend time with the church," Leland explained. "All of us need the fellowship of other Christians, and we need the teaching from the Holy Scriptures in order to grow. You are a very young Christian, Lidia."

"I want to come," she said softly. "I'm just so scared."

Lidia's hand fidgeted with a paper on the edge of the table. Esther put her hand over Lidia's, and Lidia relaxed a little. "Okay, I'll come if you promise to bring me back in your car. Is it okay, Papa? I could leave Alberto here with you and Mama."

"I don't feel good about it," her father persisted.

"Señor, I will take care of her. There will be people all around. I assure you I will bring her back safely," Leland said.

Churchyard Showdown

"Okay," her father said finally. "I guess you can go if you really want to—as long as you won't be alone on the road at any time."

The following Sunday, Lidia sank into the back seat of the mission Blazer. Esther smiled at her and closed the door. "We'll be back in a couple of hours," Leland called to Lidia's parents as they waved goodbye.

It seemed almost silly to drive the short distance to the meeting, but as the Blazer bounced and whined up the hill to the church house, Lidia's eyes darted about, checking one side of the road and then the other for Conrado.

When they arrived at the church house, Lidia joined gratefully in the singing, glad and relieved to be there again. When the meeting was over, Lidia turned to greet the ladies behind her, who welcomed her warmly and inquired about the baby.

Benigno's daughter Milagro hurried up the aisle toward Lidia. "Conrado is outside. He wants to talk to you."

Overhearing, Esther slipped out the other end of the bench and scurried to where Leland was chatting on the men's side. "Leland," she said, her voice urgent, "Conrado is outside asking to see Lidia." She watched apprehensively as Lidia made her way toward the double doors at the back of the room.

"Go out and stay with her," said Leland. "I can't forbid him to talk to her; he is her husband. They aren't alone out there. She'll be okay."

Esther moved toward the doors, pausing here and there to shake a hand held out in greeting. As she reached the double doors, Milagro exploded through them from outside, her eyes as big as tomatoes. "Conrado is pulling on Lidia!" she exclaimed.

"Go tell Leland right away," Esther said. As she burst through the doors into the sunlight, Leland's promise to Lidia's parents pounded in her mind. Her heart lurched at the scene outside. Conrado was gripping both Lidia's thin arms behind her back, shoving her ahead of him toward the road.

Lidia was bracing herself. "Let me go! Let me go!" she screamed.

Esther hurried toward them, praying that God would keep His protecting arms around Lidia and that Leland would arrive quickly. Conrado paused when he saw her, then his eyes shifted beyond her. Following his gaze, Esther felt her knees go weak with relief. Leland was striding toward them.

"Conrado!" Leland called.

Conrado glared at the young pastor, never loosening his grip on his wife's arms.

"If you want her to go home with you, get in the car with us, and we'll take you to talk to her parents," Leland said. "I promised them I would bring her home. Get in the car and let's go down there."

Conrado glanced scornfully from Leland to Philip Ebersole, who had appeared at Leland's side; then he tightened his grip on Lidia's arms and resumed tugging her toward the road.

Lidia struggled. Her cries rang over the churchyard. "He's . . . he's going to kill me! Someone help me! He's going to take me over the hill and kill me!"

Leland leaned toward Esther. "Get the car and bring it right up here beside them," he said. Esther hurried to obey. Why did the car take so long to start, so long to back up? Finally she pulled up beside Conrado. The veins in his forehead bulged behind beads of sweat, and his hands gripped Lidia like a vice.

Esther scooted into the front passenger seat, leaving the driver's seat open on Leland's side. The church house had emptied into the yard. The adults watched with concern, the children with frozen fascination.

Praying hard, Leland pulled open both driver's side doors. Conrado was strong, but small. Together Leland and Philip could overpower him. Leland shook off the thought. Physical force was not an option even to protect another. Christ's way is love. Leland trusted in the presence of his Father.

Lidia strained toward the Blazer. One of her arms broke free. In a flash, Leland chopped his hand over Conrado's other wrist, breaking his grip. Lidia was free. She dashed toward the car and jumped into the back seat, and Leland slammed the door.

Conrado's eyes bulged, and his face was red. His words were measured and ominous. *"Nobody* hits me and gets away with it."

Right now Leland didn't care. Lidia was safe in the car. He slid behind the wheel and pulled the door closed behind him.

Churchyard Showdown

Conrado recovered his wits. Legs set apart, he planted himself in front of the Blazer. Leland shifted into reverse. Conrado leaped like a tiger onto the hood. The crowd in the churchyard gasped. Leland hesitated, then shifted into first and eased toward the road. Conrado slid off the hood and threw himself in front of the tires. Leland quickly braked and shifted into reverse. Conrado was back on the hood.

Leland idled the engine, considering his options. As he looked at Conrado, lying across the hood in front of his windshield, his heart was touched. Lidia wasn't the only one hurting; this nineteen-year-old boy was full of pain and confusion too.

Leland knew what he had to do. He put the Blazer in park and opened the door. Conrado slid from the hood onto his feet and braced himself as Leland walked toward him.

"Conrado," Leland said gently, "I'm sorry I hit you. I really am. But we don't want to see you do something worse to your wife. If you take her over the hill and kill her or something, things will be much worse for you than they are now. But I'm sorry I hit you. It was not right." Leland felt peace as he looked into Conrado's stony stare. "Here I am. If you want to hit me, go ahead."

Slowly, Conrado's hand slid backward along his side, then inched into his pocket. Leland felt his heartbeat quicken, but he stood quietly. Surely Jesus would do the same in his place.

Conrado's face was a cold mask as he closed his hand on something in his pocket and began sliding it out. Esther, watching through the windshield of the Blazer, prayed as she never had before. Every eye in the group was fixed on the edge of that pocket as Conrado's hand emerged, gripping—a small notepad.

Deliberately Conrado pulled a pen from his shirt pocket, squinting at the Blazer's license plate and scribbling something on his paper. Then he wheeled and stalked away.

Reina was at home the next morning when Conrado marched into the kitchen and selected a large knife. Checking the steel edge with his thumb, he said, "I'll be waiting for Leland when he walks home from school today." He reached for the sharpening stone.

Reina had heard about the incident at church, and she had no doubt Conrado would do as he said. She yearned to help him—to reach his troubled heart somehow. Surely if he knew how much she loved him, how much *God* loved him, how much potential for good there still was in him . . .

Every purposeful hiss of the stone on Conrado's knife grated across her heart.

Reina could not let this happen. If she left now, cutting across by the shortest route, she could reach the schoolhouse before Leland started home.

Reina hurried up the steep trail, the faces of Leland, Esther, and the little children before her, the sun hot on her back. She pondered the magnitude of the love the Seibels had poured out on her family over the years. *How could Conrado even contemplate this evil deed?*

The schoolhouse was in sight now, and there was Leland, latching the door behind him and whistling as he strolled across the schoolyard.

Reina paused to catch her breath. "Good afternoon, Brother Leland," she called.

"Good afternoon," he answered cheerfully.

"I'm sorry to bother you—but Conrado got a butcher knife out of the kitchen, and he says he is going to kill you on your way home from school. I came to walk home with you. I'm sure he won't hurt you if I'm with you."

"So you think he really meant it?"

"I'm sure he meant it. Don't walk home alone."

"Okay, sister. My life is in God's hands, but I'll be glad to have you walk with me if you think it is best." They walked in silence most of the way, Leland wishing he could feel as calm as he had sounded. What would Conrado attempt in his anger?

When they parted at the Seibel home, they had seen nothing of Conrado. Leland thanked Reina warmly. He opened the door to his house, releasing the welcoming scent of frying chicken.

Sighing in relief, Reina turned her steps toward the woods and home.

Had Conrado really been waiting and decided to keep out of sight, or was it all a bluff? It was impossible to know. Either way, she thanked God for His protection over Brother Leland.

Thwarted today, perhaps Conrado would cool off before he found another opportunity.

CHAPTER 31

Papa Leaves

"You're nothing but a no-good drunk!" Conrado's voice carried from the other side of the house. Dionel felt his stomach twist. Didn't Conrado care what his father was going through? Dionel wrapped the ewe's tether rope around a sapling near a patch of good grass, fighting tears as he jerked the knot tight.

It was right here on this patch of grass that Papa had nearly died a couple of months ago. He had groaned, clutched his chest, and stretched out on the ground, losing consciousness for a few moments. It had been different from his drunken falls, and anyway, he had been sober that day. Was it a heart attack? A stroke? Dionel had stood gazing down helplessly at his stricken father, agonizing over what he could do for him, wondering whether there was time to do anything—aching with love, loss, and longing.

That was when a hard voice had spoken behind him. "Leave him alone. Let him die!"[1]

Dionel had been seized by a terrible loneliness in that moment. Did no one else care that Papa was dying? Did others despise Papa so much that they

---

[1] Years later, Dionel remembered the words, but not the identity of the speaker.

just wanted him out of the way? Dionel was seventeen and could work like a man, but some loads are too heavy even for a man. Dionel had broken down and sobbed for the papa he loved and needed, the papa who didn't have the strength to be there for him and who now seemed to have been abandoned by the last people who might have been able to help.

Now, as he finished tying out the ewe, listening to the loud argument on the other side of the house, the memory brought tears to his eyes.

A yelp of pain jerked him back to the present.

That was Papa!

Dionel raced to the other side of the house. Reina was screaming at Reynaldo. Conrado was brandishing a tree branch and hollering something Dionel couldn't understand. The little ones stood around them crying in terror. Papa had been yelling earlier, but now he was strangely silent, a terrible expression on his face. A large red welt was rising on his forehead.

As Vicenta hurried down the hill toward them from her place, Reynaldo turned without a word and entered the house. Outside, everyone looked at each other, sick at heart. The little ones were still crying.

Papa reappeared, a small bag slung over his shoulder. He moved through the cluster of children outside the door, his shoulders slumped, his face haggard, his eyes dull and hopeless. He rounded the side of the house and walked down the trail without looking back.

Reina watched him go. Was he really leaving? She felt a flicker of relief, followed by panic and then a storm of remorse and confusion.

A few minutes later, Reynaldo staggered into his cousin Amalia's house, slumped into a chair by the table, and buried his face in his arms. Amalia finished the tortilla she was forming and flipped the others off the hot steel. It was nothing new for Reynaldo to drop by her house, discouraged and needing to talk, but today the look in his eyes and his whole manner was different.

Dusting her hands on her apron, Amalia sat down across the table from him.

Reynaldo looked up, his cheeks streaked with tears. "Amalia, I have come to say goodbye. There is no reason for me to stay any longer. I am going to live with my father." He lifted his hand to the thick red bruise on his forehead. It was seeping a little. "Conrado hit me with a branch."

"What was it about this time, Reynaldo?"

Reynaldo poured out his story. He had been leaving the house in search of another drink, and his wife had blocked his way, furiously reminding him that he had been drunk only the night before. Conrado had stepped in, disrespectful and determined to stop him. When Conrado hit him on the head, it was the last straw.

"All we do is fight," Reynaldo said. "My wife doesn't want me, and my family doesn't want me. They are better off without me."

Amalia wanted to say something to make a difference. The man needed hope. But she had said it all so many times already. What difference would it make now?

Reynaldo rose to go. "Amalia," he said, turning back with one hand on the door latch. His voice was hoarse and tragic. "Don't . . . don't forget the children."

"I won't, Reynaldo, and I'll pray for you every day."

He went out, closing the door behind him. Amalia watched through the window as he trudged down the trail. Forty-two years old, the father of nine children—walking away from it all. "Oh, God," she groaned. "Don't leave him alone. And remember those fatherless children."

CHAPTER 32

The Kiss of Belonging

If only I could eat grass like the cow, I wouldn't have to be hungry anymore. Ten-year-old Juana, her hair a tangled mass of dark curls, sat by the spring hole, clutching her tummy. The cow's head was down, ripping at the clumps of fresh grass. Watching her made Juana even hungrier. She imagined a plate full of rice and carrots and greens tossed with scrambled eggs. Closing her eyes, she could almost smell the garlic and cilantro and hot lard.

There had been no breakfast this morning. Grandma said there was no food in the house. She had taken her basket and gone to ask the neighbors for food. Maybe someone would give her something for them to eat.

When I get big, I'm going to the city. There is lots of food in the city. Juana leaned down to drink from the trickle of water where their spring had once been. The water helped a little, but it didn't still the gnawing hunger. She was reminded of the huge clear pool that used to be here, spilling over its edges in noisy foam, splashing down the hill, rushing away in the riverbed below. Since Papa and Mama had decided last summer to sell the spring, the place where the river used to be looked hungry too, as though there was never enough.

The men who bought the spring had dug a hole and put a big concrete tank in the ground. From the tank, long pipes took the water far away where it quenched other people's thirst and watered other people's vegetables. The poor river would be dry and empty forever now, she guessed.

Water still came out of the pipe by the kitchen. Someone from the mission had given Mama the money for the pipe to bring the water from a little spring way up on the hill. Papa and Conrado had strung the pipe all the way down the hill to the house. Mama said she would pay them back as soon as Papa's corn was sold, but they said she didn't have to pay them back.

So now, whenever the dishes needed washing or the baby needed cleaning up, nobody had to carry water from the spring. It was already in the house.

That little spring was almost up at the place where the bus stopped, where Papa would get off when he used to come home from the coast.

Papa used to go down to the coast to work while everybody in the mountains was waiting for the corn to grow in their fields. Many other men also worked at the coast. At the coast there was lots of work, and flat fields where Papa could grow food any time of year.

Juana had all day to think, and if she thought really hard, remembering all the good times, she didn't have to think so much about how hungry and lonely she was. She thought about how she used to sit out here with Sonia and Marixa, waiting for the bus to bring Papa home from the coast. As the time drew nearer and nearer for the bus to come, the girls would get so excited they couldn't even think of anything to talk about. Juana couldn't say how they knew when the bus was almost there. Since it growled along the high road at exactly the same time each day, they could just feel when it was time.

All three girls would try hard to be the first one to see Papa step off the bus. Then they would watch, squirming with delight, while the bus helper climbed around on top of the bus, throwing the big bags down to Papa.

Then he was with them, their very own Papa, beckoning from the top of the trail, calling them to come on up. They would bounce up from the deep grass, calling back to the older ones to come and help, leaping up the trail between the tall corn, too glad to notice the steepness of the trail. Even Aide didn't cry about the steep path those times, as she did when they

The Kiss of Belonging

walked to school.

Papa didn't go to the coast anymore—or come home either. Juana wasn't sure which hunger was worse—the hunger in her tummy or the hunger in her heart. She looked across the fields, high and ragged with wild grasses and weeds. They were as empty of food as Grandma's kitchen, as empty as her own tummy, and she wondered why nobody planted. If she would be big enough, she would plant.

Before Papa drank all the time and Mama went to the city, they all used to work together, cutting the wheat, piling it in shocks with the heads all set the same direction to keep the rain off as it dried. When the wheat was dry, the big threshing rig would come, and they would all watch as it separated the beautiful wheat kernels from the straw.

The cow was grazing next to Juana now, and she could feel her grassy breath and see the green juice on the black lips as she yanked mouthful after mouthful of grass, her wobbly chin jerking toward her knobby knees. At least the cow had plenty to eat.

Oh, Papa, we need you. Don't you know how much we need you?

Juana squeezed her eyes shut, reliving her most precious memory of Papa. There had been an extra nip in the air that night. Juana was nearly asleep, sprawled in her thin nightdress on her wheat straw mat on the floor between the beds. Papa entered the sala, a blast of chill following him in as he opened and closed the door. Juana heard his steps as he approached, preparing to step over her as he always did before getting into his own bed.

Then the footsteps stopped, and Papa was drawing the cover up over her. She felt his fingers brush her shoulders as he tucked the edges in. Juana held perfectly still, mesmerized by the tenderness in his touch. He finished covering her, and for a moment she felt his lips against her forehead; she breathed the woodsy, sawdusty, smoky smell of his hair. She lay perfectly still, trying to freeze the moment, to keep it forever.

Juana had never doubted that Papa loved her, but Papa didn't kiss his little girls. That touch, that single kiss—it had ached all through her. Now, as she sat by the dried-up spring, feeling it all again, hot tears slipped out and rolled down her cheeks.

After Papa had kissed her, she heard him stepping across her bed, shuffling about, removing his shoes. Slowly, slowly, she had pushed the blanket away from her shoulders, bunching it down to her waist, exposing her bare arms to the chilly air. Maybe Papa would see that her cover was off again. Maybe he would come back to her. Maybe he would lean over her and cover her—and kiss her, just once more. She hoped it so hard it hurt.

When she heard Papa's bed creak under him, she relaxed. Still feeling the print of Papa's lips on her face, she relived the kiss over and over until she fell asleep, the blanket still scrunched around her waist.

Sometime, surely, Papa would come back. Then there would be corn in the fields again, and food in the kitchen. Maybe some night when the cold settled into the canyon, some night when her tummy was full of tamales, Papa would tuck her in again and kiss her forehead.

CHAPTER 33

The Wrong Army

It was National Armed Forces Day, June 30, 1987, and the towns were dizzy with parades, marches, food, music, and recruiters.

President Cerezo had come to power in January of 1986, promising to work to strengthen peace in Central America. He claimed he would reestablish respect for human rights and try to start talks with the guerillas.[1]

The army was putting on a great display of cooperation. They were the defenders of the nation, stronger than any institution in the country, stronger than the government itself and subject to no one. But beneath the festivities, unrest simmered as human rights organizations made plans to march in protest of army brutality, and the army prepared to break up the protests with tear gas.[2]

---

[1] *Annual Report of the Inter-American Commission on Human Rights 1985–1986,* September 1986, <http://www.cidh.org/annualrep/85.86eng/toc.htm>, accessed on January 23, 2017.

[2] *Annual Report of the Inter-American Commission on Human Rights 1986–1987,* September 1987, <http://www.cidh.org/annualrep/86.87eng/chap.4b.htm>, accessed on January 24, 2017. During these years, elements of the Guatemalan army, backed and trained by the U.S., were responsible for widespread disappearances and killings of civilians. A human rights organization, Grupo de Apoyo Mutuo (GAM, translated as Mutual Support Group) had documented hundreds of these abuses. On June 30, 1987, on Armed Forces Day, the GAM announced that it would demonstrate publicly in large numbers. The army deployed a column of troops firing tear gas to break up the GAM demonstration.

SONG OF THE SHEPHERDESS

Dionel felt the influence of the charged atmosphere as he approached the army recruitment booth. The recruiter smiled broadly, "We need fine young men like you. The army pays well, and food and lodging are provided. When you put on that uniform, son, you will have joined something greater than yourself: an organization committed to protecting the peace and prosperity of our nation and the lives of our countrymen. This mission and ethic will give you purpose and direction."

The recruiter repeated part of his earlier speech which, shouted through a bullhorn, had drawn Dionel to this side of the crowded street. "The army exists to protect the Guatemalan people and all our marvelous natural resources. Good things are ahead for you as a soldier in the Guatemalan army." He slapped a sheaf of papers onto the stand erected on the sidewalk and held out a pen.

"I won't be eighteen until the middle of July," Dionel said, stalling.

"Not a problem," said the recruiter, smacking the table as if the objection were a bothersome fly. "Our new guidelines allow men as young as sixteen to join, for a limited time. We'll get you signed right up today."

Dionel shook his head and stepped back. Though the recruiter's face kept smiling, his black eyes flashed with a cold, threatening glint.

"I—I really need to think about it," Dionel stammered.

He did think about it. He thought as he walked up the street past the blaring music of marimbas[3] and guitars, past other army recruiters trying to beckon him in, past stalls where the smoky smell of roasted corn and *paches*[4] taunted his empty stomach.

I need to go home. I don't want to be one of them.

Dionel remembered the nights of terror he had known as a child after the army had come through La Cumbre, near his grandpa's house. They had been pursuing the guerrillas like bloodhounds, grilling everyone: "Which of your neighbors are sympathetic? Which houses let the guerrillas in? Who

---

[3] A percussion instrument consisting of a set of wooden bars struck with mallets to produce musical tones.

[4] A type of tamale made with potatoes.

might have fed them?" In an act of brazen terrorism, the army rounded up and murdered several entire households who had been forced to feed the roving guerrillas the night before. Episodes like these were occurring all over Guatemala. No, he didn't want to be part of that brutal machine. He just wanted to go home.

Home? *Oh, God, what is there to go home for?* Loneliness threatened to swallow him alive as he headed out of town toward La Laguna. *Mama is gone. Papa is gone. I don't really have a family anymore.*

The enemy of his soul pounced on the moment. *Your home is nothing but an illusion, a memory. If you want to help your abandoned siblings, make a decent income so you can fill their stomachs and buy them clothes respectable enough to go to school in. It's just a job, Dionel, and there are no other jobs available that pay as well as the army. Why all the scruples when you aren't living like a Christian anyway? You have nothing to lose and so much to gain.*

By the time Dionel broke out of the woods into the clearing against the mountain, he had nearly made up his mind. He detoured to his Uncle Mariano's house to have a talk with his cousin.

"Sergei, what do we have to stop us? With both my parents gone, I don't really have a family anymore. The pay is really good."

They had talked about this before. Sergei gazed across the terraced cornfield, considering. "Why not? We aren't making any money worth our time around here. It might not be that bad if we have each other."

A few weeks later Dionel glanced at his cousin as the heavy gate of the army base clanged shut behind them like a taunt. Sergei was hanging back, letting Dionel lead the way. Dionel's heart thumped. What had they gotten themselves into?

Led by a guard wearing military fatigues and shouldering a machine gun, they crossed an open area heavily guarded by more uniformed soldiers and entered the building where they would register. Some kind of initiation exercise was in progress, and the officers in charge were cursing and hollering, kicking and hitting any new recruits who performed less than perfectly.

Sickened, Dionel realized he had made a horrible mistake. He had joined the enemy, he thought, the same criminals who had slaughtered his grandpa's innocent neighbors and spread fear and hate across the country. But it was too late to turn back now. He had signed himself away, and he was trapped like a rabbit in a snare. He would have to survive it somehow.

Within a couple of days, the cousins from La Laguna experienced the cruel initiation ceremony they had watched on their arrival. The boys tried hard to follow every order, but the event was rigged to be brutal. Every missed cue or imperfect response brought a barrage of kicks, punches, and curses. The pain was intense, but the humiliation was worse. Even a dog didn't deserve this. The term of service ahead of them stretched long and hopeless.

Dionel was glad at least to have Sergei in a bunk nearby, and the boys stuck close to each other for the first week. Then Dionel was assigned to a separate barracks and training group, and after that they saw each other only for a few minutes at meals.

Soon after their arrival, Dionel woke at 2 a.m., blinking groggily into the glare of a searchlight that blazed from the bunkhouse doorway. "Out of bed, everyone!" barked a voice. "Stand at attention!"

The thickness of sleep gave way to a stumbling alertness. The boys were ordered out into the bitter cold of the highland night, where they all ran as the officers shouted curses and threats. Dionel's legs ached, but slowing down was not an option. Often an anguished cry would pierce the night air above the cursing of the officers. Someone had been struck yet again for not keeping up.

Finally, an officer barked, "Go in and get your showers!" They took turns in the showers by groups. Dionel recoiled from the shock of cold water on sweaty skin, and afterward he lay shivering in bed a long time before falling asleep, only to be awakened in minutes by the rising bell.

That must be some sort of initiation, he guessed. But it turned out the night runs were part of the regular routine. Some nights were even worse: they were ordered onto their hands and knees and forced to creep along the cold ground for hours until their elbows and knees bled and Dionel could hear crying in the night all around him. Then they returned to the ice-cold showers and the frustrating interim of rest before the rigors of daytime training.

For three weeks Dionel kept up the pace. The endurance exercises were tough, but the hard-muscled Monterroso cousins found they could swim, run, climb, and jump with the best. There was a thrill in learning to avoid bullets, taking cover behind trees, buildings, or machinery, and to hide in cornfields or other concealment where cover wasn't available. Though the two cousins stayed quiet, trained hard, and generally did well, they continued to be sickened by the brutality inflicted on the less athletic trainees.

The worst sufferers of all were the new recruits. The older recruits would join the guards and officers in the bloodthirsty beatings as the victims cried and begged for mercy. Often the violence would escalate into an insane frenzy, completely out of proportion to whatever had triggered it, like a wind-whipped fire, pulling in more and more bystanders, leaving the boy victims terrified, traumatized, and sometimes broken and bloodied.

Dionel had gazed in horror at the limp, bloody body of a boy who had come in that afternoon. *That poor guy doesn't even look old enough to be here. He had no idea what he was getting into. They don't even care that he is a person! Could I become just like them by the time I am done here?* The possibility was unthinkable. He wanted to run as far from this place as he could get.

Dionel lay awake a long time that night, turning one way and then the other. The musty mattress, the snoring of his roommates, and the dread of the bell kept his body from relaxing. His mind was tormented by the memory of the day's training and of the screams of the boy who had been beaten almost to death.

Thank God he could still feel. But he hated what he felt: the cold smoothness of a grenade in his hands, the finality of the pulled pin; the click of the safety on his automatic rifle, the pulsing thunder in his body as he fired. This fourth week of training was all about how to shoot, detonate bombs, and throw grenades—how to mutilate the enemy while staying safe yourself.

It was all just practice now, but Dionel could already picture the real, thinking, feeling person who would someday be standing in the way of the grenade as it left his hand, arcing toward the kill—probably another boy just like him.

"My kingdom is not of this world: if my kingdom were of this world, then would my servants fight." [5]

What difference does it make? You don't live like a Christian anyway.

"Love your enemies, bless them that curse you . . ." [6]

But you don't even love these men around you. Jesus said if you hate your brother, it is the same as if you killed him. If you hate already, you may as well learn to kill. One is no worse than the other.

As Dionel fought the age-old battle between the truth of the Master and the lies of the enemy, he found himself remembering Brother Carl's eyes as he admonished him to be a man of integrity, a man God could use. What would Brother Carl think if he had seen him hurling grenades today?

This isn't right. I am a Christian. This isn't who I want to be. I've got to get out of here, but how?

Dionel was ordered to a new detachment, where his duties involved cleaning up and doing odd jobs in camp while the rest of the group trained in the mountains. His only chance to see Sergei now was in the mess hall for a few minutes at breakfast.

Entering the mess hall one morning, Dionel scooped up a handful of cloudy water from the metal bowl near the door and splashed it over his face, trying to wash away the grime of the morning's drill. Judging by the appearance of the soldiers ahead of him, he was probably making things worse. But the water felt good, and besides, washing was required. He wished he could wash from his mind the curses of the trainers, the sounds of deafening explosions that rang in his ears, the violence and hate that had pounded him all morning like a mud storm.

Turning toward the food line, Dionel saw Sergei approaching the washbowl. Sergei brushed close to him, mouthing the words, "Sit with me."

---

[5] John 18:36
[6] Matthew 5:44

Good, Dionel thought, *there is still room at the far table.* Quickly they sat down together at the end of the table away from the others. They might have a few seconds to talk before the table filled down to where they were.

"Dionel, I want out of here. Are you going with me?" Sergei kept his voice low.

In the light of day, the conviction that sometimes troubled Dionel at night seemed less compelling. "I don't know, Sergei. It isn't as bad for me as it was, and you know what would happen to us if we got caught trying."

"Well, nothing has changed for me. This place is like hell."

Every time he had an opportunity, Sergei begged Dionel to leave with him. "I have a plan all figured out. I'm sure we could do it." Still Dionel stalled. He wasn't ready to face it.

Then the rest of Dionel's detachment returned from the mountains, and the constant yelling and beatings began once more. On the third day after the return, an older soldier kicked Dionel in the back. That night he could not get comfortable in any position.

The next morning at breakfast, Dionel chose the spot next to Sergei and set his plate of rice, beans, and tortillas on the table. The tortillas didn't look or taste anything like the ones Grandma made, he thought. A thrill of anticipation shot through him at the thought of Grandma's tortillas. He decided to take the plunge.

"Sergei, if you really think you can get us out of here alive, I'm ready."

Sergei's eyes lit up for an instant, then he slouched in his chair again, looking bored. "Fine," he murmured. "Two in the morning. Probably no drills tonight. Meet me outside this building, by that corner." He motioned with his eyes. "I've studied how to avoid the lights."

Someone approached the table and the boys fell to eating. For a moment, they had forgotten they were hungry. A few minutes later as they left their soiled trays on the high stack by the kitchen, their eyes met once more. The escape was as good as done.

At a little after two the next morning, they met at the corner of the mess hall. The security light at the corner of the building swept in slow arcs across the open grassless area between the barracks and the fence. That beam seemed longer and wider this morning than ever before. They might die out there.

"Keep flat against the wall," Sergei whispered, and Dionel wondered for the hundredth time why he had ever thought this was a good idea. "As soon as the light's past, run. When it comes back, drop and don't move till it passes."

After several bursts of running, punctuated by breathless, frozen pauses, the boys knew they had only one more dark run to reach the fence. "Keep track of the fence," Sergei hissed. "We'll clear it on the next run and take cover in the corn."

They scrambled over the fence and hit the ground, running fast, listening for the chatter of machine gun fire behind them, grateful for the high corn that swallowed them up. They ran and ran, pausing to catch their breath, then running again, as far from that hated place as possible. The bitter cold two o'clock runs had trained them well for this moment.

Hours later, they emerged from a cornfield and saw before them the road by which they planned to travel home. The first bus of the morning wouldn't arrive for an hour, but if no one had seen them escape, they wouldn't be missed until later at roll call, after showers, breakfast, and cleanup. Lying on his back on the damp ground among the cornstalks as they waited for the bus, Dionel felt more relief than fear. He wanted to thank God. He wondered if God still heard him.

When they heard the bus growling toward them around the curve, the boys stood. Stepping onto the road, they waved the bus to a stop and climbed on, shaking inwardly but looking as casual and calm as they could manage.

When they reached home, Vicenta looked up from her sweeping, her eyes filling with love and concern as she recognized them. As Sergei headed down the hill to his house, Dionel sat down and let the sweetness of home wash over him. He had told himself he had no home, but it sure felt like home today. He picked up Joel and cuddled and tickled him. Benjamín stood by shyly, smiling up at him. Dionel grabbed and tickled him too. Most of the girls were away at school.

Vicenta stirred the fire to life, heating leftover tamales and setting coffee to boil. While Dionel ate, she sat down across from him, waving a cluster of flies off the stack of tamales and covering the dish with a cloth. "I can go to Xela and pick up your first month's pay," she said, "but don't you dare show your face out there. I'm glad you're home, but they'll come here looking for you first thing. The quicker you get out of here, the better. They kill defectors, son."

Reina was still in the city. Dionel wished he could let her know that he was out of the army and safely home, but then the thought struck him that she may not even have known he had enlisted. Reynaldo probably didn't know it either. He shook off the thought; there was nothing he could do about it.

He would head down to the coast for a while, until the army had moved on to more pressing matters than the search for two runaway boys.

CHAPTER 34

A Solution

Before dawn one Saturday morning in late July 1988, Reina walked briskly down the street, snugging her sweater around her shoulders with one hand and feeling with the other for the purse in her right pocket. She glanced over her shoulder. She had thought for a moment she heard footsteps somewhere behind her, but the street appeared deserted. She glanced to the right, where a warehouse threw a black shadow into an alley that met the street.

Reina was used to this morning errand down to the corner store for milk, but she never liked it. Early morning in Guatemala City was different from early morning in the mountains where she had grown up.

The headlights of a truck approaching from behind illuminated the street for a moment before it rumbled past, plunging her back into darkness. There was that sound again, as if someone were following her. Probably just her own footsteps echoing off nearby buildings. Still, she would feel better when she had turned the next corner onto a street with more light.

A hard hand hit her lips and stifled her sudden gasp. Her teeth ached, and she tasted blood. "Don't fight or I'll kill you!" It was a man's voice, a hoarse whisper.

He had her firmly, shoving her into an alley and throwing her to the ground. Facedown in the dirt, a chunk of adobe block gouging her shoulder, all Reina could see in her mind were her small children. Little Joel, Benjamín, Marixa, Juana, Sonia, Aide, and Eliza. Nothing mattered except that precious crowd of trusting faces. She had to tell him.

"Sir, I have children." Her voice didn't sound like her own. "Do whatever you want, but please don't kill me. My children need me. Please, sir, I have nine children." She felt a knife against her skin. *Please, Lord, the children need me. Let me live.* Time stopped as she steeled herself against what was happening.

Finally her attacker stood to go. "Look behind you and you're dead." She lay, frozen, as the slap of shoes on pavement faded and gave way to the pounding of blood in her ears, the rasping rattle of a steel security grate opening in front of a store across the street, and a burst of dawn birdsong.

Reina got up, brushing herself off. The dress Esther had made for her was ruined, slit jaggedly all the way down one side. She groped for her purse. It was gone. It held her wages from the last two weeks.

Tears stung her eyes as she stumbled over the trash between the buildings and peered cautiously around the broken adobe wall at the end of the alley. The street was clear except for a few parked cars and some hens scratching for breakfast. She hurried home, glancing over her shoulder again and again. Her employer would understand about the missing milk, and Reina wouldn't be wanting any breakfast this morning.

The following week she moved through her usual tasks and errands like a machine. Her mind was haunted with questions. Who was she anymore? Where was God?

Thirty years ago, when God had heard her prayer and opened her blind eyes—on that day she knew she was heard and loved. God Himself was her light. It was hard to remember the clarity she had felt that day, except as a contrast to the confusion and turmoil roiling inside her like a muddy, flood-swollen creek at the end of the dry season, sweeping up the trash in its path, forcing its way through narrow channels. The wide-eyed, trusting little girl she had been was far behind her now.

A Solution

She thought of the afternoon Carlos had left her trembling at the cheese kettle, the day she could sense the nearness of protecting angels. It was hard now to ponder that miracle of deliverance, yet it kept flashing across her memory uninvited. In one way, she had felt God's protection after Saturday's encounter—she was alive, wasn't she? But in another way she felt used, violated, rejected—not worth the angels' time anymore.

Who was she anyway? Reynaldo's wife? God knew how much she had adored that man, how determined she had been to make him happy, only to have her love slowly drowned in the jugs of *cusha*. Yet despite her hopes, dreams and ideals—despite her genuine grief and disappointment in Reynaldo—she knew with an aching sense of regret that not all the blame was his. She had helped make him miserable.

Was it all over for their family? Try as she might to strain some nugget of hope out of her muddied thoughts and emotions, she could find nothing. Probably Reynaldo was even now staggering drunkenly over the hills of La Cumbre, even now stealing some clothes off some hardworking woman's clothesline. He had said he was not coming back. She would always be his wife, she supposed, but there was no purpose for her in that identity. Only pain.

Was she even God's child anymore? Reina had loved being a member of the new, faithful church in El Edén. She had thrilled to the privilege of seeing her children in a Christian school, learning to love and fear God. She had felt she truly belonged in that little body of believers—for a while.

The last time she had been home, Brother Leland had come to visit, accompanied by the overseers from Pennsylvania. They had pled with Reina to reconsider her priorities. Though she still attended the Mennonite Air Missions church in Guatemala City, she did not attend local church meetings when she was home. Reina's attitude and priorities, the leaders said, indicated a lack of concern for following Jesus in righteousness. If she was unwilling to acknowledge this and repent, they could no longer consider her a sister in the church.

Reina had felt their love and sorrow, especially Brother Leland's. Yet she had sat through the meeting feeling strangely cool about the whole matter. Though the preachers didn't know it, she never read her Bible anymore. Her frustration and confusion had grown into a kind of barrier against God. With the mess her life was in, how could they expect her to make it to church every Sunday she was home? Nobody but God Himself—not even her own children—knew the pain she had faced in her relationship with her husband.

Anyway, she was no longer a part of the little church in El Edén, and she avoided thinking about it more than she had to.

Sometimes Reina felt almost as if she belonged in Guatemala City. She liked having an indoor shower with hot water and fragrant soap. She liked living near a doctor's office, a large market, and a post office. She liked the affirmation of her boss's approval. Still, she doubted she would ever feel truly at home stepping smartly in and out of executive offices. This life was empty and pointless to her, except as a means of feeding her children.

Ah, yes—she was a mother. This identity alone made sense. It superseded all her other identities, and she never questioned it. Being a mother gave her life purpose. She had children who were counting on her to not drown with them in their ocean of need, but to climb out and throw them a rope. She loved them fiercely. She would find a way to solve their problems, whatever it took.

Well, *almost* whatever it took. The last time she was home, someone had had the nerve to suggest she should resume making *cusha* to sell. Reina had smoldered at the thought. Looking levelly into her neighbor's eye, she had declared, "If my children and I have to eat dirt, we'll eat dirt. I will never again make *cusha* under any circumstances."

Reynaldo had tried that, and he had duly proven that the solution may be worse than the problem.

"Señora! Señora!"

A Solution

Reina turned, startled.

A tall, striking woman was hurrying up the street toward her, heels clicking. "Señora, stop."

Reina hesitated. *Should I know this person?*

The woman was smiling down on her. "I'll tell you what will take care of your problems. You need to go to Los Angeles, California. There you could make plenty of money to provide for your children."

"But—but we are poor," Reina stammered. "I can hardly buy our food and clothes. I could never get enough money to go to Los Angeles."

"Poor?" The strange woman waved the thought away. "You have *land!*" The word seemed to expand on her tongue. "Pawn it!" Then she swept down the street and around the corner.

Shocked, Reina stood still for a long moment. *Who was that woman, and how does she know about me and my needs?*

Uprooting each foot in turn, Reina walked mechanically down the street. If she hurried, she could reach the post office before it closed. Her employer was counting on her getting these packages into the mail today.

As the bus groaned up the mountain and around the last curve, Reina collected her bags from around her feet, stood up, and shook her daughter's shoulder. "Wake up, Aide. We're about to get off."

Aide stared blankly around for a moment. Someone was playing a radio behind her, and in the seat ahead a baby was wailing. She looked out the window. La Laguna. They were home.

A wave of anticipation swept over her. Grandma was in the little house nestled down there in the valley—Grandma and her whole dear family. And Mama had said they weren't going back to Guatemala City anymore.

She followed her mother down the steps of the bus, waiting while the attendant opened the big door along the bottom and pulled out a couple of bulky boxes. After a bit of juggling and stacking, the whole load was balanced on the heads of the woman and girl or draped over their shoulders.

As they made their way down the familiar trail, Aide noticed that Reina was unusually silent. Mama had something big on her mind for sure.

Several days later, Vicenta squatted by the fire, humming as she stirred the chopped greens that sizzled and snapped in her skillet. The children's gift for finding green things this time of year made cooking much easier. And the garlic patch was threatening to overtake the place. *Mmm!* Even at seventy-seven years old, Vicenta salivated at the smell of garlic and greens and pine smoke.

It was a blessing to have enough. Reaching out with a wrinkled hand, Vicenta lifted the lid off the steaming tamales. Nearly heated through. She broke an egg over the bright, limp greens, giving the yoke a quick jab, watching the white cloud up around the edges. She reached for another egg.

Footsteps sounded in the doorway. Vicenta glanced up. "Reina! So good to see you! You've hardly been in the house since you came back from the city. What new project are you working on now?"

"That's what I came to talk about, Mama. It looks like I'll be leaving for a long time."

Something in her voice checked Vicenta's good cheer. "What do you mean, dear?"

"Remember the lady I told you I met in Guatemala City? I'm sure she was sent from the Lord. Surely you can see that. We're so poor, and then out of nowhere, here is the answer we've been looking for! I have it all arranged, Mama. One of the neighbors wants to pay me for the use of our land. He will graze his sheep here, and the children will watch them; then he'll divide the lambs with you to pay the children for their help. I can't believe how perfectly it's all working out."

"So you're really going to do it." Vicenta dropped a bent lid onto the iron skillet with a clatter and pulled the pot of tamales to one side. She picked up two-year-old Joel, who had toddled over and wrapped his arms around her leg, and held him close, settling her small frame heavily on a block of

A Solution

wood. "Well, I don't suppose it's any harder to mind the children with their mama a couple *thousand* miles away than a couple *hundred*. You have to do what you have to do, I guess. This old lady won't stand in your way. I hope you've prayed about it, though."

Vicenta eyed her daughter for a moment. "Reina, have you thought about where you will go to church?"

Something squeezed at Reina's heart. Didn't Mama know she'd been skipping church for quite a while already? Though she had attended the Mennonite Air Missions church when she first went to Guatemala City, lately she had missed more often than she went.

That would change, though, if she went to Los Angeles. She had always wanted God, and if He worked this out for her, she would have a reason to hope again. "Mama, there are thousands and thousands of people in Los Angeles. I am sure it will be no problem to find a church to go to." Her ignorance gave her words conviction. "I'll find someplace as soon as I get settled."

CHAPTER 35

New Beginning

Reina crept toward the barbed wire fence, the coyote's final instructions echoing in her head. "Stay out of sight. Keep your eyes open, and when no cars are around, move fast! Once you cross that fence, you're in the United States. You're on your own after that, but you're smart and resourceful. Get in touch with your relatives. You'll figure something out." He grinned. "You're the best. ¡*Dios la bendiga!*" [1]

The trip so far had been smooth and uneventful. Reina's cousin Dinah, who lived in Los Angeles, had put Reina in touch with a brother-in-law who was a guide, or "coyote," directing Central Americans seeking to cross the border into the United States.

Reina had traveled by bus to Mexico City and flown from there to Tijuana, where a fleet of cars brought the band of immigrants to the border. Dinah's brother-in-law had been fair and generous, even buying her food on the way.

The forty who gathered at the fence in Tijuana, Mexico, that day in August 1988, were only a handful of the thousands of Guatemalans who fled north during those bloody years of civil war. Seeking respite from fear, tension,

---

[1] "God bless you."

abductions, and slaughter, weary of the relentless struggle for survival, they left their families and fell on the mercies of the United States—the same government which, in too many cases, was sponsoring the oppression, bloodshed, and injustice in their beautiful homeland.

Reina watched as several people made a dash for the fence and clambered over in slow motion, like clumsy cats in a brushy tree. Despite her many longings and emotions, at this moment she felt nothing but determination. She was a small woman, and she must get across that fence. That was all.

She peered through the bushes until the road was clear of cars as far as she could see in both directions. Several more of her companions moved forward. It was now or never. She rushed toward the fence, stretching the wires apart and shoving her bag between them. She clutched the steel post and scrambled up the taut wire, ignoring the barbs. Getting over was all that mattered. Her shoe caught on the wire and she pulled her bare foot out of it.

Someone behind her hissed, "Quick. A car is coming!"

She was at the top, teetering in the warmth of the early sun. Somewhere nearby, a dog began barking. Bunching the back of her skirt, pulling the wadded fabric around to the front of her trembling knees, Reina jumped. Someone thrust her bag into her hand. Her deserted shoe wobbled for a moment in the wire before dropping to the ground in Mexico.

The sound of the car engine was much closer. Reina glanced about frantically. There, the bushy cedar tree against that building. She ducked behind it. From the prickly space between the cedar tree and the block wall, she listened to vehicles braking, idling, and revving up again. A search was underway. Someone must have tipped off the border patrol.

In twos and threes, the officers rounded up her traveling companions, barking commands, brandishing guns, forcing them into several cars that had gathered at the scene. Reina scarcely breathed. If they caught her, she would have to go back—or worse. This was the scene she had refused to let herself imagine during the long days rattling through Mexico on the crowded bus. "Please, God, please. My children are hungry," she pleaded silently.

She listened as the cars circled the area three times, then revved their engines and departed in a line. Reina became aware that she was sharing her prickly refuge with a couple from El Salvador.

"Are they really gone?" she asked.

"I think so. I can see the road from here. I think they got everybody but us."

They waited a long time before creeping from behind the cedar. They looked around. What next? Reina pondered her remaining shoe. Which would arouse more suspicion: one shoe or none? She kicked her left shoe off, tossing it behind the bush, and the three began walking. Since she seemed to have lost Dinah's phone number, Reina stayed with the Salvadorans.

They walked for a couple of hours, hiding behind buildings or sagebrush at the sound of approaching cars. Eventually they approached a residential area, where tidy houses overlooked stretches of irrigated lawns. A man turned a mower around at the far edge of a lawn and headed toward them. No one else was in sight. They walked as naturally as possible toward the edge of the lawn. The man from El Salvador called to the groundskeeper, who drove over to them and shut off the lawnmower engine.

"We are looking for someone to drive us to Los Angeles. Do you know anyone who could help us? We can pay," the El Salvadoran man said.

The groundskeeper glanced around quickly, then looked back at the three fugitives. "I can take you," he answered in perfect Spanish. I suppose you want to go right away?"

"Yes!" they replied in unison.

After parking the mower, the man led them to his car. They climbed into the back seat. Reina reached into her pocket, pulling out the last of the money the neighbor had given her for the grazing lease. She handed it all to the driver.

CHAPTER 36

Los Angeles

Reina wrung out the dishrag and flopped it over the edge of the sink. Beyond the bars protecting the window glass, traffic streamed by. It was a monotonous, roaring flow she no longer noticed. Her mind was home in the endless hills around La Laguna. Eliza would be washing dishes in the *pila* this morning, with a sponge and a bright ball of orange soap, to the cries of highland birds, the bleating of sheep, the crowing of roosters—and the laughter of children. Reina's children.

Tears misted her eyes. This city could never be home to her unless her family was here.

She was glad to be with Dinah, at least, and the other relatives and friends who shared Dinah's apartment. Because Luisa had lost her phone numbers, the lawnmower man had let her stay at his sister's house until she got the next steps sorted out. Without money or a home, it was several days before Reina tracked down Dinah's phone number and managed to call her. Dinah came for her as soon as she was off work that evening and drove her to the apartment in the Oxford building. The others already living there crowded together cheerfully to make room for one more in the cramped space.

Reina had gone to the immigrations office the Monday after she arrived at

Dinah's apartment. An officer had looked at her over his glasses and sternly asked, "So why are you here?"

Standing as tall as she could manage, she had answered. "Because I was hungry, sir, and my family is hungry."

The man had not hesitated. He had prepared a little green card and handed it to her. On it was printed Reynalda Luisa Barrios. The card gave her permission to work for pay in the United States. Reina was amazed. *Thank you, God!* That was the day she decided to be called Luisa. Dinah thought the name would be easier for Americans to say and remember.

From the beginning Luisa had hoped her family could join her in L.A., but a recent conversation with Dinah had kindled another hope in her. Drying her hands on a damp towel that hung from the oven door, Luisa turned from the sink and rummaged through a drawer for a pen and paper.

She cleared a space on the tiny table and sat down to write:

> *My dear husband,*
>
> *I am living with Dinah. She has been very kind to me.*
>
> *I found work right away keeping house for a lady Dinah knows.*
>
> *I have enough work to pay my expenses and a little left to send to the children.*
>
> *Dinah tells me there are places here in Los Angeles where people addicted to alcohol can get help. The staff at these places are trained to help people with addictions. Many of the people who run the programs were alcoholics themselves but have been free for many years. She says you are welcome to come and stay here in her apartment with me. Maybe you could get help at one of these places.*
>
> *If you are willing to come, I think we could soon have enough money together to pay your way. I know we could find work for you here.*
>
> *Reynaldo, I believe this may be God's answer to bring our*

family back together. I cannot tell you how much I long for you and the children to be here with me. I miss all of you.

Luisa dropped her pen and lowered her face into her hands. The pain in her heart almost suffocated her. Reynaldo must be hurting terribly too. She could picture him as clearly as if she were with him. He was the man she had loved, who had handled an *azadón* with grace and strength; who had labored long hours raising food for his family; who had laughed in love and delight over the antics of his little ones; who had patiently taught his sons how to plant, how to harvest, how to care for the animals and the crops, how to take lumber from a tree. Sometimes he had even prayed with his family, and for a few sweet years they had attended church together. Now he was wandering over the hills, stealing whatever he could find and peddling it for a pittance—anything to get his hands on another jug of *cusha*.

Perhaps even now he was waking up in his own vomit on a lonely roadside somewhere, retching, head pounding, hating himself for what his life had become. Who would go out now and bring him home?

The hope that tried to bubble to the surface of her heart this morning broke through in a torrent of tears. *Please, God! Please heal our family and bring us all back together again. Oh, God, have mercy. Have mercy!*

Much later, Luisa pulled a tissue from the box on the table and wiped her face. Picking up her pen, she resumed:

Please write and let me know what you think. Reynaldo, I know God wants to set you free.

She paused. *Is it only Reynaldo who needs to be set free?*

In the past few weeks, painful memories of her own actions kept forcing themselves into her mind. Angry, condemning words. Coldness. *Why wasn't I more loving and encouraging? Why wasn't I more patient and forgiving? But, God, it was hard. What could I do when my children were starving and he drank up the little I could get for them? What could I do when he stole my pots and*

SONG OF THE SHEPHERDESS

pans to support his vice and blamed his problems on me?

Regardless of what she had done wrong, she knew Reynaldo needed help beyond what she or anyone around him could give. Their whole family needed help. *Oh, Lord Jesus, please give us another chance. Give me another chance to show him how much I love him. Give him another chance to be the man you want him to be. Make us whole.*

Luisa wrote the address on the envelope through a blur of tears. She missed Reynaldo intensely.

Several weeks later, Luisa wrote another letter:

> *Bring the family and come. Dinah's brother-in-law will see to it that you all make it safely to the border. There is help for you here.*

She waited hopefully for several weeks, but there was no answering letter. Why did he never write? Surely he would come. It could mean everything to their family.

The money Luisa was able to send to her family from her housekeeping job hardly seemed to compensate for the long months she was forced to be away from them. She watched constantly for opportunities to earn a little more.

Dinah told her she could get five cents for cans and bottles by turning them in at the grocery store. One morning Luisa went for a walk with a grocery bag, determined to pick up every can and bottle she saw in the gutters, roadsides, and trash cans. Twenty cans would bring a whole dollar, and she knew she could find several times that many within a few blocks of her apartment.

As she filled her third bag a couple of blocks from home, Luisa became aware of a man watching her. She stayed focused on her task, wishing he would move on. She still wore her modest cape dress and pleated mesh head covering. *Maybe he wonders what a Mennonite is doing in Korea Town.*

Luisa jumped when he spoke in gently accented Spanish. "So why are you gathering cans, when you could be working for me?"

She looked up. The stranger's eyes were blue, like the Guatemalan skies

Los Angeles

she missed so much in hazy Los Angeles. Friendly creases sprouted from the corners of his eyes toward neatly combed graying hair at his temples. He was well dressed and groomed from the top of his head to the soles of his expensive leather shoes.

"I might want to work for you, sir, depending what it is."

He laughed. "You could do it. Come with me and I'll show you."

His name was Mr. Moss, he said, and he was a Persian Jew. With his partner Hamit, he was building apartments in Beverly Hills. Luisa quickly accepted his job offer, serving as housekeeper for his wife and cleaning up debris at the construction sites. Mr. Moss appreciated Luisa's diligence and honesty, and he treated her kindly and fairly. Luisa thanked God for leading her to such an employer in this lonely place.

And then there was Marco, another of Mr. Moss's workers. Most people in the company spoke English or Persian, but Marco spoke Luisa's language. He was a good listener, and he made her laugh. Though he worked hard, he always took time to answer her questions and explain aspects of California life that bewildered her.

Marco never tired of hearing Luisa's stories about her mother and the children she had left behind in Guatemala. Luisa told him about her letters inviting Reynaldo to come. "Have you heard from your husband yet?" he often asked.

"Not yet," she replied, "but I'm sure he will write. Maybe the first letter got lost in the mail. That happens sometimes."

"You are lucky you can write to your children," he told her once. "I don't even know where mine are."

"Oh, I can't imagine! What happened?"

"Their mother took them across the border into Mexico, and I have no idea how to contact her. She doesn't want me to have anything to do with them."

"So you were married?"

"No, I was never married," Marco said, "and now I'm glad I wasn't."

Moss and his partner's plans for the Beverly Hills project called for seven apartment complexes of twenty-four units each. Marco and Luisa stayed busy with the heavy work of cleanup, lugging leftover lumber and blocks to huge dumpsters by the street. When the construction debris was cleared, the sidewalks needed to be swept and the interior of the buildings cleaned to prepare for furnishings and tenants. Two nights a week, Luisa helped Marco sweep shopping center parking lots.

None of the work paid well, but by putting in long days and some nights as well, Luisa could pay her share of the rent, take care of her own needs, and mail a check for one hundred dollars each month to her family in Guatemala. She trusted her mother to use the money wisely, but she wished she could be sure it was getting into Vicenta's hands. If only there was a way to give it to her mother directly without having to rely on others to bring it home from the bank. People had reported that Conrado, and maybe others too, sometimes made off with the money before it ever reached home.

One Sunday, with the day off and a few dollars in her pocket, Luisa remembered a store she had visited with Marco one day on an errand for their boss. She needed a few things. She would take a bus down there herself and do some shopping.

Luisa dressed carefully, still unused to the pleasure of choosing from several changes of clothes that were pressed and smelling of scented soap and fabric softeners. Then she headed down to the corner to wait for the bus she remembered they had taken the other time they went to the store.

Before living in California, Luisa had never experienced a whole day off. Staying in bed all day sick hardly counted as a holiday, and although the church in Guatemala had discouraged unnecessary work on Sunday, it could hardly be called a day off. Animal chores, caring for the children, getting everyone out to church and back, and all the other duties had crowded in on her like flies to a hen yard.

The bus pulled up to the curb, and Luisa climbed aboard amid a crowd of hurried, unhappy-looking people. Here in Los Angeles it seemed few had time to smile or give a greeting. Feeling strangely alone, she dropped her change into the box beside the driver and headed back the aisle, sinking into an empty seat. She was almost relieved when her seatmate deliberately turned and looked out the window. The lady probably didn't speak her language anyway. Sometimes she felt like a crow in a flock of pigeons. Why didn't more people understand that a smile works in *any* language?

What were her children doing this morning? Vicenta would surely be walking out to church with the littlest ones. Luisa hoped Aide was still going to church; she knew Eliza and Dionel had stopped altogether. She tried not to let it bother her; after all, she wasn't going to church herself anymore. She had also given up wearing her covering in public, though she still wore it for prayer.

Luisa had visited a couple of churches in the L.A. area, but she never felt at home in them. None of the people at these churches seemed to understand why they had come. They looked and acted like everyone else in the world, as if they had done their whole duty to God by attending church once a week. Luisa had seen plenty of such religion in Guatemala, and she was certain it was not true Christianity. Would she ever find a church that believed in being holy because God is holy?

Thinking of the warmth and order in the little church at El Edén made her homesick, and it made her unveiled head feel bare and vulnerable. Maybe days off were not such a good idea. One had too much time to think.

CHAPTER 37

Temptation

A few hours later Luisa was once again aboard a city bus, her arms full of packages. She had been sure this was the bus that would take her back to her street, but nothing around her looked familiar. Maybe she had gone too far. Making her way to the front of the bus, she tried to ask the driver for help, but struck a familiar dead end—he did not speak Spanish.

She got off at the next stop, clutching her packages. Daylight was fading quickly, and she seemed to be in a part of the city she had never seen. She scanned the sidewalks for someone who might be able to help her find the right bus. But no one made eye contact with her, and she didn't have the nerve to stop someone and ask for help. They probably couldn't understand her anyway, and she didn't like letting strangers know she was lost. She slumped against a wall, clammy fingers of fear squeezing her heart. A street lamp flickered to life, then another.

Luisa spotted a phone booth on the corner. Marco had told her to call if she ever needed him, and she surely needed *someone* now. Though her predicament was embarrassing, she made up her mind quickly. She couldn't stand on this dangerous street corner all night. She stepped into the phone booth and closed the glass door behind her, fishing in her purse for the paper on which she had written his number.

When Marco answered the phone, Luisa had to squeeze her eyes shut to keep from crying. A familiar voice, and in Spanish! Pulling herself together, she read Marco the street names on the nearest signs.

"Wait right where you are," he said. "I'll be there in a few minutes."

Luisa stepped out of the phone booth and leaned her head against its cold glass as tears ran down her cheeks. Marco was coming for her. She had not felt so protected and cared for in a long, long time.

Cars came and went in the shimmer of street lamps, lights dimmed in the store fronts along the sidewalk, and security grates rolled down over doorways.

There was Marco. Pulling up to the curb beside her, he hopped out and hurried around the car to where she stood. He smiled down at her, his heart in his eyes. She tried to look away but gave it up. It felt so good to be loved, to have someone share her burden. Marco hugged her close for a moment and then opened his car door to let her in.

Riding home through the early winter evening, Luisa had a fierce talk with herself. She had made a commitment. She was Reynaldo's wife, and nothing but death could change that—not *cusha,* not thousands of miles, not loneliness or betrayal. Though she was desperately lonely, and it felt like Marco was her only real friend in Los Angeles, she would never be unfaithful to her husband.

When Marco pulled up to her building a while later, he asked her gently if she wanted to come home with him instead, but that battle was already fought and won. Luisa thanked him sincerely for his help, gathered her bags, and stepped into the street.

He got out, locked his car door, and came around to her side. "I'll carry your things for you," he offered, reaching for her bags. As she prepared to object, he cut in, "I'm going with you to your floor. It isn't safe for you to be out here alone at night."

The graffiti on the heavy door in front of her was lit with flashes of blue and white light; two police cars were pulled up to a curb half a block away.

Temptation

Luisa handed Marco her packages. A Styrofoam cup crunched under his shoe as he stepped back to let her walk ahead of him.

They climbed the stairway in silence beneath the glare of the single bare light bulb. Luisa heard shouting as they passed one door, and she shuddered at the painful memory of Reynaldo's drunken rages. The people in these apartments had enough to eat, they had running water, and they were never cold in the winter, but they were as destitute as anyone anywhere who was a slave to alcohol.

At her door, Marco handed Luisa her bags. "Good night, Luisa. Always let me know if you need me for anything." His eyes sought hers in the dimly lit hall, but she turned toward the lock on the door.

"Thank you, Marco. Goodnight."

Luisa pulled the wide squeegee down across the window, the new glass shining behind the rubber blade. In the newly laid brick beds along the street below, landscapers dug holes and planted trees and shrubs. This would be a beautiful place.

Hamit, her boss's partner, pulled up to the curb, jumped out, and walked up the sidewalk to the landscapers. After speaking to them for a few moments, he disappeared into the front doors of the building.

Luisa moved to the next window, sprayed the glass, and began to wipe it dry. She was stretching to reach the top of the window with her squeegee when she jumped at the sound of someone calling her name. Glancing over her shoulder, she saw Hamit.

She drew the rubber blade firmly to the bottom of the pane and turned around to face him. "Good morning!"

"Luisa, Mr. Moss and I have watched your work, and we are really pleased. You show up for work on time, and you finish the job. We can trust you. That's rare these days."

Luisa smiled and thanked him. It felt good to know she had won their trust and approval.

Hamit continued, "Would you consider staying here nights for a few weeks until we have the security system in place? We just had 150 refrigerators and 150 ranges installed yesterday, all brand new. Vandalism and theft can be a real problem at this stage of the project. We need someone to stay here, turn lights on and off, and let us know if anything suspicious is going on. I would pay you to stay here nights, and when this building is ready for renters, we may need you at another one."

Luisa didn't take long to decide. By living here she would not only make some extra income, but also save the money she was paying for rent. "I would be glad to stay here," she answered.

"Could you make it tonight?"

"Sure. What time do you need me to be here?"

That evening as Luisa prepared to leave for her apartment to collect her things, Marco offered to take her out for supper. She accepted gladly.

While they waited for their food, Marco told Luisa he'd accepted an offer from Mr. Moss to stay in one of the new buildings until it was ready for renters.

"I'll be staying there too," Luisa laughed. "I was going to get my things together tonight."

"Ah, then we'll be seeing more of each other." Marco winked. "I'll take you to get your stuff with my car." Luisa didn't have much to bring, but she was glad for his help. What would she do without Marco?

On their days off, Luisa and Marco often visited the Alameda Swap Meet, where they wandered among the booths, enjoying each other's company. Sometimes they bought huge Salvadoran *pupusas de queso*. The thick, filled corn tortillas, a foot across, reminded Luisa of the ones Mama used to make from Don Feliciano's corn. Those had been so huge that she and Mama and Chilolo all shared just one for breakfast. These *pupusas* were filled with thick, melted cheese, and everything was prepared fresh right there at Alameda.

Luisa tried not to think of how God felt about her friendship with Marco.

Temptation

She hoped God understood that she was lonely and needed someone to be with, someone who spoke her language. She tried not to admit to herself that the friendship had become more than that. Marco was in her thoughts more and more, even when they were apart.

The months stretched on, and still Luisa's letters to Reynaldo all went unanswered. The total silence seemed unlike him. She had written at least four times. Surely if he cared, he would have replied. There was still hope for them if Reynaldo would be willing to try again. If only he would write to her!

But when flowers opened to springtime, when birds carried bits of twig and string into budding trees along the busy streets, preparing homes for their coming families, Luisa's hope began to wane. If the restoration she longed for was never to happen, at least her friendship with Marco helped her forget it.

CHAPTER 38

Out on the Mountains Cold

They found Reynaldo's body in the dust beside the road.

No one could say what had happened. He may have passed out as he staggered along, his liver too toxic to keep on. He may have died of exposure. He may have fallen at the hands of someone who resented his thieving. The Monterrosos would never know.

As the sun rose over Reynaldo's broken body that morning in late February, only one thing was sure: the Shepherd was out on those hills that night calling His lost sheep, yearning over him, and calling him back to the fold. Could it be that Reynaldo wandered over those hills that night, crying from the depths of his soul, "Lord Jesus Christ, have mercy on me, a sinner"? The Shepherd who seeks His lost sheep knows.

Chano purchased a coffin. Relatives came. They helped Chano wash, dress, and arrange his son's body. When his wife, Magdalena, had died several years ago, Chano had set up an arch, a table, and candles. He had let the candles burn for a week and had prayed to the spirits to leave her in peace.

He had no heart for those rituals this time. Reynaldo wouldn't want them. Chano had betrayed his son often enough in life; he may as well be true to him in death. Reynaldo's church could take charge. Chano felt as if a mountain of sin was settling on his shoulders, crushing him. What an awful darkness!

Reynaldo's baby—Joel, he called him—how old is he? About four? Chano groaned.

Chano thought of another coffin he had purchased forty-five years before. God knew he had loved that woman. God knew he had been drunk when it had happened. When he saw how badly he had hurt her, Chano had sobered up quickly. He had fought for her life then with the strength of a man and the tenderness of a woman. He had fought for her day and night—and lost.

Gazing in despair at the broken body of his wife, Chano had wrapped his great arms around their three-week-old son, no bigger than a plucked chicken. He had clasped the baby tightly to his chest and pressed his face into its soft neck, sobs wracking his body. She had adored this baby. She had named him Reynaldo.

People would be coming for the wake tonight. Chano went through the necessary motions, and that evening when Larry Weaver walked through the low doorway into the crowded sala, Chano pulled him aside and asked him to say a few words to everyone gathered there. Then he sat down with his head in his hands.

At La Laguna the next morning, Dionel paused, resting his ax head on the ground and wiping his left arm across his sweaty forehead. He and Aide had been chopping firewood since the sun came up. He would give a lot for a good cold drink of water now.

Someone seemed to be coming up the path in a terrible hurry, taking shortcuts through brush and ferns at the sharp corners. He could hear the person panting, frantic to reach him. What had gone wrong now? Dionel's hand tensed on the ax handle, and then Eliza was running toward him, her face tear-streaked, her black eyes tragic.

"Papa's dead," she gasped.

A dull pain burst through Dionel. Aide let out a small cry like a kitten someone had kicked. Eliza collapsed onto the log Dionel had been chopping, dropping her face on her knees, her thin shoulders shaking with rending sobs.

Through his aching confusion, Dionel wished he could hold her, the way he held Joel when he fell too hard. He wished he could turn back this inky black reality that threatened to swallow up what was left of their fragmented world.

Eliza caught her breath quickly and calmed down. "They are burying him this morning," she said. There was no time now to sit around and cry. Even if they hurried, the morning would be nearly gone before they could reach La Cumbre. What if they put Papa in the ground before his own children even got there to tell him goodbye?

The three hurried down the mountain, willing the steep, twisting path to shorten itself. For too long already they had been child-parents to two motherless little brothers and a tribe of little sisters, working harder than most grownups do. But somewhere deep in their hearts they had always nourished an unspoken hope that it all was temporary. Even Dionel, though at eighteen he had mostly given up the hope, had dreamed that somehow, someday, they might all be a family again. Mama and Papa would come home. They would go to church together. Corn and wheat would grow in their fields, and the care of the family would no longer be up to him. All would be right again.

That dream was dead now.

They burst into the open and approached the house. Oddly, the small adobe buildings that used to be home stood there just like always, clustered desolately above the breast of hard-packed earth that still sloped down in little terraces toward the languishing river bed. They came around the house from the back, and there stood Grandma in the doorway, surrounded by the tear-streaked faces of the fatherless little ones, her own face lined with concern.

Vicenta was the children's tower of strength, the one human constant in their torn lives. As long as she lived and moved on this plot of earth, it would be home.

But Vicenta, for once, had nothing to say. She handed them a bag of warm tamales. Dionel, Eliza, and Aide turned away from the little huddle in the doorway and headed down the hill, their minds grasping for any thread of hope. Maybe it was all a mistake, a rumor. Things like that happen sometimes. They would know for sure when they got to La Cumbre.

An hour later, thirteen-year-old Sonia was descending through the empty cornfield, returning from school in Sibilia, when she saw her cousin hurrying toward her.

"Did you hear that your father died?"

"What?" Sonia exclaimed. Surely she misunderstood.

"It's true," her cousin insisted. "Someone brought the message this morning. They are burying him today."

When Sonia burst into the house a few minutes later, wild-eyed and breathless, Grandma put her arms around her and held her face against her bosom. So the news must have been true.

"Dionel, Eliza, and Aide have gone to his burial," Vicenta explained.

Sonia jumped up. "Then I'm going too!" She headed for the door, but Grandma shot out an arm, blocking her path.

"Sonia, they are already too far away. You can't walk all that way by yourself."

Sonia flung herself across the bed and cried as she never had in her life. Juana and Marixa joined her, sobbing as though their hearts would break.

Meanwhile, the three on the trail hurried, hoping to get to their grandfather's house before the burial was over and Papa was gone forever. Twice they passed a family fanned out over a field, working together, their planting sticks jabbing at the earth like the proboscises of so many mosquitos, intent on extracting sustenance from the dry brown terraces. They were dropping corn kernels into the holes and covering them again, going on with their lives as if the whole world had not just ended, as if they expected the rain to come again, as if they assumed they would all be together to harvest this corn nine long months from now.

Weary of walking and weary of thinking, the Monterroso children arrived at last at Chano's house and looked around in dismay. Nobody was there.

Out on the Mountains Cold

The cemetery in La Victoria where Reynaldo was buried.

Chano's fat pigs grunted at them complacently through the stick fence.

"They have already gone to the cemetery in La Victoria," said a neighbor, Don Leon.

La Victoria! So they were too late after all. Walking there would take another hour. By the time they got to the cemetery, it would probably all be over.

"Don't worry," said Don Leon. "I'll take you down in my car. They just left a bit ago. Get in."

They climbed into Don Leon's car, drawing strength from each other's nearness. The car wound down the mountain, bumped and rattled through town, and turned at last into the driveway of the cemetery.

Looking like an elaborate arrangement of bright blocks such as the mission children sometimes played with, the cemetery sprawled up the hillside toward the purple mountains. It seemed unreasonable that this spot should put on such a cheerful face.

The colorful tiny house tombs had rows of window-like openings in their ends. Behind each opening was a space for a coffin. Some of the spaces already had bodies in them. Those windows were plastered shut. Other openings still gaped, waiting blackly for someone else to die.

Just ahead, they saw a crowd huddled with heads bowed. A couple of cars stood in the driveway. As Don Leon pulled to a stop and the children opened the car doors, the sound of a hymn floated across to them. The three Monterrosos approached, stepping around whitewashed mounds heaped over the remains of other people's loved ones, and the small crowd parted to let them through to the front.

Poor people couldn't afford tiny house tombs for the dead. Reynaldo would be buried in the ground. The hole was already dug, the dirt heaped beside it.

Larry Weaver read from the Scriptures, the cadence of the ancient words blending with the distant lowing of a cow and the cry of a rooster.

Someone opened the coffin. Dionel and the girls were standing where they could see the faces of the guests as they filed by and looked inside. Most of the people there were from the church. The children felt unsteady and alone. If only Mama would be here with them, or Grandma. Finally, Chano stepped forward and beckoned the three to approach the coffin.

It was six months since they had seen their father. They had always imagined that if they saw him again, he would be coming home to make things right—to start over, like he always had before.

Dionel looked at the face he had loved more than any other—the face of the man who had patiently taught him nearly everything he knew: how to plant and harvest, how to saw a straight log, how to earn and how to spend. This was the father who had once led them all in seeking God. Somehow, though, Dionel had always felt protective of him. Now he found himself still feeling responsible for his father, as if he and Eliza ought to do something— maybe help him onto his feet and bring him home. Maybe tread softly so he wouldn't get mad and depressed and take off for another jug of *cusha*.

Dionel was used to standing on his own feet, and he had thought he was pretty grown up. But to stand here looking down at Papa for the very last time—he didn't know how to do that. He wanted to be strong for his sisters who were sniffling beside him, but he could barely muster strength for himself. God seemed far away.

A robin hopped between the white-washed mounds, cocking its head to one side, bracing its feet, leaning back, stretching a worm from the earth. The robin disappeared, with the worm, into the pine woods beside the cemetery lane, heading toward an unseen nest, a nest brimming with open beaks.

Dionel didn't want to think about it, but there it was: his own beloved father had traded off all nine of his children for his addiction. And his mother was two thousand miles away, cleaning rich people's houses, deluded into thinking her children needed a check in the mail more than they needed their own mama.

Mama doesn't even know Papa is dead. Oh, God, this is all so wrong. Papa! Mama!

After the coffin was closed and the gathering dispersed, they returned to Chano's house, where Leland sat down with Dionel, Eliza, and Aide. He opened his Bible. " 'When my father and my mother forsake me, then the Lord will take me up,' " he read. " 'I will never leave thee, nor forsake thee.' "[1]

Dionel yearned to trust God again, to find comfort in that great Father heart, but it seemed too late; and he and his sisters could not quit crying.

In a corner of the room, Chano sat with his head in his hands. Once, he lifted his haggard face to the ceiling and struck his breast, groaning in a voice so low that only the few nearest him heard his words.

"Why? Oh, why didn't I give him her letters?"

---

[1] Psalm 27:10; Hebrews 13:5

CHAPTER 39

Hope Gone

Mr. Hamit and Mr. Moss were kind. The day the news came, they offered to let Luisa take the day off. But she had to stay busy. She couldn't quit crying. Each chunk of concrete, each board or scrap of steel that thudded into the dumpster pounded her empty shell. *It's all over. What is the point of keeping on? It's over. For all your risks and sacrifices and work, you've only been able to send a pittance to your family, and now your family will never be whole again.*

Her bosses were building their dreams, even as they built homes for families to live together. She was cleaning up the messes—throwing away what no one wanted.

Sometimes a small distraction relieved her, as when some extra-large piece of debris needed moving and someone came to help, but always her thoughts returned to the same point. Reynaldo was gone. He would never respond to her letters. She would never see him again. It was all over.

Why, why didn't he answer my letters? The children—did they make it to the funeral? If only I could be with them and hold them close. If only we could cry together. No one in this whole huge city even knows Reynaldo. No one cares about my children but me.

By the end of the day, Luisa was exhausted. Her face hollow-eyed and puffed, her dress worn and dusty, her shoes pinching her feet, she turned to leave the job site and return to her apartment before sunset. It wasn't safe for a woman to be alone on these Korea Town streets at night, people kept telling her, but this was a better block, and her apartment was clean.

But oh, so empty.

A pickup pulled up beside her. "Luisa, get in. I'll take you home." It was Marco's voice.

She turned and looked at him. The concern in his dark eyes washed over her soul. She stepped off the edge of the sidewalk as he sprang from the driver's seat, walked beside her around the front of his truck, and opened the door on the passenger side.

In the comfort and shelter of his pickup, Luisa felt her shoulders relax a little. All day at work she had sensed his concern, heard tenderness in his voice whenever he spoke to her. After all, maybe she did have one real friend in Los Angeles.

"I'll order some pizza and we'll eat in my room. I don't want you to be alone tonight," Marco said.

Luisa was relieved to let someone else think for her, to let someone else take charge. For once she didn't have to hold it all together alone. Marco was here for her.

"Do you want to talk about it?" Marco asked softly, back at his apartment. He lifted a slice of pizza and held it out to her, trailing a sheet of shining cheese.

"There isn't anything to say." Luisa didn't reach for the pizza, so Marco set it on her plate. "They found him in the morning. Two days ago. That's all I know. I wish so badly I could be with the children right now." She was crying again. "It hurts so much to think what they're going through."

Luisa stared out the window across an expanse of flat gray rooftops. Four pigeons lined up along a rain gutter to wait out the evening, and a violet sunset tinged the yellowish smog. She saw nothing.

Marco handed her a tissue and she took it. His eyes were wet too.

"Joel and Benjamín are so little. I doubt Joel remembers his father at all. He's barely four years old now." Luisa picked up her fork and laid it back down again; the pizza looked like cardboard. Marco leaned closer to hear her words, barely audible.

"I was three when my father died," she said. *"Cusha* killed my father too. I'm sorry, Marco, I can't eat. Maybe you can save it until tomorrow. It was kind of you to think of me." She dropped her face into her hands. Marco came around the table and sat down beside her.

"It's okay, Luisa. I know it's tough."

"We were married for twenty-five years, Marco. We had nine children together. Too many of those years were wasted, fighting and drinking. But we had good years too. We had happy family times. But so much pain . . . so much pain. I prayed we'd have a chance to start over. The children loved him. They don't deserve this."

Luisa lifted her face, still looking at nothing. Her voice cracked. "Nine children lost their father. What was he thinking?" Her face dropped to Marco's shoulder. "Oh, Marco, how can I do this alone? If only he had come. If only he had gotten help before it was too late."

"You aren't alone, Luisa. I'm here."

His nearness was a comforting warmth, like a cozy fire on a freezing night.

"Luisa, just stay here with me tonight. I don't want you to be alone."

I'm no longer Reynaldo's wife, Luisa reasoned blindly. *God knows how lonely my apartment is tonight. Surely nothing could be wrong with staying here, just this one night.*

CHAPTER 40

Hamit

A nurse breezed into the birthing room, radiating competence and efficiency. She leaned over the bed, lowering a snugly wrapped baby into Luisa's arms. "Doctor says you can go. You're both doing great," she beamed. "Do you have someone to come and get you?"

Luisa nodded. As the soft weight of her newborn son sank onto Luisa's chest, every nerve in her weary body, every corner of her aching spirit, relaxed and absorbed his sweetness, his littleness, his need.

The baby nuzzled at her breast, and she smiled—but only briefly. That touch of perfect happiness was like a wave crashing against a sea wall of reality, rolling back again, leaving an uncrossable expanse of naked sand between her life and the joy of home and family that she longed for. It was always like this: some pain, some memory, turned back any wave of happiness that tried to reach her.

Will Marco care about him? Luisa had stayed at Marco's apartment those first weeks after Reynaldo died, and when Marco had found out a baby was on the way, he had been pleased until another woman he was dating had convinced him the baby was not his. Then he had asked Luisa to leave his apartment, and the other woman had moved in.

Luisa had returned to the Oxford building and fit herself back into the small apartment shared by ten other Guatemalans. Space was tight, and at night their small cots filled the tiny quarters wall to wall like a puzzle. They each took turns cooking in the tiny kitchen for the rest.

Since Luisa had moved back to the Oxford building, Marco had stopped to see her only a few times. *Do I even want him to come? If he could believe that about me, if he didn't care enough to be there for me during the pregnancy, do I want him involved with Hamit?* Her racing thoughts coasted to a weary conclusion: *Yes, I want Marco to care. A little boy needs his father.*

She didn't want to admit to herself that she was lonely. Today, in the afterglow of childbirth, she felt her weakness and vulnerability. She had put Marco's name on the birth certificate as the baby's father. Maybe now he would believe her.

Luisa had paid for Eliza's passage to the United States a few months before. At eighteen years old, Eliza had wanted to come, and her arrival had been a comfort. The other Guatemalans in the apartment had crowded a little more and found space for her. She would be coming to the hospital soon to pick up Luisa and the baby.

As Luisa waited for Eliza, her thoughts rambled on. *What will become of this little one? Is there a church anywhere in this city that loves and obeys Jesus? Would it make a difference if there were? If none of my children have held onto God at La Laguna, with a church nearby to teach and encourage them, what hope does this tiny one have in the bowels of this wicked city?*

Aide had been the last of the children to leave the faith, the last of the family to leave the little church they had loved. For two and a half years, Aide had known the peace that comes from walking with Jesus, denying oneself, and living a holy life. She and Vicenta had been the only ones in the family still persevering with that commitment, and the bond between them was strong. Luisa had hoped and prayed that Aide at least would grow up to live the values and ideals she and Reynaldo had cherished for their family.

The most recent chapter of Aide's story had played out two thousand miles away, and only trickles of news had reached Luisa.

Back at La Laguna, Aide's mother had become only a bittersweet memory, a meager monthly payment, and an occasional package of fashionable shoes and dresses. Papa had left them too, surrendering himself to his addiction. Still, Aide had never stopped praying for Papa. Like her mama, she had cherished an unshakable hope, a belief that one day Papa would return and their family could be whole again.

The day the children had walked over the hills to La Cumbre to gaze into the beloved face of their dead father, Aide's hope had finally fractured. In her desperation for human comfort and sympathy, for respite from the grief that haunted her, Aide, like her mother, had turned from the Shepherd who alone could heal her and had fallen into an immoral relationship.

Brother Leland had admonished Aide, urging her to repent of her unfaithfulness to Jesus. He had pled with her lovingly, as he had done so often with her parents.

"Jesus was a man of sorrows. He was acquainted with grief," the pastor explained. Like the heart of the Good Shepherd, his own heart ached with Aide's pain. "The prophet Isaiah said that Jesus bore our griefs and carried our sorrows. He died to restore you to His Father, to comfort and heal you completely. There is no sin too big for Him to forgive, no life too broken for Him to restore."

To Aide it just didn't seem worth trying be a Christian anymore. A few months later, after their admonitions brought no change in Aide's life, the church leaders sorrowfully terminated her membership.

That had been only two months before Hamit's birth.

Now, none of the family but dear old Vicenta was walking faithfully with God.

Only five years had passed since those early days of hope. Those five short years had swept up changes like floodwaters sweep debris from trashy shores. Five short years had left Luisa's family ravaged and scattered. If only she could talk to Reynaldo about it.

I'll fill this little one's mind with Scripture, Luisa resolved. *I'll teach him to pray. This child must know there is a God of love and holiness in heaven.*

She fell asleep with the tiny boy in her arms. When she awoke an hour later, weak but refreshed, Eliza stood by the bed, looking down at her mother and her little half brother. As she touched the baby's silky head, then picked him up and held him against her, her mind flooded with memories of Joel, the brother she had practically raised on her own. How she missed him.

Eliza sighed, bending to kiss Hamit's soft head just below the silky hairline. Life would be very different for this brother. It almost made her angry; but no, she would love him just like the others. It wasn't this baby's fault that her little Joel didn't know his mama. That was Mama's fault. A hot tear skidded down Eliza's cheek.

Two weeks later, Luisa bound Hamit to her chest and returned to work. The bills had to be paid. Another building was almost ready for renters. She spent hours behind a vacuum cleaner, dodging in and out of closets, plodding slowly down miles of hallways, winding back and forth across acres of new carpet. Each time she changed the bag, there would be nothing inside but a huge wad of carpet fuzz mixed with a few bits of wood and plastic and scattered tacks. She washed construction dust from newly installed countertops and wiped down brand-new bathrooms that were already cleaner than most kitchens in the mountains of Guatemala. She rarely saw Marco even at work these days; he was doing the heavier outdoor cleanup.

One Friday evening when Hamit was two months old, Marco strolled into the crowded apartment in the Oxford building.

Luisa stiffened. What was he here for?

Marco set a huge bouquet of roses on a little table, handed Luisa a large package, and reached for the baby, smiling from ear to ear. Dazed, Luisa let him take Hamit from her arms. As she unwound the paper package, several baby boy garments slipped out of it.

Marco was exclaiming in delight over his chubby little son, but Luisa didn't look up. *Where has he been all these months? He never returns my calls. For two months he couldn't be bothered to visit his son, and now he comes in here and crows over the baby as if he owns him?*

Shaking, she wadded the baby clothes into a ball and flung Marco's gift back in his face. Then she pulled Hamit out of his arms. Marco hastily tried to explain what had kept him away so long: he'd been busy, he really did care, he just couldn't get here until now. Finally he went away, leaving the bundle of baby clothes on the bed, the flowers on the table, and Hamit in Luisa's trembling arms.

Undismayed by her chilly treatment, Marco returned the next weekend and the next. As he showered her and Hamit with gifts and attention, Luisa's animosity began to break down. When he offered to drive her to and from work, Luisa was relieved. Before long, they were once again spending much of their time together.

Twenty-year-old Dionel swung his machete at the standing corn, mopping his face with his sleeve, his determination mounting with every *zing* of the blade against the cornstalks. This would be the last time he would slave from dawn to dusk for a few dollars a day. Soon he would be making that much an hour in Los Angeles.

The coyotes were charging a thousand dollars to take someone to the U.S. border. Mama had sent for Eliza and paid her way north because Eliza had cried and begged to go. Conrado had gone too. He simply stole things and sold them to raise the money. Dionel had asked his mother to help him get to Los Angeles too, but she had never sent the money. Fine—he would make his own way.

Dionel found a couple of friends who had also caught Los Angeles fever. Together they cut and sold firewood and picked up any other odd jobs they could find, working hard and saving every penny. Today's job was his last.

When the job was finished, the farmer paid Dionel the two hundred pounds of corn they had agreed on. He loaded the corn onto a bus and headed to La Laguna, where he unloaded it for Vicenta and the children. Then he hugged each of them and left for a new life in the United States.

SONG OF THE SHEPHERDESS

Dionel dug through his bag again, unfolding and refolding each item. Again he rooted hopelessly through all his pockets. The paper with the phone numbers was lost.

He and his friends had made it to the home of a nice old lady one of them knew near the Mexican border. Dionel had been stuck here for weeks as his traveling companions one by one had crossed the border successfully, been expelled from the house for drunkenness, or had given up and gone home.

He didn't know how he could proceed without his mother's phone number. Had he been crazy to start out on this journey?

Other questions haunted him: *Why did I leave the church? Why didn't I keep my commitment to God?* The questions tormented him as he lay in bed at night, shouting at him over the nocturnal urban din of barking dogs, honking horns, whining engines, music, and voices. *What am I doing with my life? It's too late to go back now. I could never face Brother Leland. I could never confess everything I've done. What would he think?* Though Dionel had felt crushed when he heard of Brother Carl's death from cancer, he was glad Brother Carl didn't know what he was doing with his life now.

Fortunately, Dionel's elderly hostess was kind and appreciated his good manners and respectful ways. "You may live here as long as you need to," she said, "and go whenever you are ready. May God go with you."

Dionel found temporary work making shrimp cocktails in a Mexican restaurant for scanty pay. Finally he figured out a way to contact his mother, and after saving money for a month, he bought a train ticket to Tijuana, crossed the border, and arrived at last in Los Angeles. There he plunged into the social life and the craze for wealth that pervaded the L.A. Guatemalan community.

His mother might maintain that she had to move to L.A. to care for her children, but Dionel had always suspected that it was a clever lie of the enemy to distract them from living for God. Mama was still in a relationship

Hamit

with Hamit's father, and Dionel saw no evidence that God made any real difference in her life anymore.

Dionel missed God—when he thought about Him. So mostly he didn't think about Him. If he worked hard and played hard, there wasn't room for much more. It was easier to forget.

CHAPTER 41

Los Angeles for Jesus

One afternoon in June 1990, the smog had cleared over Korea Town, changing the sky from its usual sickly yellow to an amazing blue. Drifts of fragrance sweetened the air where brilliant flowers spilled from window boxes and planters along the sidewalks like whispers from God amid concrete, steel, and asphalt. Birds fluttered among the branches of the huge trees lining the streets. Here, as in the mountains of Guatemala, they opened their little throats and sang as if everything on earth were always good.

If one paid attention to the beautiful things on a day like this, one could almost shut out the diesel exhaust fumes, the constant humming and revving and whining of engines streaming past, the trash in the gutters along the street. One might look away from the eyes—empty eyes, worried eyes, haughty eyes—of fellow pedestrians.

Still, the future looked bleak to Luisa as she walked home in the evening, dog-tired, the last building cleaned, Hamit sleeping on her back, his fat soft weight both comforting and painful. Comforting because he was there, painful because the others were not, and because she remembered how they had suffered—especially Benjamín. She could still see those big dark eyes in that peaked little face, still hear the tiny barking cough, the thin crying.

Luisa thought of Joel, the baby she hardly knew. He had been just the age Hamit was now when she left him to go to Guatemala City. Benjamín was seven now, and Joel was five. It had been almost two years since she had seen them. Would they know her anymore? Would they understand that she had left them because she loved them? She had to take care of them, didn't she? Wasn't that the loving thing to do?

She thought of the morning when Hamit had been only a few weeks old, and she had been hurrying to finish the glass on the big entrance doors of an apartment building. Snugly wrapped in a soft blanket, Hamit lay near the brick edging of a bed of Persian tea, and he was crying hard. Luisa swiped the glass faster, reaching up to buff a final smear or two. She would have to take Hamit inside and sit down somewhere to nurse him before polishing the elevator.

She collapsed her squeegee's extension handle and turned to pick him up—then she sprang toward him with a cry. Ants! Ants everywhere! Like an evil spill of living black pepper, they crawled all over his soft skin. Luisa snatched Hamit from the seat and dusted the ants off his face. She reached into his squalling mouth and swiped out ants. Tenderly she undressed him, took a soft cloth from her bag, and whisked him all over. The ants had come from under the lacy Persian tea and up the brick border as if they knew he was there.

On her way home that evening, Luisa stopped at the pharmacy. She held Hamit out for the pharmacist to see and made crawling motions with her fingers to try to make him understand about the ants. He nodded, looked thoughtfully at Hamit's speckled body. Then he called a Hispanic lady who was placing little white bags on the shelves behind him.

"They're ant bites. Do you have something that will make him feel better?" Luisa asked her.

The salve the pharmacist recommended had healed the splotches in a few days.

Luisa sighed, remembering. If only problems were all so easily solved. She reached back and adjusted the baby's bottom a bit. That was better.

Sometimes her attempts to fix her family's problems seemed to create so many more problems, she wondered if it was worth it.

A pigeon hopped out of the way as she passed, its gray suit pressed and clean. In contrast, Luisa felt ragged inside—kind of all dirty and used up, more like the jagged crack in the concrete where the pigeon pecked a seed. *How did I get here, so far from God, so far from my family, so far from everything that mattered to me?*

As Luisa approached the dingy front door of her apartment complex, another renter was crossing the street, a talkative woman who usually had gossip to share. "I saw the most interesting group of people today," the woman began after the routine greetings. "They were singing on Broadway—a whole bunch of them—right near the intersection by McDonald's. The ladies all had long dresses and little net caps on their heads. And the singing! It was amazing, professional. And no instruments at all! I've never seen anything like it."

Luisa snapped to attention. Pleased at the effect of her news, the neighbor plunged ahead with the story. "Amish, I think they were. Or Mennonite, maybe." She consulted the back of a paper tract in her hand.

Luisa caught her breath. "Did they give that to you?" she asked.

"Yeah, one of the women handed these to me when she saw me standing there gawking. One is written in Spanish."

Suddenly Luisa was back in a little galvanized-metal church house off a rutted road among misty mountains. On all sides of her were voices resonant in lovely four-part harmony. She had been one of them—she and Reynaldo and their children, Juan and Amalia, and all the others. It felt like a lifetime ago. Surely no Mennonites would come to Los Angeles. It must be someone else. She looked hungrily at the leaflets. "Do you need them? I mean, may I look at them?"

Hamit stirred and let out a wail. Luisa bounced a bit to quiet him, holding her breath as she waited for her neighbor's answer.

"You want them? Sure, I don't need them," the woman said, handing the leaflets to Luisa.

Inside the door, Luisa's hands shook as she fumbled to fit the key into the lock. When she reached the apartment, she was relieved to find no one else home. She laid the leaflets on the table, washed her hands, and unwound Hamit from her back.

At last she was settled into a chair, Hamit nursing contentedly, the papers beside her. She felt a breathless anticipation as she picked up the leaflets.

That night the Shepherd came into a city teeming with pain and loneliness, like a hundred other cities; into a district called Korea Town, dismal and wicked like a thousand other districts; into a building, huge and creaking like ten thousand other buildings; into an apartment, dinky and cheerless like a hundred thousand other apartments. The Shepherd entered the room where Luisa sat with her baby—this child of a man who was not hers. There the Shepherd wooed His beloved, calling her by name, and she recognized His voice.

Luisa knew what she had to do. She dialed the 800 number printed on the back of the tract. A voice answered in Spanish.

Marlin Wagler's gaze was riveted on the littered street forty feet below the steel-framed window. He bit into his sandwich—a mission lunch—compressing thin white bread against cheap bologna. Mom's bread was fragrant and textured, and he didn't even want to think of the summer sausage and garden lettuce Dad was probably eating in his sandwich today.

Still there was no reason to complain, he knew. Their group's breakfasts and dinners at the Valley Motel were good, prepared by James and Joann Smucker and Rich and Sandy Kraybill. If mission fare was good enough for those people down on the street, he could handle it once a day for a week.

A woman on the sidewalk below rose to a crouch, rearranged a blanket on her slab of cardboard, then settled down to wait—for what, he didn't know. It seemed all these people did was wait. All along the street, men and women lay on pieces of cardboard, small heaps of clothing and possessions piled beside them on the ground or in rickety shopping carts. Tarps propped on pipes or cart handles provided a scrap of shade for the luckier ones. The staff at the Fred Jordan Mission said these people lived on the street year round.

Remembering the piles of human excrement they had walked around yesterday as they handed out tracts, Marlin shuddered. And that pervasive smell of old urine—would his shoes ever feel clean again?

Some seventy-five of those people had come into the mission for lunch today. They had trickled in and out throughout the day, asking for drinks of water. As long as he could remember, Marlin had known what Jesus said about giving a cup of cold water in the name of a disciple. But as he watched the mission staff cheerfully filling cup after Styrofoam cup, placing them in dirty-nailed hands, Jesus' words became more than a vague, clichéd appeal to his compassion. The words became flesh—and grimy flesh, at that.

As Marlin thought of his parents, home on the farm waiting for his return, he felt rich and protected.

Marlin Wagler and his friend Rich Denlinger were part of a team of about forty-five people, led by Gerald Kilmer, who had traveled to L.A. on a nine-day evangelistic campaign called "Los Angeles for Jesus." This was the second year the event had been held.

The whole experience had stirred Marlin: the soul-searching times of prayer and sharing around God's Word in the mornings at the motel; the rich estates in Hollywood; the disdain and indifference of the wealthy who turned away from the team or took their tracts and tossed them directly into trash cans; the stench of urine along Fifth Street between San Pedro and Los Angeles Avenue, where the homeless lived; the pure notes of the team singing "There is a God, He is alive!" above the roar of traffic; the gang of gun-toting little boys crossing the busy intersection on their way to who-knew-where; the range of human emotions, or the lack of them, in the faces everywhere. Marlin knew he would never be the same. If he and his teammates chose to, he thought, they could go home and eventually forget about these people; but Jesus never would.

Pulsing music pounded through Marlin's musings, and he watched as a huge man sauntered around the end of the block and started down the street on the north side of the mission. He balanced a boom box on his bare shoulder above a muscular, black back that glistened in the sun. The many pockets of his cargo pants bulged. As he approached, people rose off their cardboard slabs, digging in ragged jeans pockets. Was that money they were pulling out?

The boom box man was fishing in his pockets too, fishing out a little bag of something. Someone shoved a fistful of cash toward the bag, and the man with the boom box slid it into his pocket and released the bag to the waiting hands, scarcely breaking stride. He continued down the street, music throbbing, exchanging needles, syringes, and small plastic bags from his amazing pants in exchange for crumpled cash from outstretched hands.

Marlin felt sick. *This is happening right in front of me—and Jesus, you have to watch this every day? You knew these people's names before they were born. You watched them grow up. You know all their individual hurts and disappointments and betrayals. You know their anger, bitterness, and hopelessness. You died to redeem these men and women. Have we made any real difference for you in these nine measly days?*

CHAPTER 42

Home at Last?

It was the team's last full day in Los Angeles. Most of them would return to their homes the next day. Gerald Kilmer made a final call to James Roth in Woodburn, Oregon. James, a long-time missionary to Mexico and fluent in Spanish, had offered his phone number as a contact, and they had printed it on the backs of the Spanish tracts.

"Just checking to see if you've gotten any calls," Gerald explained when he heard James' quiet voice on the other end of the line.

"A Guatemalan lady called," James answered. "She read one of the Spanish tracts and wants to connect with you. She says she used to be part of a Mennonite church, but left her family in Guatemala to come to L.A. to try to support them. She has fallen into sin but seems repentant."

That was how Gerald found himself pulling up to the curb in front of the Oxford building the next morning, the last Sunday morning the team would be in L.A. Luisa was waiting on the sidewalk, wearing the most modest clothes she could find in her closet and with a kerchief tied over her head. She and Hamit got into Gerald's car, and they made introductions as well as they could without a shared language.

Luisa was sure she wouldn't know a soul at the Sunday morning meeting, yet she felt strangely like she was coming home. Hadn't she been here before? Blind and confused? Trusting the sheep to lead her home? Trusting her heavenly Shepherd to be her light? She closed her eyes tightly and pressed her face against Hamit's silky head. She had been barely ten years old. Marixa's age. *Oh, God, can you bring my family back together again? I want them to know you. This world is so dark, so hopelessly dark without you.*

When Gerald and Luisa arrived in Santa Monica that Sunday morning at the Valley Motel, the team was finishing up their morning devotional time.

Luisa slipped in quietly and sat in the back of the room. The team members were singing their theme song: "Can the world see Jesus when they look at your life?" She couldn't understand the words, but the harmony washed around her like a healing balm.

After the closing prayer, a tall, thin woman with reddish hair and a wide, friendly smile came over to shake Luisa's hand. In halting Spanish, she introduced herself as Joann Smucker and invited Luisa to her motel room to talk. Joann's two sons, Brian and David, spoke more Spanish than their mother and went with the ladies to interpret.

Alone with the Smuckers in the motel room, Luisa opened her heart, summarizing her story for their sympathetic ears, wondering again how she could have strayed so far from God. She ached for the peace she had known on the day she and Reynaldo were baptized.

" 'If we confess our sins, He is faithful and just to forgive us our sins, and to cleanse us from all unrighteousness,' "[1] Brian said, "He *wants* to forgive you, to cleanse you, and to set you free."

"I want to come back to God, but I have sinned so deeply against Him. It can't ever be like it was before. Maybe it is too late." Ugly scenes paraded

[1] 1 John 1:9

Home at Last?

before her closed eyes. She cried as she had not let herself cry in a long time.

"It is never too late, Luisa," Joann said. "God loves to make us new again." She put her arm around Luisa. "Do you want to pray?"

Luisa nodded, and they knelt together by the bed. "Oh, God, I have sinned. Can you forgive me? My sin against you is so huge. Can you make me clean again? I only want to live for you. I'm sick of the life I've been living. Please make me clean and take me back into your family."

As the love of her heavenly Father surged through her broken spirit, Luisa dropped her wet face onto her arms and cried some more. She knelt there for a long time.

When she rose from her knees, she felt an unspeakable relief, an incomprehensible peace. Joann, wiping her own eyes, hugged Luisa, as Brian and David beamed and angels rejoiced. Luisa took Hamit from Joann and followed the Smuckers back to join the others. All was well. There would be much in her life to unravel, and much to put back together, but she knew she was not alone. Her Shepherd had promised to never leave her nor forsake her.

They rejoined the others for breakfast. In the bustle of their last day in Los Angeles, most of the team took little notice of the Hispanic lady sitting quietly among them with her baby. Everyone was busy, some leaving for the park to pass out more tracts and some loading suitcases into cars and hugging each other goodbye. When the Smucker family invited Luisa to ride with them to the airport, she accepted; there was really no one else to talk to. David and Brian Smucker were flying home to Oregon that morning, and the rest of their family would follow in the car the next day.

On the way to the airport, Brian interpreted as Luisa shared more with the family. "I need to be with a church again. If there is work in Oregon, I would like to move there. I don't want Hamit to grow up in the city." They talked about it awhile, and James decided to discuss it with the remaining team members in the evening.

Back at the motel that evening, James and Joann Smucker approached Marlin Wagler and Rich Denlinger after supper. "You're headed to Canada from here, and you'll be traveling up through Oregon tomorrow, right?" asked James.

SONG OF THE SHEPHERDESS

"That's what we planned," Marlin said.

"Could you leave a day later and bring Luisa with you? She wants to come to Oregon, but she needs a day to notify her boss and get ready to go."

"Well, I don't know. We don't speak any Spanish," said Marlin. "We'd be glad to help her, but I don't know how well it would work."

Joann hurried to her room and brought back a dog-eared Spanish-English dictionary. "Here, you should be able to get by all right with this."

James had thought it through. "If you boys would take her home tonight, she could show you the way to her place. Then you could go back on Tuesday morning to pick her up."

"Well, I guess that could work," said Marlin. "We'll stick around and give her a ride."

When Marlin and Rich dropped Luisa off at the Oxford building that evening, she hardly felt Hamit's weight on her back as she sprinted up the dark stairs. She felt as if someone had suddenly unlocked the ball and chain she had worn ever since she had drifted away from God. Snatches of the hymns she used to sing ran through her head. "Peace, perfect peace, in this dark world of sin. The blood of Jesus whispers peace within!"

Things were shaping up fast. Marco had not been around for a while, and if everything went as planned, she would be settled in Oregon before he even knew she was gone. The two young men who brought her home tonight would come by on Tuesday morning, help her load her things, and take her and Hamit to Oregon. There she would be with a church at last. The people of the church would help her find a job and a place to live.

Luisa had said nothing to these Mennonites about her longing to bring her family to join her. After all, she had met them only this morning, and she would be enough of an imposition by herself, following them home like a stray dog, she thought—though she knew by their kindness and concern that they saw her as a sister in Jesus. The main thing right now was to get back with God's people, to learn to live like a child of God again, and to trust Him with the rest. She would make herself useful, working hard wherever she found an opportunity. There would be time enough later to think of

Home at Last?

plane tickets and legal expenses.

Luisa knocked at her apartment door, and Eliza opened it. "How was it?" Eliza asked, taking Hamit from her mother's back.

So much had happened in this one day, Luisa hardly knew where to start. Eliza had just married and seemed happy, but still Luisa feared she would be upset. "I'm going to Oregon," Luisa said.

Eliza's head whipped around. She stared at her mother. "What did you say?"

"I'm leaving on Tuesday." Luisa's eyes begged Eliza to understand. "I have to, Eliza. There is a church there, a church that teaches holiness and obedience to the Scriptures, like our church in Guatemala. Don't you see, Eliza? I have been far from God. I have been miserable. I have tried so hard to make it work. I have prayed every day. I have read my Bible. But I have missed God's people terribly. I've missed God too. I haven't been obedient to Him, and I've had no peace. I have been in sin."

Eliza put Hamit in his baby seat and hoisted it to the center of the bed. "Are you leaving Hamit?" she asked softly.

Through a sheen of tears, Luisa saw Eliza gazing toward Hamit and knew she was thinking of something else: two skinny, dirty little boys running barefoot around a mud hut in the mountains of Guatemala. *Oh, God, how did I do it? I was out of my mind.* With a pang, Luisa realized those little boys might be missing Eliza, but they would not miss her, their own mama. She ached to hold them, to look into their clear, dark eyes, to feel their little arms around her neck, to know they loved her—and forgave her.

"Of course I'm not leaving Hamit, Eliza." Luisa had not meant to sound so sharp. "I can keep him with me. I can work with him on my back there as well as here. And . . . Eliza? When I get settled, I want all of you and the little ones to come and join me in Oregon. Maybe Mama can even come, and we can be a family again. A Christian family."

Luisa lowered her voice. "Eliza, you know leaving Hamit in California wouldn't bring Joel and Benjamín any closer."

Eliza sighed and went into the tiny kitchen to find something to eat.

Luisa tried to focus. There was a lot to be done. First, she called her boss.

To her relief, he was understanding. "When you come back, know that you can still get work with me," he said. Though his kindness was touching, Luisa hoped she would never be back.

She slept soundly that night. Even the excitement of the upcoming trip could not overcome the deep peace that filled her soul. When she told Dionel her plans the next morning, his face was a mask.

"Will you come with me, Dionel?" she asked hopefully.

Dionel felt a brief tug, but he steeled his mind against it. The night before had been a barrel of fun. Now to give up everything when he was just learning his way around, and leave Andrea behind too? No way. He had tried being a Christian in Guatemala.

"No, that's okay, Mama. I'll stay. I hope it works out for you, though."

On Tuesday morning Richard Denlinger parked his Jetta in front of the Oxford building, locked the car, and climbed the stairs with Marlin, peering at doors along the hall until they found Luisa's apartment number. They helped her carry her bags, her baby, and her car seat down to the street. It was surprising how much could be accomplished without sharing any words.

The miles passed speechlessly as they headed north. They were making good time. They would stop for the night and not push it too hard. For a few hours the baby traveled well, sleeping, looking around wide-eyed, and sleeping some more, but after a while he became fussy. Luisa began saying something in Spanish, making motions toward her baby's mouth and tummy.

After several fruitless attempts to figure out what the lady might need, Marlin's eyes lighted on the dictionary on the dashboard. He picked it up and handed it to Luisa. She leafed through it, then handed the book back, pointing to a word.

"*Leche!* It's milk! She wants milk for the baby." Berating themselves for their thoughtlessness, the boys took the next exit and found a grocery store.

That night at the motel, Rich and Marlin worried about how to tell Luisa when they wanted to leave in the morning. They searched the dictionary, managed to find a few words that might get the message across, and hoped for the best. The next morning at precisely the appointed time, Luisa stood

Home at Last?

quietly outside her room waiting for them, her baby in her arms and her suitcase beside her. Life in L.A. had made Luisa adept at the speechless communication required to work around language barriers, and she appreciated how the two kind young men tried to understand and communicate with her.

When they exited the freeway hours later, the sun was low in the sky. Luisa strained to see this countryside, this place of homecoming. Nurseries, vineyards, and berry patches surrounded modest farmhouses framed by clipped hedges or wooden fences. Each farm sang hope to her heart. Here was work—work for her and for her family. Surely the church would want to help her bring her family here to this Garden of Eden, far away from the perilous concrete wastelands of Los Angeles.

The wide valley was almost as flat as one of Mama's tortillas, but against the darkening sky, Luisa could see the striking outline of a distant mountain—Mt. Hood, Marlin said—cold and white even in June. Mt. Hood was not so tall or symmetrical as Tajumulco back home, yet it spoke the same strong comfort. "Therefore will not we fear, though the earth be removed, and though the mountains be carried into the midst of the sea."[2] Like Tajumulco, Mt. Hood was not going anywhere; but even if it did, God would be her refuge and strength. She rejoiced in the freedom, peace, and hope she felt. It had been so long!

Dark was settling in and Hamit was asleep when they turned at last onto a narrow gravel lane lined with evergreen trees. A huge shaggy fir along the road reminded Luisa of the great old trees on La Laguna. She watched each house as they passed, wondering which would be her new home.

At the end of the lane stood a cluster of tumbledown buildings surrounded with tall grass and weeds. Light struggled out through broken windows. The car slowed down, and Luisa's heart sank. Was this to be her new home? No, they rounded a sharp, hidden bend beyond the derelict buildings and continued into the woods, stopping at last at the very end of the lane.

Luisa peered through the deepening dark. On her left, neat curtains framed

---

[2] Psalm 46:2

lighted farmhouse windows; on her right, the dim silhouette of a huge barn rose against the night sky. Marlin opened the car door. The interior light came on, and Luisa looked down into Hamit's sleeping face through a blur of tears.

It was June 19, 1990.

They were home.

CHAPTER 43

Starting Over

The next morning Luisa watched as Marlin and Rich loaded their suitcases into the car. She tried to express her thanks to them the best she could.

When they were gone, she helped wash dishes, sweep the porches and kitchen, hang and fold laundry—the things women do to bring a household back to order after two weeks away. But she soon ran out of jobs suited to a stranger, and Joann was feeling too ill to provide more work for Luisa. Luisa was relieved when Joann's oldest daughter, Caroline, offered to take her along while she did a little shopping.

Caroline drove to a small thrift shop, where she introduced Luisa to the proprietor, James Roth, the man whose number had been written on the back of that Spanish tract and whose gentle voice had answered her phone call—was it only three days ago? Luisa and Hamit stayed at the thrift store, visiting with the Roths, while Caroline did her other business in town.

The next day more of the Smuckers were sick. Hamit threw up and cried a lot. Glad of her housekeeping experience, Luisa helped in any way she could.

The awkwardness of her new circumstances would wear off, she knew. Already she loved this place, with its simple house and old farm buildings nestled on the edge of a plateau, grassy slopes descending from the house to the valley floor on the west and north. From her bedroom window, Luisa could see far across the Willamette Valley.

Within a few days Joann had recovered from the virus that had struck the family, and Luisa was glad to help as they launched an all-out attack on the housekeeping, rugs flapping, dust flying, mops squeaking. Luisa tried to observe how Joann wanted things done, which wasn't always easy, as Joann knew little Spanish. Frequently Joann had to call for assistance to explain things. "Caroline, could you come here and explain to Luisa how to shake these rugs without hanging onto the tassels?"

By Saturday evening Luisa understood that the family had a tradition of moving to their farm in Harrisburg each summer to work in the grass seed harvest, returning only on weekends. During this year's harvest, they suggested Luisa stay behind to tend the house and chickens until they returned.

On Sunday morning Luisa could hardly wait to get to church—it had been so long. As she rode with the Smuckers past vineyards, nurseries, and orchards, every scene and thought became a prayer. *God, please let my family come here. Please let us all get out of the city, back to the land. Please let us be part of a pure and holy church.*

The car slowed and pulled into the gravel parking lot of a stately old church house. Between the road and the imposing concrete stairway at the building's entrance, a sign read, "Welcome—Hopewell Mennonite Church." Families flocked from parked cars and from houses on both sides of the church lot, moving in little clusters up the stairs.

Luisa sat in the back of the meeting room with Hamit on her lap, absorbing the sights and sounds of a Mennonite meeting. She drank in the simplicity and modesty of the women's dresses, their makeup-free faces, the peace, the joy, the sense of belonging—and then the singing began. Luisa closed her eyes and bathed her spirit in the ringing four-part harmony.

After the benediction, as the friendly church members approached her one after another and introduced themselves, Luisa learned that many of them spoke Spanish, as if God had chosen the church especially for her. She also gathered that work was easy to find in the local fields and packing houses, where hundreds of Latino migrant workers were already working.

Luisa hugged to her heart her hope for her family. She would ask the Smuckers about it before they left for the lower valley to harvest grass seed.

On Monday morning Luisa picked strawberries under a clear sky. The berry farm was within walking distance of the Smucker home. The earth was dry and soft, the strawberries huge and sweet. Luisa's hands flew, filling one little berry-stained hallock after another. The hallocks were small boxes, about six inches square, made of wood veneer. Twelve hallocks fit into a flat wooden crate, six on each side. When a crate was filled, Luisa carried it to the long plank table at the edge of the field, where the farmer's wife and daughter weighed it on a big scale.

Unlike her job cleaning up construction debris, the farmer paid her by the weight of the berries she picked, not by the number of hours she spent in the field. Luisa was a fast picker, so the pay—given to her as each crate of berries was taken away—was reasonably good. The work was pleasant too.

Hamit sat on the ground between rows of strawberry plants, his shiny little lips pursed, strawberry juice oozing from the corners of his mouth. He clutched a broken hallock Luisa had given him, whacking it against the nearest strawberry bush. "No, Hamit. Do it like this." She pushed his hand away from the berries and showed him how to whack the hallock on the ground. He grinned as it crackled. Hamit was a patient baby, and when he wasn't eating berries, he made strawberry mud in his hands or went to sleep in the row. At first, Luisa tried to keep his chubby hands wiped clean, but she soon gave up.

Luisa liked these quiet days under the wide skies. She felt at home here in a way she never could in the commotion and concrete of Los Angeles. Even better, she liked returning to the Smucker home in the evening. She loved the big grassy lawn with the sprawling trees, the welcoming porch, the lighted windows—and the family. The family who sang and prayed and read Scripture together. Someday—*oh, God, please*—her family might be settled into a home like this, together in this wide, verdant valley, far from the hard-fisted, fast-paced city.

On one of these peaceful evenings, Joann answered the phone, then handed it to Luisa. "For you," she said. "Spanish."

Luisa put a folded towel on top of the stack, lining up the corners. Who could be calling for her? *It must be Eliza. She's the only one who has this number. I hope everything is okay.*

She took the phone from Joann. *"Hola,"* she said.

Her heart sank as a man's voice answered. It was Marco, all kindness and sweetness. "Luisa, I miss you, and I miss Hamit. You've got to come back, darling. I can't live without you. We'll get married, and I'll make you a home. We'll be a family."

"But Marco, I want Hamit to be raised in a Biblical church. I want him to know God. I need a church for myself too."

"Luisa, be reasonable. Of course you can go to church. There are churches all over Los Angeles. Remember, he's my son too. A boy needs a daddy."

His voice softened. "I love you, darling. I want our family together. We'll bring your children from Guatemala too."

Luisa felt her heart skip a beat or two, but her newfound peace was too real and precious to be knocked off-center so easily. "I'm sorry, Marco. I can't come back. I want to live my life for God. I need to be near a church that practices what the Bible teaches."

Marco's voice turned brittle, calculating. "If you won't marry me, I'll marry some other woman. I'll get custody of Hamit, and *she* can raise him for me. Stay there if you like, but I'm getting Hamit."

Luisa felt cold, and her ears rang. She could think of no answer. Across the room, Joann tugged on the string to lower the blinds, glancing toward Luisa with worry in her eyes.

More gently, Marco said, "That's not what I want to do, Luisa; I want to marry you. I want us to be a family. I'll only take Hamit from you if you force me to. It's your choice. I plan on raising my son."

"I'm sorry, Marco." Luisa was shaking when she hung up the phone. She picked up Hamit and hugged him. Pressing her face into the flannel sleeper over his fat shoulder, she cried, her scalding tears salted with the pain of her whole tangled life.

Things looked a little less dark the next morning, however. Likely Marco would get over it. He surely had not paid much attention to Hamit when she was in Los Angeles. She prayed about it a lot and tried not to worry, but it gnawed at the back of her mind. She thought of Jacob of the Bible: "If ye take this also from me, and mischief befall him, ye shall bring down my gray hairs with sorrow to the grave."[1] *Oh, God, surely you won't ask me to give up this baby too.*

During the week, while the Smuckers worked in the harvest near Harrisburg, the little house on the edge of the valley was Luisa's domain. She cooked and cleaned and cared for the chickens. She mowed the lawn and tended the garden. On weekends the big family returned and the house was busy and full, and they all went to church together on Sundays.

All summer, Luisa cherished her dream of bringing her family together in this place. However, she noticed that when she spoke of it, people listened kindly but said little or changed the subject. A few who knew her best urged her to return to her family in Guatemala.

Lord, Luisa prayed, *I am willing to go back if that's really what you want me to do, but it would be so hard. You know how much I want my children to come here.* She remembered the hunger, the dirt, the rags, and especially the suspicions and strained relationships in the church in Guatemala. *Oh, Lord, work a miracle to bring my family here to be with me. It would be a small thing for you. Please, Lord.*

At the end of August and grass seed harvest, the Smuckers returned home from their farm in the lower valley. After they unpacked and life in the farmhouse resumed its normal routine, James decided the time was right to put a new roof on the house. Glad to be needed, Luisa hauled load after load of old roofing by wheelbarrow across the lumpy yard and barn lot and dumped it all on a pile near the woods. Hamit bounced on her back, swaddled and content.

---

[1] Genesis 44:29

SONG OF THE SHEPHERDESS

By the end of September, with the new roof on and the summer work past, Luisa's help was no longer needed around the house. She knew she needed to make a decision.

One evening in October, Luisa accompanied the Smuckers to the lower valley. They had a supper invitation from Henry and Gwen Hertzler, the schoolteacher and his wife who had lived for a time at El Edén. Their home was only a few miles from the Smucker farm.

The evening was pleasant, their home peaceful and welcoming. Luisa pondered the difference between the orderliness of this home and her own life, a fragmented, impossible puzzle. Included among the Hertzlers' six children were two adopted sons from Mexico. Pondering this on the couch after supper, Luisa wondered if she saw a ray of hope.

"I am going back to Guatemala," she told the Hertzlers. They seemed pleased, but she could tell they had no idea what that decision meant for her. She pondered her idea until it was time to leave. It was now or never. Partway through stuffing Hamit's chubby arms into his coat sleeves, she paused and looked up at Henry and Gwen.

"If—if Hamit's father won't give permission for me to take him to Guatemala, would you keep him for me? I want him to be raised in a Christian home."

Henry and Gwen glanced at each other and looked thoughtful. "I'm sure we would consider it if you need us," Henry answered. "We'd need to pray about it."

"I hope you can keep him," Gwen said as she hugged Luisa. "A baby belongs with his mama. We will pray, and surely it will all work out."

As the Smucker vehicle, with Luisa and Hamit in the back seat, headed north toward Woodburn on Interstate 5 that night, the approaching headlights taunted her: "We're on our way home," they seemed to breathe as they streamed past, one after another, morphing into a long line of red pinpoints in the rearview mirror before vanishing into the darkness. As she neared the Smucker home, passing now-familiar farmhouses and hedges silhouetted in moonlight, her heart screamed silently, *Where, oh where, is home?*

She longed to be with her children in Guatemala, especially now that she knew she was going back. But she had cherished the hope that Oregon would be the home she sought for all of them, and it was hard to think it was not to be.

Worst of all was the specter of losing Hamit. Marco had not dropped the idea as she had hoped. He had called the Smucker home a couple more times, demanding that she return to L.A., alternating between threats and coaxing.

Luisa had found a measure of peace with the separation from her children in Guatemala. They were with their godly grandmother, after all. But how could she leave her baby with a man she did not trust and a woman who was a stranger? If her baby were forced from her arms, no place would feel like home. She would have to figure out some way to get Marco's permission to take Hamit to Guatemala for a visit. Then, somehow, she would find a way to keep him there.

That weekend Joann drove Luisa to the home of Judy Headings, a young mother who lived beside the Hopewell church. Luisa needed dresses for the return trip, dresses suitable for nursing her baby, and Judy Headings was about her size. Judy handed Luisa several dresses to try on, noted a few small adjustments, and promised to order the dresses Luisa needed. They would be finished within a few days.

So it was really happening. The train ticket had been purchased, the dresses had been ordered, the kindhearted Smuckers had given Luisa a generous check, and she had called ahead to let Eliza know she was returning to L.A.

Everything appeared to be in order. Still, Luisa thought, no one around her knew how it really was. A few days before, Eliza had called to tell her that Aide had had a baby girl. Aide named the baby Suledi. Luisa looked down at Hamit in her arms, then closed her eyes and looked into the face of her heavenly Father. *God, we wanted our children and grandchildren to live holier lives than we lived. We wanted them to know and follow you, to be strong and pure, and to raise godly families. Oh, God, have mercy on us.*

Would little Suledi, too, grow up without a daddy? She begged God to be with Aide and Suledi.

Luisa also prayed for Lidia and her baby. After Conrado's attempt to take her from the churchyard, Lidia's parents had moved away, taking their daughter and her baby with them. No one knew where they had gone.

As Luisa boarded the train to return to Los Angeles, the one unchanging thing in Luisa's life was the deep peace in her heart. Since the day she had confessed her sins at the Valley Motel, nothing had shaken her quiet knowledge that she belonged to the Shepherd, that she was found and forgiven, and that finally He would lead her home. But when would it happen, and how?

CHAPTER 44

Going Home

Luisa leaned toward the small oval window, drinking in the wild, craggy scenery below the plane. Never had she imagined her homeland like this. Those thousands of peaks, slopes, and canyons, like crumpled blue paper—families lived there. In those tiny folds were barefoot girls in colorful, faded dresses herding sheep, boys and men in ragged britches wielding *azadones* on terraced hillsides, tired mothers bending over cooking fires or nursing skinny babies. In those creases were children laughing and playing with sticks and stones, and drunken fathers staggering stupidly home or lying along the road in their own vomit.

Sin and righteousness, love and betrayal, laughter and sorrow—they were the same everywhere, she had discovered, regardless of poverty or wealth.

"You can take him if you stay just one month," Marco had told her. Luisa tightened her arms around her sleeping baby. Once she was home with little Benjamín and Joel, Marixa, Juana, Sonia, and Aide—and Mama—she would never leave again if she could help it. She was going to stay in Guatemala as long as she possibly could. She would figure out the details when she got there. *God, please make a way.*

As the seatbelt light blinked off, Luisa shifted Hamit to her hip and slipped her arms through the straps of her bags. As passengers began to deplane, fragments of small talk drifted around her. *Spanish!* It sounded good. Now if she could figure out how to get off this plane and through the airport . . .

Following the porter as he maneuvered her luggage through the terminal, Luisa remembered a small bag tossed over a fence, a single shoe dangling and left behind. Stepping through revolving doors onto the street, her senses were filled with the sights, sounds, and smells of home—especially the smells: wood smoke, diesel fumes, fried food. She wanted to cry.

Here where every sign and every word of conversation were in Spanish, finding the bus she wanted was almost as easy as tying her shoes. She belonged here.

On the bus, Luisa settled into an open seat, hugging Hamit. Flowers, a dazzle of magenta and vermilion, shaded closed courtyard gates as the bus rumbled through the streets, braking occasionally to take on more riders. Large painted signs and boys with carts shouted offerings at passersby. As the bus growled out of town, Luisa looked through the legs of billboards into a yawning ravine, its sides barnacled with tier on tier of dismal structures. Tiny figures threaded their way along impossibly steep trails that snaked between the shacks.

As the bus passed into the open countryside, memories rose like ghosts at every twist of the road. Two little girls, sticks in hand, sat on the bank watching a handful of sheep grazing the grassy roadside. Three black pigs, hams jiggling atop small hooves, ran ahead of a small boy who trotted behind them, his brown body straining backward as he held the ropes taut.

A colorful house clinging to the side of a terraced mountain reminded her of home, so prosperous in comparison to the slum she had just passed through, yet so meager and destitute in comparison to the life around Beverly Hills.

As Hamit drifted to sleep, Luisa pulled her scarf over her head. She needed to think. She needed to pray.

She woke an hour later. On the distant horizon, Fuego's volcanic cone posed grandly, white steam billowing from its summit into a hazy blue sky—pressure and turmoil transformed into beauty and majesty. Praise and peace filled her soul.

As they entered Chimaltenango, the bus slowed in heavy traffic. Passengers got on and off. The bus puffed on through town and climbed the winding road into the mountains. Two hours later it hissed to a stop at the top of the path to her house on La Laguna.

As the driver pulled the lever to open the door, Luisa struggled with a big bag on the shelf above her. Moving to the front, she made her way down the steps. Dust was thick around her shoes as she waited for the porter to extract her largest suitcase from the belly of the bus. She wasn't prepared for the tempest of emotion that swept through her, the weakness in her legs as she turned to scan the wide canyon. The warm updrafts flowing past her, heavy with the dry season's afternoon haze, the panorama of terraced fields, the towering trees, the cluster of adobe huts surrounded by toy-like figures—those were *her* children!

Luisa stood still, her eyes riveted on the children below. Suddenly she whirled around. Fumbling through a sheen of tears, she looped the straps together on her two biggest suitcases, heaped a few smaller bags on top, tightened the strap on Hamit's carrier against her back, and turned toward the steep trailhead. The path was worn and smooth. She had only to reach Conrado's house; someone would help her take her things the rest of the way down.

No one was at home at Conrado's place. Luisa left her largest bags there and moved more freely. The figures in the yard below became clearer. The biggest one stopped and turned toward the hill. Suddenly three children were running toward her along the mountain.

They met in the fava bean field. Luisa dropped her bags and stretched out her arms. Juana ran into them first, then Marixa.

"Mama, Mama!"

"Oh, Juana, Marixa! My girls, my little girls!"

While the girls cried and exclaimed, a seven-year-old boy stood quietly apart and looked her up and down with big eyes.

"Benjamín," Luisa called when she unwound herself from her girls. She unfastened Hamit from his pack and handed him to Juana. Going to Benjamín, she knelt and put her arms around him. He smiled a quick, shy smile. She leaned her face against him, inhaling the sweet, sweaty smell of a small boy in early spring.

As the girls headed up the trail to bring down the suitcases, Luisa continued down the mountain, Hamit on one arm and Benjamín following, her efforts at small talk with him making little headway.

Vicenta met them at the edge of the courtyard, a baby girl on her hip. Setting Hamit on the dusty ground, Luisa walked into her mother's free arm, weeping, feeling the weight of the past two and a half years roll off her shoulders while her mother held her, swaying, crooning, and clucking. *Oh, Mama, everything's all right in your arms.*

When Luisa finally stepped back, she saw Joel sitting in the dirt beside Hamit. Confident and bright-eyed, he was showing Hamit how to push a crude little car along the ground. Benjamín still stood nearby, watching.

Luisa squatted down next to the boys. "Did you make this car, Joel?"

"No, Benjamín made it."

She smiled up at Benjamín. "It's a nice car, Benjamín." Luisa examined the little carving of chechen wood. She had carved chechen herself as a child, but not this well. "You're a good wood carver." Benjamín almost smiled.

"Give your mother a hug," Vicenta instructed Joel. When Luisa wrapped her arms around him, she wanted to hold him forever. Finally she pulled him away a bit and gazed into his little face.

Oh, Reynaldo, he looks just like you.

As Vicenta squatted down and clucked to Hamit, Luisa took tiny Suledi from her. She was still holding her when Juana and Marixa arrived with the suitcases.

Everyone gathered around as Luisa opened her big suitcases, revealing gifts and wonders. This was the time, too, for opening a couple of large cardboard boxes Luisa had sent ahead to await her arrival. One of the most amazing things in the boxes was a baby-sized seat with a little table at the front, all mounted on a wheeled frame. Juana and Marixa had seen things like that at the gringos' houses, but never dreamed one would make its way to the packed-earth courtyard of their high mountain home. It looked too white and clean to set down there in the deep dust of late February.

By suppertime, Aide and Sonia had returned from their work on neighboring farms. They hugged Luisa and admired Hamit.

My little girls are women.

"See, Mama, here is garlic." Sonia handed a bag of papery bulbs to Vicenta.

To these children, Luisa realized, eighty-year-old Vicenta was more mother than grandmother.

"Just what I needed. I had run out completely cooking up this feast."

Everyone traipsed into the little kitchen, where eight stools sat in a smoky semicircle near the fire. They bowed their heads while Vicenta prayed for them all, asking God to bless the food and thanking Him for His goodness.

Vicenta had prepared chicken and rice with her fragrant tomato sauce over all, and tamales on the side. How good it felt to be home—and how strange.

That evening after supper, Marixa and Benjamín took the cows out to graze. Vicenta had a nice little herd of five. But it didn't look like anyone had worked the fields or planted corn for a long time.

CHAPTER 45

Life at La Laguna

Luisa tried to fit back into life at La Laguna. Vicenta still went faithfully to church every Sunday with Benjamín and Joel. When Luisa accompanied her once, she felt like an outsider. She sensed she was also an outsider among her neighbors. The lady who had mooched off the foreigners had returned with an illegitimate baby, flaunting all manner of fancy baby equipment. Old prejudices raised eyebrows. Gossip tittered through the hills.

Then there was Carlos, who still lived next door. Vicenta and the children were constantly getting into arguments with him. If it wasn't the property boundary, it was the animals. One day Marixa came home crying after Carlos had hollered at her for letting her sheep wander into his corn. The fury Luisa felt toward Carlos at such times scared her.

Luisa wanted to stay with her family, to be true to God's will for her life, but it did not seem to be working. Did no one understand that it had been love which had taken her to Los Angeles? Had it really been so terribly wrong? She wished she could know for sure. *You know we were hungry, Lord.*

One morning Luisa climbed the hill to be alone with her Bible. As she passed through a weedy area near the house, something caught on her shoe—a bit of trim and fabric, trampled and dirty. She reached down and picked it up. She recognized it as a dress she had sent her family just six months ago. A little farther on, a shoe lay on the path. It appeared to have been in good condition when it was left there, but now it was ruined by exposure to rain and sun. Had her long hours of work in Los Angeles really done her family any good?

It was true that Luisa's girls wore nicer dresses than before, and they all had shoes. Although the hundred dollars a month Luisa had sent barely reached around, it had saved Vicenta from begging. Leland and Esther still helped, and the older girls had jobs that paid about a dollar a day, unless their employers paid them with food instead. The past years had not been easy for any of them, including Luisa herself.

Luisa prayed a lot these days. She had hoped the confusion would clear, that God would open a road through the wilderness when she chose to follow the counsel of the brothers and sisters at Hopewell Mennonite Church. But now that she was in Guatemala, nothing was clearing up. Two dollars a day was all she could hope to earn at a job, even in the city. Besides, a job would take her away from her family again. Still, she was determined to make it work somehow.

One day Luisa went to discuss Hamit's legal status with Santiago, a brother in the church. "He is a U.S. citizen," she explained over coffee, "because he was born in the United States and his father is a citizen. I need to find a way to get permission for him to stay in Guatemala."

"There's a lawyer in Xela who works on things like that," said Santiago. "I don't think he charges too much, either. I'm going to Xela tomorrow, and I could look into it."

"Could you take Hamit's papers to that lawyer? I saved a little money, and it might be enough. I can't stay here unless we can get papers for Hamit."

When Santiago saw the lawyer the following week, the lawyer took Hamit's birth certificate and passport and told Santiago to return in two weeks.

When Santiago returned, the lawyer shuffled through his files for a bit and then shrugged apologetically. "I'm sorry, it will take a little more time. I can't find the documents. Come back in two weeks and I will have them. But although Santiago checked back several more times, the answer was always the same. One day the lawyer finally admitted that, although he was very sorry, the papers were lost and he had no hope that they would turn up again.

Slowly the realization dawned on Luisa that she no longer had a choice about staying in Guatemala. Barring a miracle, she would have to return to the United States.

One May afternoon Benjamín and Marixa arrived home from school with shining eyes and ran straight to Luisa. "Mama, I have something for you!" Marixa sang. "Happy Mother's Day!" With a hug, she handed Luisa the card she had made in art class.

Benjamín stepped nearer. "Mama," he said in a little breathy voice, "I made this for you." He handed her a little card. She looked at the neat drawing on the front. "It's beautiful, Benjamín!" she exclaimed, pulling him in for a hug. He was warming to her presence at last.

Benjamín was a gifted young artist, but for a long time he'd had no mama or papa to admire his work. Though his grandmother loved him, she was too busy to pay much attention to his many projects. However, a kind old neighbor lady who lived between their home and the school had befriended Benjamín, and he had formed the habit of stopping in at her hut every Friday on his way home from school, clutching his latest art project. He would call *"Buenas tardes"* as he walked across her level, gritty courtyard, where chickens cocked their heads at him and small black pigs grunted and played. She would come to the door beaming, stacks of crinkles at the outside corners of twinkly black eyes, her lips sunk back in little creases against toothless gums.

"Come on in, my boy. I'll have a drink for you in just a minute. Sit right down here at the table." The old lady would hold Benjamín's latest work up to the pale light from the window. "Well, look here," she would cluck. "Did you do this all by yourself?"

As his friend fussed and admired his work, Benjamín sat at the table, drinking in her affection and approval as eagerly as he drained the tall glass of sweet, hot *atole* she placed in front of him. He would leave his treasured art projects with her, and the next time he dropped by, he would see them pinned up on her whitewashed adobe walls. Always she had time for him, and always she treated his offerings as though they were nuggets of gold.

But Benjamín had never given his old friend a Mother's Day card like the one he gave today to his very own mama. For a few enchanted weeks, his own mother was there when he got home from school each day. She was there to wash his and Joel's knees when they were skinned. But Joel always ran to Grandma first. It was a little confusing, since they all called Grandma "mama." And although they had all thought their mother was going to stay, she was already talking of leaving again.

"Juana, I want to take you back to California with me," Luisa told Juana one day when she found her alone watching the cows.

Juana looked up in amazement. "Really, Mama? To Los Angeles?"

"You aren't getting along well with your older sisters, and you argue with Grandma. I think it would be easier for everyone if you came with me."

Juana was indignant: "We didn't have these problems as long as Dionel was here. He was always fair."

"Do you want to come with me?" Luisa asked.

Juana thought about it for a long time. Although she often fought with the family, she loved them all, especially Marixa. She and Marixa did everything together, and she protected Marixa when the older girls picked on her. She and Marixa and Sonia all slept in the same bed. How would Juana survive without her sisters and Grandma? Tears gathered in her eyes.

"Do I have to go, Mama? Can I think about it for a few days?"

"You can tell me tomorrow, but I will need to make arrangements soon.

I plan to leave in two weeks. I really want you to come with me, but it is your decision."

That night in bed, Juana whispered in Marixa's ear: "Mama wants me to go to California with her. Will you be all right if I go? I'm afraid there won't be anyone here to stick up for you if I go away. You would have to take care of yourself."

"It's okay, Juana. I'll be all right." Marixa fought back tears in the darkness. She had just had her tenth birthday, and Mama had been here to help celebrate it. She had thought Mama was home to stay.

Two weeks later, a sad little group stood in the yard. Luisa had her bags packed and Hamit fastened to her back. Juana clutched a bulging bag and looked around at her beloved family, not knowing whether to smile or cry.

"We have to go now if we want to catch the bus," said Luisa. She looked into two little-boy faces close to Vicenta's skirt, one on each side, and knelt to kiss the sun-browned cheeks. She kissed Marixa, whose soft dark eyes brimmed with unshed tears. She kissed Sonia, gentle and beautiful. She kissed Aide, who held Suledi in her arms and looked aloof. Last of all she bid farewell to her mother, concerned, brave, and tired. Luisa steeled herself against the tears that threatened to interfere with her goodbyes. Her emotions felt like they might strangle her. *You have to do what you have to do,* she thought.

As Luisa and Juana turned and started up the trail, Marixa ran into the house, threw herself across the bed she would never share with Juana again, and cried as she had not cried since Papa's death.

CHAPTER 46

Another Return

Poised between two worlds, Luisa stood on the crest of a desert ridge. Arizona lay to the north, a small Mexican town to the south. Farther south—behind her, thank God—lay a vast stretch of trackless wilderness. Just beyond the border she could see the twinkling lights of the storefront to which the coyote had directed her.

"This stretch of border will be no problem," he had said. "Mexicans often cross the border to shop in the market. No documentation is required. Just act confident. Go in broad daylight, walk directly to the store, pick things up, look them over, and put a few things in your basket."

Unlike her first trip north, when a bus had delivered her almost to the border, this trip had been grueling, requiring many bus changes and several hours of hiking through the mountains. Those desert mountains; the tufts of sagebrush and mesquite rising from the bleak slopes, casting shadows like gray rakes on the sand beside them; other travelers squatting on rocks, tilting their dry water bottles into their mouths in hopes of tasting a few more drops—it was all behind her now.

How had she come to this—sneaking over the border again, this time with an undocumented baby who was a U.S. citizen, and with a twelve-year-old daughter wandering somewhere along the border with strangers? Luisa had hated to leave Juana, but on such missions, one does not argue. One does what one is told.

In a hotel room a few miles away, Juana listened nervously to her instructions. "We'll have to get under the fence to cross into Arizona. Until then, everything has to look as natural as possible." The guide pondered Juana, squinting a bit. "How old are you? Twelve?" He turned to an older woman who hovered nearby. "Do you have something she could wear—some makeup, maybe—to grow her up a little?"

"Come on in here, honey, and I'll fix you up," the lady said to Juana.

The woman led Juana into the bedroom, where she rummaged in her suitcase, gray head bobbing, earrings swinging. "This will do, I think," she said at last, snatching a pair of denim overalls from the chaos. "Take your dress off, honey, and try these on."

Reluctantly Juana pulled her dress over her head, and the lady shoved the overalls into her hands. Fumbling, she put them on. Scrunching the last snap together, she frowned. "Do I have to wear them? They're too tight."

"If you want to see your mama again. They'll do fine. Now sit down here on the chair and I'll put a little color on you. We'll have you looking sixteen in no time."

As she stood to return to the living room, Juana caught a glimpse of herself in the mirror and recoiled at the bold countenance that looked back at her. But the coyote nodded his approval. "Much better. Here, have a few chips before we go."

Juana looked warily at the bag of tortilla chips. She was hungry, but she had never eaten anything like that before. She picked up a chip and crunched it between her teeth. Yuck! It did not taste like food, but she supposed she should eat something. An open jar of salsa stood on the table. Imitating the guide, Juana took a handful of chips and dipped each in the jar of salsa before crunching it down.

"Let's go," said the guide at last. "Your mom will be at the meeting place in an hour or so."

Another Return

As Juana stepped into the street, in tight overalls and bedecked with makeup, she felt embarrassed and exposed. "Okay," said the guide. "Now we're going to walk along holding hands so people will think you're my girlfriend. That way they won't be so quick to get suspicious."

Reluctantly Juana let him take her hand. The young man chatted pleasantly, pointing out a child struggling with a goat by the road, laughing easily, leaning in closer to her to make small talk. He was doing a good job of pretending, making everything look as natural as possible, and Juana appreciated it, though it felt strange. *What would Mama say?*

Smiling easily down at her, the guide murmured, "Now we're just going to take a stroll out of town, somewhere to get alone, you know." He winked, and Juana laughed in spite of herself. "We'll watch for our chance, and when no one's around, we'll go through the fence. If anyone sees us on the other side, we're still just a couple in love, see? Now stay relaxed, act normal, don't ask questions, and do whatever I say. You'll be fine."

To her surprise, Juana felt safe with the young coyote. She would have a story to tell Marixa! A breath caught in her chest. When would she ever see Marixa again?

"Now!" said the coyote, unlacing his fingers from hers and lifting the wire. "Get under the fence."

Juana slid under, and the coyote followed. "Okay, you are in the USA! Just take my hand and keep walking as we were before."

Ten minutes later they approached a house standing alone in the sand, surrounded by a few junk cars. The coyote knocked at the door and someone opened it, letting them into a small room, its air heavy with sweat and breath. The door closed quickly behind them and someone locked it.

Mama! Juana rushed across the room to where Luisa stood against the wall with Hamit on her back. Suddenly remembering her benefactor, she turned to thank him, but the two guides were already slipping out the back door.

In the crowded room, Juana kept close to her mother. One lady kept tugging the blinds back a little and peeking out a window. After what seemed like hours, an engine hummed outside and the lady by the window murmured,

"They're here."

An unsmiling man stepped inside and began giving orders. "Everyone will lie flat in the back of the pickup. When you're all in I'll cover you with a tarp. If we have to stop, keep still and don't make a sound until I give you the word that it's safe or until we are on the road again."

They walked out one at a time, scrunching themselves into the bottom of the pickup bed like cornstalks in a shock. At first, Juana felt a pleasing thrill of adventure, but as the truck shifted into gear and headed across the desert, the thrill spiraled quickly into torment. Juana was squeezed so tightly she could hardly breathe. *What if we run out of air?*

For what seemed like hours, the pickup hummed down the highway, on and on, as if it would never stop until they all were dead, squashed as flat as the laundry that came out the back of the gringos' wringer washing machines. Hamit was crying, and Mama was trying to quiet him. He must be squashed too, poor baby.

Suddenly flashing lights glared through the thin tarp, followed by the shrill wail of a siren, a sound Juana had never heard. The pickup stopped. A moment before, Juana had been sure that if this machine stopped for any reason, she would scramble up and jump out. But not now! Fear froze her flattened body. She tried not to breathe. Voices were growing louder and nearer. The tailgate creaked. The tarp was yanked off. Fresh air!

"Get out with your hands behind your heads!"

CHAPTER 47

Interrogations

Juana scooted from under the canopy and across the tailgate, struggling to get her hands behind her head as soon as there was room. Her stiff legs didn't want to cooperate. Standing so suddenly was brutal.

"Form a line and keep your hands up!" yelled the officers behind the truck. As Luisa crawled out and took her place next to Juana, she hoped desperately that merely keeping her hands exposed would be acceptable; she had to keep hold of Hamit.

"Okay, walk to the van and get in—and keep your hands up!" The officer gestured with his rifle toward the waiting van.

Luisa was surprised to find she wasn't afraid. She had permission to work in the States—her papers were in her bag—and Hamit was a U.S. citizen, even if he didn't have papers. Someone should be able to find a record of his birth. The only real problem would be Juana's status.

As they followed the others to the van, Luisa leaned close to Juana. "You're Eliza. You live in Los Angeles. Don't forget."

Juana looked at her mother in confusion, and Luisa felt guilty, even as she justified her action to herself. Had she actually told her daughter to lie? She was vaguely aware that she didn't trust God to take care of her anymore.

She prayed; she wanted to trust God; but when it came down to it, she was determined to succeed, and she couldn't afford to take chances. Some deep, buried fear drove her to clench her fingers around the broken pieces that remained of her life. The wounds of disappointment, rejection, and betrayal made her cower from the care of the only Physician who could heal her.

The buildings and streets of Indios, California, looked like a child's sand-castle on a boundless beach. Only the irregular, unbroken line of the San Jacinto Mountains, gray-blue against distant sky, suggested an end to the desolation. As the border patrol van rolled down the sand-blown streets, the passengers sweated against each other, worry lines creasing their faces.

The van pulled up in front of a huge building so bleak and sharply square that it appeared to be cut from gray ice. Luisa climbed out of the van behind the others, Hamit against her bosom, Juana stepping on her heels. At the front of the building, heavy steel doors opened and the immigrants filed into a large room with a row of desks on the far side. Behind the desks was a row of doors. Down the middle of the room were rows of chairs on which sat rows of tired-looking people. Looking down on them all were rows of windows. Trash was strewn about the tile floor in disregard of rows.

The driver motioned for the newcomers to line up in front of the desks. When she and Juana reached a desk, Luisa signed their names on the paper, careful to write in Eliza's name for Juana's.

Each would-be immigrant was given a number and sent to the chairs to wait. Juana scooted her chair as close against Luisa's as possible. In the next row a small boy spotted a partly inflated balloon on the floor. His black eyes shone as he picked up the balloon by its tail and held it out to show his mother. She nodded at him without smiling.

They sat waiting a long time. Luisa could not remember when she had last eaten. Hamit was hungry too and getting fussier. At last an officer walked toward them briskly, a pistol secured against the wide black belt that circled her waist, dividing her olive-green shirt from the crisp lines of her olive-green pants. On her left sleeve was a round black badge circled in yellow, bearing an outline map of the United States under the words "U.S. Border Patrol."

Interrogations

The officer smiled at Juana, who was bouncing Hamit, then turned to Luisa.

"Reynalda Luisa Barrios?"

"Yes."

"Is the baby yours?"

"Yes."

"Come this way."

Together Luisa and Juana followed the officer through a door that led out the back of the building into a small police station. There, another lady in green sat behind a desk. She looked up and smiled when they entered. "Hello, will you have a seat?" she asked. She made a phone call, speaking in English, and a man soon entered. He interpreted as the officer addressed Luisa.

"Mrs. Barrios, it is important that you tell us only the truth. If you tell the truth, you will be fine. If you are not honest with us, you will just make more trouble for yourself. Do you understand?"

"Yes."

"Okay, first we'll need everyone's full name."

Luisa gave her name, Hamit's and "Eliza's," spelling them out. "The baby is a U.S. citizen," she added.

The lady looked up in surprise.

"His date of birth?"

"November 1989."

The lady typed rapidly, her green eyes darting across the screen in front of her. "You're right; he is here!"

She looked up. "You were found in a situation that looks very suspicious, Ms. Barrios. Can you explain why you were being smuggled into the country when you appear to have permission to be here legally?"

"A lawyer in Guatemala lost all of my baby's papers. He was trying to get permission for Hamit to stay in Guatemala. Without the papers, there was no way for me to prove that my baby is a U.S. citizen, or even that he is mine."

The lady raised her eyebrows—whether doubting Luisa's story or the lawyer's, Luisa couldn't tell.

"And your daughter? I understand she is not a citizen of the United States?"

"She has no mother or father in Guatemala, ma'am. And she has already been living with me in Los Angeles."

The lady looked up Eliza's name and date of birth. Her eyes darted from the computer screen to Juana, then back again. She tapped her fingers on the desk, pondering Juana.

"Now we have some questions about your border crossing, Ms. Barrios. This is not to get you into any kind of trouble. Remember, if you tell the truth, we can help you."

Luisa answered the questions as truthfully as she could, but she was glad when they were over.

"Now we will need to talk with your daughter alone," the officer said. She made another phone call, and the officer who had brought them to the room reappeared.

"Are you ready?" she asked, smiling at Juana.

Juana stood, looking warily from the border official to her mother.

"We're together. She's my daughter," Luisa began.

"I'm sorry, but we must talk to her separately. Don't worry, she'll be back in a few minutes."

"It's okay," Luisa said to Juana, hoping it was true. "Go with her."

In a room across the hall, the officer sat behind a desk and motioned Juana to a chair facing her. Juana tried to look confident, wondering if the wilted makeup and overalls were succeeding in making her look older.

"What is your name, child?"

Juana hesitated and then answered, "My name is Eliza Monterroso."

"Where do you live?"

"I live in California. In Los Angeles."

The lady consulted her computer and asked, "So, Eliza, since you and your mother both already live in Los Angeles, can you tell me why you and your mother and little brother were being smuggled from Tijuana in the back of a pickup truck?"

"We were coming home from visiting family in Guatemala, and we lost our papers." At least that was mostly true.

"You live with your mother?"

"Yes, señora, we live in the same house."

The lady typed some more and then looked at Juana. "Okay, a few more questions for you. Can you tell me the color of your refrigerator in your home in Los Angeles?"

Juana thought frantically. She hadn't seen many refrigerators in Guatemala, but all she had seen were beige. She hoped refrigerators were the same color everywhere.

"Beige, señora."

"And what color is your sofa?"

Juana was beginning to feel dizzy. Had she really eaten nothing since that handful of chips on the other side of the border? Why were they asking her these things? She had no idea what color the sofa was in Eliza's apartment, or whether Eliza even owned a sofa. At home in Guatemala they had no sofa.

"I don't think . . . uh . . . we don't have any sofa," Juana answered, feeling as though she were jumping off a cliff. Wouldn't Mama have mentioned something as important as a sofa?

The lady asked many more questions. Then she got up and left the room for a few minutes. When she came back, she was smiling. "Are you hungry?" she asked. "Come with me." She stood back from the door to let Juana leave the room ahead of her. Was there going to be something to eat?

When Juana and the officer returned, Luisa was sitting on a chair in the waiting area, and Hamit sat on the floor in front of her, clicking the button of a ball-point pen. "We'll need the names and phone numbers of your closest family members in Los Angeles," the officer said. Luisa gave her the phone numbers of Dionel and Marco.

As the officer left, a man came in from outside and handed Luisa two small white bags and a tray of cups with lids. Inside the bags were Styrofoam boxes and little square cartons of milk. When Luisa handed a box to Juana, she looked suspiciously at the squishy brown bun inside, then opened the sandwich and inspected it. She wrinkled her nose. What wouldn't she give right now for a baked potato? But, oh, was she hungry! Juana took the hamburger and bit into it. She managed to wash the whole thing down, bite after bite, with the odd-tasting milk.

As they ate, Juana told her mother about the friendly woman who had questioned her, and she repeated as many of the strange questions as she could remember.

"Oh no, Juana! They asked me the same questions. Whatever did you say?"

As Juana recounted her answers, Luisa listened in amazement—every one of Juana's guesses had been correct.

The officer in olive-green reappeared, smiling. "Okay," she said, "you are free to go, and everything is arranged for you. After I show you to the house where you will stay tonight, you can go into town or wherever you wish. Be up early tomorrow. A cab will be here at six in the morning to take you to Los Angeles. Your family in Los Angeles is taking care of your expenses. Be sure to get your residency taken care of as soon as you get there so you don't have to go through this again."

"Oh, thank you, thank you so much," Luisa said. Some of the tension of the last days drained from her. Tonight she was taken care of. *But Shepherd, what of tomorrow?*

CHAPTER 48

The Next Step

Crowded into the Oxford apartment in Korea Town, Juana felt like a wild bird in a cramped cage. Walls and furniture blocked her at every turn, and there was no real outdoors to escape to.

She stood for hours each day on the tiny fire escape balcony which clung high on the wall outside the apartment. There at least she could be free of the enclosing walls and ceiling. There she could breathe.

A sickly sky arched above her, and people and cars streamed by in the street below, more in one day than would pass La Laguna in a lifetime. Who were they all, and where in the world were they going?

And what was she expected to do with the rest of her life, with no sheep to tend, no corn to hoe, no carrots to pull, no greens to gather . . .

"Juana, I need some spinach for supper." Eliza's voice called her back into the stuffy space. "You can get some just down the street and around the corner. Here's some money to pay for it."

Juana was thrilled to go outside and to see some real food growing again. Today was her thirteenth birthday, and Eliza had brought home a scrumptious-looking cake covered in huge, bright strawberries. The spinach must be the final touch to the birthday meal Eliza was preparing in a clatter of pots and pans, which filled the crowded room with tantalizing smells.

Tucking the money into her pocket, Juana headed out the door and down the hallway. She had only been in Los Angeles for three days. Eliza had taught her how to recognize the arrows and exit signs that showed the way outside. Walking gratefully away from the building, Juana headed down the sidewalk in the direction Eliza had told her, then turned the corner and scanned her surroundings. No spinach. Nothing but some coarse grass in the cracks of the sidewalk.

Confused, she tried the next street, still with no luck. She hurried back to their building, skipping up the steps and down the hall.

"Eliza, I couldn't find any spinach. I looked all up and down that street."

Eliza laughed. "It's kind of hard to get to. You have to go into a parking garage, but then you just turn the corner and there it is."

Juana had seen the parking garage, but she hadn't gone into it. That must have been where she went wrong. Back outside and down the street she hurried. *Ah, here is the place.* Juana entered the garage, certain of herself now, then turned the corner as Eliza had said. She looked all around. Still no spinach! In fact, it was hard to imagine any place along these streets where spinach could even grow.

Eliza must be playing a joke on her, Juana decided. She probably knew all along there was no spinach here. Feeling foolish and peeved, Juana retraced her steps. She burst into the apartment. "Eliza, I've looked and looked, and there isn't any spinach there. There's nothing but more buildings."

Eliza sighed. "Okay, wait a second and I'll go with you." She turned off the burner and rinsed a spoon in the sink; then they set out together in the same direction Juana had just walked twice. It appeared pointless, but Eliza seemed to know what she was doing. When they turned into the parking garage and walked around a corner and back outside again, there was still no sign of spinach, but Eliza was undismayed. She walked confidently up to a glass door on a store building and pushed it open.

Juana followed Eliza into the store and past a row of counters. Suddenly, right in front of them, under an unbelievably long sheet of slanted mirrors,

The Next Step

lay piles of vegetables of every kind, glistening with dew. It was a little like the market in Sibilia, only this place was much smaller, and the vegetables lay strangely unattended under the mirrors, as if their sellers had all gone home. Eliza tore a bag from a roll and helped herself to some spinach. Then they walked back toward the front of the store and got in line at one of the counters. Juana watched in astonishment as one customer after another simply paid whatever price the lady at the counter asked. Did no one here have enough sense to haggle over the price?

Two days before Juana's birthday, Luisa had been surprised to receive a call from Brian Smucker, who was back in California with the Los Angeles for Jesus team. "We didn't know if you had gone to Guatemala yet," Brian said, "but we didn't want to miss seeing you if you are still in town."

"I did go to Guatemala," Luisa explained, "but I had to come back to Los Angeles for a while. I would be very glad to see you all."

Maybe seeing the Smuckers would strengthen her spirit in this seemingly godless city, Luisa thought. She really should be looking for a church. That had been the chief thing on Vicenta's mind when she had bid Luisa goodbye a week ago. "You must find a church, Luisa. A church where you can get encouragement and teaching, where people follow Jesus."

Yes, Luisa thought, *I need to find a church—maybe after I get all the children here to the U.S. Oh, God, please bring us all back together again, and help us find your church.*

Brian offered to take her to the team's Sunday meeting. When he arrived at her building to pick her up, Luisa felt hopeful. *God is here in L.A. too. Juana, Dionel, and Eliza are here. Conrado even comes sometimes. Only five more to go—and Mama, if she wants to come.* Luisa doubted that Vicenta would ever want to leave Guatemala. It was home to her, she was old, and probably nothing could induce her to leave her beloved church.

Luisa worried about Conrado. He had seized an opportunity to become a coyote. Smart, resourceful, and driven, Conrado was perfectly suited to such a job. He feared nothing, least of all God or the law. Luisa hated to think of the risks Conrado took every day. It seemed like gambling with fate.

When she arrived at the motel, the team was gathered in the conference room. Though most of them were strangers to her, it still felt almost like coming home. The group welcomed Luisa with hugs and asked her to share her testimony.

Shyly, Luisa stood in front of the great brick fireplace and told her story, something she had never done in public before. Brian stood beside her, interpreting. She had sought God all her life, she told them. She and her husband had found Jesus together, and they had joined a little Christ-following church in the mountains of Guatemala. Then her husband had fallen into drunkenness, and their world had fallen apart. In desperation, she had left home and found work in the city, then made her way to Los Angeles, where she had learned to ignore God's voice—until God sent the team and helped her find her way back to Him. She told about going to Oregon and eventually returning to Guatemala, only to have a lawyer lose all her son's papers, compelling her to sneak over the border once more.

Luisa told the group that God had given her joy and hope in her heart despite the trouble and complications that arose from the choices she made when she turned away from God.

A few of the ladies, especially those who were mothers themselves, dabbed at their eyes with wadded tissues. If she could spill everything in her heart, Luisa thought, there would not be enough tissues to do the job. But she would not spill everything.

When she sat down again, team member Ludlow Walker stood and preached. A lady beside Luisa tried to interpret for her. Ludlow explained about God's perfect will, and how we mess it up sometimes with our sin. Still, he said, God can make our lives beautiful. He never gives up on us. "Don't settle for second best just because you messed up," Brother Walker encouraged them. "Don't settle for flying coach fare when God wants to fly you first class."

All I've ever really wanted, thought Luisa, *is to know God and His perfect will for His people—for me. My God, my God, come closer to me, for my soul is in you, and wants to live in you.* The prayer of the shepherd girl in the rugged hills of Guatemala had become the prayer of the widow in a motel conference room in California. This time she added a plea: *And God, please help me find a church.*

Luisa, Juana, and Hamit ate lunch with the team beside the motel swimming pool. Joann Smucker pulled her chair close to Luisa's and asked the lady who had translated the sermon to join them. With the interpreter's help, the ladies spent a pleasant hour or more in conversation. Luisa left for home that day even more determined to walk with God.

More job opportunities opened in the coming weeks, and Luisa took all she could cram into her waking hours. Before long she was working for several employers, cleaning the halls and public areas weekly in twenty-seven apartment buildings, each with about twenty-five apartments. Hamit went with her to work; he was a good baby, and her employers understood her need to keep him with her.

At the end of the summer, Luisa enrolled Juana in public school, remembering sadly how she and Reynaldo had rejoiced to have a Christian school for their children in Guatemala. Even as she longed to have her children here with her, Luisa was glad Benjamín and Marixa were still in that little Christian school.

Dionel moved from the crowded common apartment into another apartment in the same building. His girlfriend, Andrea, his sweetheart since they were both teens in Guatemala, was expecting a baby in January, and he wanted to make a home for his young family.

Luisa, Juana, and Hamit soon followed Dionel to the new apartment, relieved to leave the crowded little room where Luisa had lived most of her five years in Los Angeles.

Marco began visiting more often; sometimes he stayed all night. He always brought flowers or some other gift for Luisa. He doted on Hamit and treated

Juana as his own daughter, helping her with her schoolwork, and sometimes loading up the children and driving them to a park or beach to play. Marco had a way with children, and Juana seemed to soak up his fatherly affection. Watching them together, Luisa thought of Marco's other children, whom he had not seen for years. How could their mother be so heartless, keeping them away from a father who loved them? Again Luisa began to dream of being a family with Marco.

When Hamit was born, the doctor had looked over Luisa's charts and said, "Mrs. Barrios, you say this is your tenth child? I never would have guessed it. From a medical perspective, you're good for another five or six." Luisa wanted those five or six. Maybe it could still happen.

In January 1992, Andrea gave birth to a little girl, Wendy. About this time Dionel accepted a position with an auction company. Sometimes he was gone for days at a time, setting up for auctions and delivering merchandise from city to city. And Marco began staying with the family more and more often.

After Luisa had recommitted herself to Jesus a year earlier, she had been sure she would keep walking with the Shepherd. She had wanted no more of the carnal life—the immorality, the emptiness, the covetousness—that had broken her relationship with the Lord Jesus. She would love those who opposed her. She would worship God in spirit and truth. She would dress modestly and simply, as a woman whose values were different from the values of this world, a woman whose adornment was a meek and a quiet spirit. She would keep covering her head in obedience to God as a sign that her heart was submitted to His order.

Yet almost imperceptibly she found herself slipping back into her old routines and thought patterns. How could she live in God's order when no one around her seemed to understand anything about it?

Luisa's bosses were honest, her apartment cleaning jobs paid well, and she had time left over to take housekeeping jobs of her own on the side. When she stopped at the bank to cash her checks on Friday afternoons, counted the cash in her hand, and arranged to send money to her family in Guatemala, she felt powerful. She had thrown off the shackles of poverty. For once in her life she had more than enough, and anything she really wanted she could have.

Luisa and Juana loved to go shopping. "Juana, isn't this doll beautiful? Wouldn't Marixa love it?"

And several aisles later: "Such cute shoes. Did you know I went barefoot until I was fourteen years old?" Luisa piled the shoes into her shopping cart atop an intoxicating confusion of sweaters, skirts, and toys. "I used to make my own shoes."

Juana turned from the shoe rack, her eyebrows raised. "You did? How?"

"I sure did. You know the corteza trees that bloom yellow during the dry season? I'd get thick chunks of yellow bark from a corteza tree. Then I'd take a knife and dig out the soft inside to make places for my feet."

"But how did you keep them on?"

"I broke stalks off a yucca plant and stripped the fibers out of them. I'd punch holes through the bark with a pointed stick and then lace the yucca fiber through the holes. They weren't very comfortable, but they were better than going barefoot over the stones and thorns."

"Too bad we didn't know how to do that when we didn't have decent shoes. I wonder what they would have said at school. Sister Norma would have bought me new ones for sure." Juana picked up another pair of shoes with dainty chains across the toes. "Look, Mama, Aide would love these shoes."

Luisa added them to her cart and selected several more pairs. "I am so glad you girls can finally have nice things."

Back at the apartment, Luisa, Juana, and Eliza packed everything into a giant box and prepared it for shipping to Guatemala. What excitement it would bring to the family when they opened it in the little house on La Laguna! Juana wished she could be a jay sitting on a branch at the edge of the courtyard to watch it all.

The buying didn't end with nice clothes and shoes. Luisa's thoughts were captured by the finery she saw in her employers' homes. Great glittering chandeliers hung from ceilings there, and lavish curtains graced the windows. Tables were draped with elegant tablecloths and set with crystal, silver, and gilt-edged dishes. She visited the stores where her employers bought these things. She lingered, touched, and lusted. No one in the hills around La Laguna had ever envisioned such opulence, yet now as she checked the price tags, Luisa found she could afford to buy some of these gorgeous things for her very own.

Luisa's Christian teaching had not prepared her for this temptation. Perhaps it had not occurred to Brother Leland to preach to his flock about waste and extravagance when they barely had enough food for the next meal. Or maybe he had taught it and she had not paid attention because it seemed irrelevant to her life.

The euphoria Luisa experienced in purchasing and possessing, though thrilling at first, was salt to her soul's thirst. Never satisfied, she bought more and more, and still her emptiness grew.

CHAPTER 49

Family Again

Dionel saw trouble ahead. He could not shake a deep-seated dislike for the man who was courting his mother. Marco liked women and wine, and Dionel hated to see his mother mixed up with a man who would only hurt her in the end.

Naturally, Marco and Dionel butted heads when they were together. One night when Marco came home drunk and belligerent, Dionel decided he'd had enough. He took Andrea and Wendy and moved into another apartment in the same building with a couple of cousins.

Marco moved into the space they left behind. "We needed our own space, sweetheart," he told Luisa. "Now we can be a family."

"I would love to, Marco, but according to the Bible it is sin for us to live together unmarried. I wish we could get married, have more children, and be a real family."

"Then let's get married, Luisa darling! I should have married you a long time ago." But months passed, and Marco made no move to follow through on his impulsive commitment.

June came again, and Luisa wondered if the Los Angeles for Jesus team had returned. She didn't really want to see the Smuckers again right now.

Besides, she had received a message a few months before that Joann had died of cancer. Being with the Smuckers would not be the same with lively, friendly Joann missing. It was better to just stay away.

Luisa knew she was in pretty much the same state she had been before the first time she met the Los Angeles for Jesus people. Her vision was gone and her commitment lay in ruins. Somewhere a longing for God, holiness, and peace still languished in the desert of her heart, but it was hard to focus these days. She moved dully through her days, hoping for some magical key to open the prison of her existence, but afraid to look closely for that key—afraid to acknowledge that she was afraid.

Sometimes against the dark background noises of the night, the contemplation of painful choices—past and future—felt suffocating. At those times she longed for sleep and the ability to forget. What if God told her to leave Marco? What if she lost Hamit? What if she had been wrong to leave Guatemala in the first place? Half-numb and afraid, she clung to the covers in the lonely darkness, unable to comprehend the kindness and grace of the Shepherd who pours healing into the wounds of those who make painful right choices; unable to imagine the deep comfort of His rod and staff.

Meanwhile, clustered on benches where the sloping green lawns of MacArthur Park swept downward toward a smooth lake graced by gliding swans and a tall fountain that cooled the summer sky, the remaining members of the Los Angeles for Jesus team were praying: "Lord, we don't even know how to contact Luisa, but you know where she is. Please, Lord, if she is anywhere in this city, help us find her. Help us give her some word of encouragement. Oh, God, help her to be faithful."

Fifty-five team members had gathered for the 1993 Los Angeles for Jesus outreach, and today, June 13, was the final Sunday. Many team members had already gone home.

Gerald Kilmer especially travailed in prayer for Luisa and her children, the burden following him while the team sang, preached, prayed, and handed out tracts. This was the fifth year the team had come to Los Angeles. They had met Luisa the second year and had seen her each year since, and Gerald wanted to know how she was doing.

It was a long walk to the place where they would catch a bus to take them back to their motel. It was time to be going. As the team headed toward the bus stop, they rounded a corner and almost bumped into Luisa, out walking with Hamit and Juana. Gerald inquired how she was doing and prayed for her before they parted, amazed at this miracle in a city of three and a half million people.

Luisa felt strangely comforted to see them, though the unexpected encounter embarrassed her. The last time Luisa had seen any of the team, she had been veiled and dressed in a simple modest dress. Since then, she had not only changed her manner of dress, but she had returned in almost every way to the sin and compromise she had claimed to be done with. Today she was reminded again that the Shepherd had not forgotten her. Someday she must find her way home.

Several lonely years passed after that encounter. Luisa lived with Marco, but between his intense work schedule and the time he spent in bars, he was rarely home. Sometimes he did not return for weeks at a time.

Hamit accompanied her to her work when he wasn't in school, and his presence comforted Luisa. At home, true to at least one of her resolutions, Luisa often read the Bible to Hamit, and she taught him to pray. She still pulled a covering over her head whenever she prayed, though she had long lost the courage to wear the simple dresses she had worn in Guatemala.

One day Marco brought home a needy man named Angel whom he had found somewhere on the streets. Ever generous, Marco gave him clothes and invited him to stay with them in their small apartment. When Angel disappeared a few days later, they supposed that was the last they would see of him. Many months afterward, however, Angel reappeared at their door, and they somehow knew instantly that he had changed.

"Listen, just sit down and let me tell you all about it," Angel said. His face glowing, he explained to Luisa and Marco how he had come to know Jesus. Across the table, Hamit sat playing Nintendo—and listening to the conversation with a hungry heart. He had never encountered a Christian besides his own mother, and when Angel left, the memory of his face and demeanor lingered in Hamit's mind. Time would show that Angel's testimony had made an impression even on Marco.

Soon after Angel's visit, Marco said, "Luisa, Hamit will start school this fall. The building we stayed in when we watched it for Mr. Moss is right across the street from the elementary school. I think we should move over there."

"Oh, Marco!" Luisa gasped.

He laughed. "I've already talked to Mr. Moss about it, and he has space available. We can move next week."

Delighted, Luisa began packing her things. She was leaving this place at last, with its rough streets, run-down apartments, and unscrupulous neighbors. The new building was only two blocks away, but in Los Angeles that was enough to make a world of difference.

Marco lined up friends to help move. On the appointed morning three pickups pulled up to the curb and men began tramping up the steps, returning a few minutes later laden with boxes or straining under the awkward weight of furniture. It all seemed too good to be true. Surely she would wake up and discover it was all a dream.

Luisa and Hamit followed the loaded trucks to the San Marino building, where the men reversed the loading process, hauling boxes and furniture past a fountain and shrubbery and up roomy elevators to Marco's new apartment. It was really happening! Marco was paying for this apartment. He had provided a home for them, and they would be a real family at last.

One by one, the remaining children came from Guatemala. But they were nearly adults, and having spent years away from their mother, they soon found places of their own to live. Still, Marco tried to include each one in the family. He bought a long table that crowded the apartment's small dining area, and on Friday evenings everyone gathered at Marco and Luisa's apartment, where Luisa, thrilled to share meals with her whole family again, served elaborate dinners.

Each Friday was an adventure. Luisa, Juana, and Hamit would go grocery shopping, buying whatever they pleased, always stopping on the way home at a store that sold Guatemalan specialties. Within a few hours the savor of authentic Guatemalan cuisine, plus their Californian favorites, would be escaping through the cracks around the apartment door.

By the time the children and grandchildren arrived, the table was spread from end to end with loaded dishes. On these evenings everyone tried to leave unresolved issues behind and just enjoy being a family. Marco got along especially well with Juana's boyfriend. Luisa always felt uneasy when they got out their wine after supper and sat drinking, laughing, and talking late into the night. Still, it was better than having Marco spend the evening in the bars as he often did on other days of the week.

Though Marco rarely got drunk, his drinking still terrified Luisa. Sometimes late at night when he failed to return, she took Hamit with her and drove around to the local bars looking for him. There was always an unpleasant scene when she found him. On Friday nights, however, she at least knew where everyone was. They were a family, and they were all home. Often it was early Saturday morning when Luisa closed the door behind the last of the visiting family members.

On one such night, as Luisa turned wearily toward her bedroom, she felt the crackle of receipts in her pocket and pulled them out, looking carefully at them for the first time. Sixteen dollars a pound for that special steak. Sixteen more for the shrimp in the salad. Ten dollars for two bags of assorted spring greens, and four dollars for that scrumptious vinaigrette. It seemed a pity to pay so much for the corn husks for her tamales, but one could not just shuck them off the stalk in L.A. The prices of the cheese, nuts, and fruits were outrageous, but everyone loved them.

Surely, she thought, it was fine to bless her family with this indulgence. They had been so deprived for so many years. It was a relief to splurge a little. But the totals at the bottom of the crumpled receipts gazed back at her like sad and hungry eyes, boring through the smokescreen of her excuses. Four hundred thirty-nine dollars. And that was about the usual cost of their Friday night feasts. Luisa felt a little sick.

When she closed her eyes that night, she saw the ravine outside Guatemala City, its slopes crowded with shelters of pallets and rusty galvanized roofing. She saw skinny children huddled inside those shacks around tin pots of beans and rice—or going to bed with empty stomachs. She saw mothers all over the world walking barefoot down dirt paths to beg a little corn for their families, then gathering sticks to cook it. She saw her own mother in the sparse furnishings at La Laguna, caring for the third generation of her offspring. Luisa felt miserable.

CHAPTER 50

Two Rings

As Luisa read the Bible during the next few weeks, Jesus' teaching about the sin of neglecting the poor kept catching her attention. She no longer found the same pleasure in her shopping sprees and fine meals. She began buying less expensive cuts of meat and avoiding expensive, out-of-season fruits. The Friday feasts dwindled to simple suppers, and sometimes people found more exciting places to spend the evening.

" 'Howbeit when he, the Spirit of truth, is come, he will guide you into all truth: for he shall not speak of himself; but whatsoever he shall hear, that shall he speak: and he will shew you things to come.' "[1] Luisa lay across the bed, propped on one elbow with a scarf draping her head, her Bible open beside her. "That Spirit of truth is the Holy Spirit of God, Hamit. God's Holy Spirit told men of God what to write down for us. What they wrote became the Bible. The Bible is God's story of how He has led His people and how He wants us to live. When you hear God's words in the Bible, it is the same as if God came to you and spoke in His own voice."

Once, Luisa had read to Hamit the words of the apostle Paul, teaching

[1] John 16:13

that Christians should not adorn themselves with gold and pearls and costly clothes like the people of the world. "A Christian's jewels are jewels of the spirit," she had explained. Hamit understood then why his mother never wore the jewelry Marco bought her. She believed God meant for people to obey the Bible. Later, when Marco gave him a beautiful gold wristwatch, Hamit had thanked him politely but left it in a dresser drawer, unworn.

Now Hamit lay on his back among the pillows, arms behind his head, watching Luisa's face as she spoke. "Son, don't ever forget, God is three in one. He is your heavenly Father. He came down to this earth in Jesus His Son, to show us the way to live. After Jesus went back to the Father, He came to us in His Holy Spirit to comfort and teach us, and to be with us always, 'even unto the end of the world.' He is the Father, the Son, and the Holy Spirit. This God is the most important thing in my life, son."

Hamit did not doubt that this God in three persons was with his mother, and that He had her under special protection. Just the week before he had accompanied her to her housecleaning job and seen it again. The lady of the house had switched off the light so Luisa could clean the chandelier. She had climbed a ladder and unscrewed the bulbs. As Luisa washed dust from the lightbulb sockets, the lady's daughter had come through the door and switched on the light out of habit.

As Hamit watched, Luisa had seemed to light up all over, the cleaning rag flying upward in her hand as sparks exploded from the chandelier. Standing dumbfounded beneath the ladder as the chandelier swung wildly back and forth, his mother's employer wailed, "Why are you still standing there? Why were you not killed? Who is your god?"

High on the step ladder, Luisa looked down into the black eyes of her employer, whose hijab had fallen back in soft folds from each side of her upturned olive face. "My God is the God who made heaven and earth," said Luisa. "He is the Father, the Son, and the Holy Spirit."

Hamit thought his mother was like an angel that day, testifying to the truth of the triune God in that clear, sweet voice as she looked down from above them with the sunlight from the great arched window blazing through a thousand prisms all around her.

On Sunday mornings, although Luisa was usually working, Marco and Hamit walked twenty minutes to the Catholic church, dressed in matching suits. Hamit followed his father into the pew and perched on the bench while Marco flipped down the little cushioned kneeler, lowering his sturdy frame to kneel awhile before rising to sit beside Hamit. Then the altar boy entered, his face peaceful and solemn as he held a golden cross high over his head. A little girl in a long white gown followed the altar boy, and behind her walked the priest, slowly, in ornate embroidered robes, head bowed, hands folded at his chest, measuring the distance to the altar with stately steps.

Beautiful music poured from the choir loft in the back of the building and filled the place. Maybe heaven sounded like this, Hamit thought—but in heaven Jesus would be alive and smiling, not carved in brass and hanging naked and cold like the figure on the brass crucifix high on the front wall.

The deacon stood on a little platform to the right at the front and read a passage of Scripture. When it was done, the priest said, "The Word of the Lord!" and the congregation replied, "Thanks be to God." They read lots of Scripture, but no one explained it, and it was hard for Hamit to tell what it all meant. He watched the light play behind the stained-glass windows, imagining stacks of little, odd-shaped colored panels before they were fit into the metal cames, colors running together, molten glass flowing into the drapery of Christ's robe . . . Hamit felt a gentle shake and awakened with a jolt, blinking in confusion as he lifted his head from his father's shoulder. Marco rose to join the line filing forward to receive the Eucharist while the choir sang "Amazing Grace."

When Marco returned to the pew, Hamit knew the service was almost over. The priest drank the last drops from the brass chalice, then wiped it out with a cloth. Hamit was getting hungry, and the priest seemed to take ages to fold the cloth napkin and drape it over the chalice just right, but Hamit understood that such things must be done with utmost reverence. When the priest was finished, the altar boy carried the tray to another little table at one side. Marco had said Hamit might be able to be an altar boy when he was old enough; it wouldn't be long anymore.

The altar boy held up the golden crucifix again and started back down the aisle with the little girl following him. Again the priest, his hands folded in prayer, walked slowly behind them. Then it was time for the worshipers to leave the pew. Marco folded the kneeler under the bench ahead, and then they merged into the crowd flowing down the aisle to the doors.

Marco always stopped at the back of the cathedral to take his turn at the fount of holy water. He stretched out his hand, palm up, catching with his fingertips the stream of holy water that trickled from above into a brass basin and then, with his eyes closed, used his dripping fingers to sign the cross over his forehead, face, and chest.

Marco had explained to Hamit that the only sin that could cause a man to be put away from the Church and the Holy Communion was the sin of speaking evil of the Church and its teachings.

It was after shaking hands with the priest at the doorway and stepping out through the great doors into the sunlight that the best part of the day began for Hamit—a lunch of tacos, followed by a long, leisurely afternoon, just him and his father.

It seemed Marco poured out a lifetime of fatherly love on this one son. His ideas for keeping a boy happy and occupied were endless. Together they explored all the museums and family attractions in that part of town, as well as many in other parts of the city. They rode bicycles or scooters to Santa Monica Beach, where they pedaled along the shore for miles. Often Juana's son, Oscar, went along, and then Marco planned activities suitable for small boys. Wherever they went, Marco answered questions, pointed out objects of interest, and explained the science and history behind the things they saw.

Marco took time to tutor Hamit each evening when he returned from work. Marco especially loved math, though he had his own approach to the subject. "But Dad," Hamit said, "that's totally different than the way they teach us in school."

"That's okay, son. This is the right way to do it. If you know both ways, you'll always be able to find the answer one way or another."

Two Rings

One day Angel visited them in their new apartment, accompanied by a group of Christian friends. Luisa sat beside Marco, holding his hand, while Angel led them all in a Bible study. Marco and Hamit seemed to hang onto Angel's every word, and Luisa prayed hard as he unfolded Bible truths—explaining them so much more clearly than Luisa seemed able to. The way Angel brought the Gospel to life made his listeners want what he had.

When Angel invited the family to come to church with him, Marco and Hamit drove half an hour across town to attend, but as usual, Luisa had to work. For a month or more, Angel and his friends frequented their apartment, and Marco drove faithfully to Angel's church. Hamit watched in amazement as his father joined in the singing and chatted with the other men after the meetings. Marco began to talk of God as a person he was beginning to know, not just a religious figure. Hamit had never heard his father talk of God that way.

Then Angel left town to work in a distant ministry, and Marco quit attending the church. When Luisa begged him to find a church for them to attend together, he steadfastly replied, "I have my Catholic church to go to." They never saw Angel again, but Hamit would never forget this man and the things he taught them about the goodness of God.

Marco or Luisa always made sure one of them walked Hamit the one block to school each morning. When it was Marco's turn, he would leave a little early and stop for breakfast at an enchanting sidewalk booth which served seven kinds of tamales. "Choose whatever you want, son," Marco said, and Hamit chose a different kind of tamale every morning until he figured out his favorites. He loved pulling his chair up to the little round table across from his dad, drinking *arroz con leche* from a tall glass between bites of hot tamale.

"How's school going, son?"

"Fine, Dad. But I wish I could have some decent clothes like the other students wear."

"What in the world is wrong with your clothes, son?"

Hamit looked down at his suspenders and high-waisted, floppy pants. "No one else at school dresses like his dad."

"Who cares what they say? You look fine!"

Hamit's round eyes narrowed. He would talk to Mom about his fashion problems. She would understand.

Luisa did understand. She bought him cargo pants that hung low at the hips, with cuffs down on his shoes like the other boys wore. Marco didn't like it, but Mama was Mama. "Always respect your mother, Hamit." If Hamit had heard it once, he'd heard it a hundred times.

Each morning after they finished at the food booth, Marco would walk with Hamit all the way into the school building, leaving him at the doorway of his classroom.

Marco supplied Hamit with a five-dollar bill each day to buy lunch, go to the pool, or whatever else came up at school. Knowing he carried a little cash, other children often begged Hamit for snacks, and he enjoyed being able to buy them chips or ice cream.

During these years, Luisa's life consisted mostly of going to work and coming home again. Three things consumed her: first, Hamit must come to believe in God the Father, Son, and Holy Spirit; second, Mama and the children in Guatemala must be well cared for; and third, all nine children must come to join her in the United States. *Please, God, please bring them all.*

In 1996, Dionel returned to Guatemala with Andrea and Wendy. Conrado continued coming and going, smuggling bands of immigrants north over the mountains and deserts. Though Luisa was glad to see him now and then, she worried that one of these dangerous missions would be the end of him.

A kind of impotent desperation began to pound in Luisa's heart. If only she could get them all together again. Maybe it could happen if she and Marco could just marry. *And when they all get here, I'll look for a church. Until then I have to work. I have to bring them all.*

Benjamín was fifteen when he arrived in Los Angeles, and Luisa knew it was not a homecoming for him. He hardly knew his mother, and though she yearned for a relationship with him, there seemed to be no way to reach his heart. While Hamit had been with one or both of his parents every day of his life, Benjamín had only had Grandma and Eliza. Luisa had not been there to admire his carved toys and his artwork, or to comfort him when he was afraid in the night. The money she had faithfully sent down each month, the boxes filled with more clothes than they could ever wear, would never buy back those lost years.

One day when Marco came home from work, he presented Luisa with a giant bouquet of flowers. He often brought flowers, but never this many. And after he kissed her, he gazed into her face for a long time, his eyes shining. Then he handed her a little black velvet box.

Why does he keep trying to give me jewelry? Luisa wondered. *He knows I never wear it.* Trying to look grateful, she set the flowers on the kitchen counter beside her empty coffee cup and opened the box. Then she caught her breath, and in the moment of silence that followed, she heard her heart beating in her ears. Wedding rings! Could it be true?

"Oh, Marco!"

He wrapped her in his arms. "It's time, Luisa. We've waited long enough."

Luisa buried her face in his shoulder, crying. This was the moment she had dreamed of for years.

"I have an appointment with the lawyer tomorrow," Marco said. "He will have the papers ready, and I'll bring them home for you to sign."

Treading on clouds, Luisa finished cutting the lettuce for supper, then scooped steaming fried potatoes into a bowl. Rings had never entered her mind when she thought about marriage; like most of the Guatemalan hill people, she and Reynaldo had been too poor even to contemplate such an expense. If rings were symbols of fidelity, she thought, it was ironic that marriages back home had seemed more durable than marriages here in California where everyone wore rings. And then there were the Mennonites, who never wore rings and never divorced.

Regardless, she hoped Marco would change his loose ways once he wore a wedding ring. He really was planning to marry her! They would be a family at last. It might be too late to have more children, but they would be a family. Surely he would be faithful to her then.

Luisa fluttered through the evening and into the next day, trying not to keep her thoughts from straying to prayer. Marco was planning to marry her!

CHAPTER 51

Wedding Day

Luisa heard Marco unlock the door and slip into the kitchen in the wee hours of the morning. His job of sweeping parking lots had to be done at night when they were empty. She had waited all day for this moment when he would return with the papers that would make her his own. Her heart skipped a beat as he entered the bedroom, his broad silhouette black against the weak street light seeping through the window blinds.

"Do you have the papers, Marco?" she whispered.

"They aren't quite ready," Marco answered, pulling off his jacket and hanging it behind the door. A dizziness buzzed in Luisa's head, and she felt a sinking feeling she knew too well. Marco leaned over her, kissing her forehead.

"The lawyer says to come back next week. If you go with me, we can sign the papers right there in his office by the courthouse, then go across the street to the Justice of the Peace. Don't worry, sweetie; by this time next week, you'll be my wife."

Luisa relaxed a little.

"We can pick up Hamit and Oscar afterward and go to a restaurant to celebrate with a bowl of seven seas soup." He laughed softly.

The following week, Luisa was dressed and combed, a tingling eagerness enchanting the simplest things: the aroma of morning coffee, the trailing pink blooms on the Christmas cactus, the solid smoothness of good coat buttons. This was her wedding day.

When she had walked eleven-year-old Hamit to the stop sign by the school this morning, they had shared an intimate wordless exuberance, and Hamit's happy face filled her heart as she left him. This precious son was a big reason why this marriage mattered so much to her.

The happiness in which she basked this morning was not like the pure joy she had felt thirty-three years ago when her Reynaldo, young, gentle, and handsome, had ridden up to La Laguna with his father. That experience had been as different from this as the skies above La Laguna were different from those in Los Angeles.

At seventeen, she had felt limitless hope for the home she and Reynaldo were beginning. Today, though she was glad they were marrying, she was no fool. A deep pain had ravaged her heart and moved in to stay.

This morning, waiting for Marco to arrive and drive her to the lawyer's office, it was easy to forget the times he had cheated on her. They loved each other, and they had Hamit to live for, as well as the rest of her family, whom Marco seemed to have taken into his heart. A woman must make a home the best way she can.

If Luisa was honest with herself, what she most anticipated about marriage was to be free from the guilt of living with a man who was not her husband. Year after year, she had suffered under the knowledge that their relationship was forbidden, that it could never be blessed by the God she claimed to love. Tonight at last she would be Marco's wife, and all would be well.

Early that afternoon they parked the car and walked up the sidewalk toward the towering courthouse building. Its rows of dark, square windows were set like an expanse of tiles against the yellowish sky. How different from the small, elegant block courthouse in Palestina where she had gone on horseback to marry Reynaldo.

Luisa of Los Angeles, she thought, was a different woman from Reina of La Laguna. Reina was part of a different story—a story in a book with broken

Wedding Day

binding whose loose pages kept fluttering out, demanding to be reckoned with but impossible to sew back inside its covers. A book strangely sealed, yet too tattered to hold what used to be.

Marco was looking at her with a puzzled frown. "Luisa, I've spoken to you twice, and you seem to be somewhere else. You aren't changing your mind, are you?"

She smiled and reached for his hand. "No, Marco. I want to be your wife. You know how long I've wanted this."

Together they entered the tall door and walked across the cold marble floor to consult the long directory on the wall. Hand in hand, their synchronized footsteps echoing in the big hall, they made their way to the elevator that would take them to the fifth floor. Hand in hand, they rose silently through the building, stepped off the elevator, and found their way to the lawyer's office, where they approached the long marble counter.

The secretary tipped her head back, glasses low on her nose. "May I help you?"

"Marco Domínguez," Marco said.

"Oh, yes. I remember you." The secretary spun her chair away from them to pull open a file drawer, and two pointed heels peeked at them from above the chair's wheels. Her bright red fingernails ticked against the filing tabs, working through the first four letters of the alphabet. Then she slid a file out and spun her chair back around to face them.

She laid the file open on the desk, balancing her pen between two fingers and swinging it above the paper as she read, her mouth curved downward thoughtfully. She looked up. "I'm very sorry, Mr. Domínguez, but before we can proceed with this request, you will need to divorce your wife in Mexico."

Luisa gasped, and Marco's hand tightened on hers, his fingers twitching. "But señora," he said, "that is impossible. I don't even know where she is or how to contact her."

"People can usually be found. If she has cut off contact with you, she is probably eager to end the marriage. You will have to decide how important it is to you to marry Ms. Barrios."

Marco tried to argue some more, but the lady merely handed him his application and repeated, "It is impossible for you to marry in the state of California unless you secure a divorce from your first wife."

Luisa thought she might faint. *Whatever is going on? Marco was never married. There must be some mistake.*

She had long since pulled her hand from Marco's, and now she found herself desperate to get outside and breathe fresh air. She said nothing as they retraced their steps in and out of the elevator and down the long hall. She didn't dare ask Marco the questions that whirled in her mind. His heavy brows were lowered into a deep scowl.

It isn't fair. It must be a mistake. Surely there's some way to appeal it.

Marco opened the car door for her, and she slid into her seat. He climbed into the driver's seat, backed out of the parking area, and stomped the accelerator, squealing the tires as the car shot through the gate. Then he braked hard at the stop sign. Luisa stared at him; Marco never drove like that.

As the car merged into traffic on the freeway, he reached out and took her hand.

"What did she mean, Marco?"

"I have no idea. I guess because I have children they think I was married. I don't know what to do. I don't even know where that woman is. We'll figure out some way around it."

There would be no flaming bowl of seafood for them at the restaurant tonight. Instead, they drove back to the apartment, where Marco stopped at the front gate and dropped Luisa off instead of coming in. "I'll be home a little late tonight. I'm sorry, Luisa."

In a daze, Luisa entered the building and made her way to her apartment. The neighbors who greeted her in the hallway seemed to be from another planet, seen through layers of fog. Suspicion bombarded her mind. Surely the lawyer was mistaken. She had known Marco for twelve years, and he had no wife. But how could she ever know for sure?

Luisa hung her coat behind the bedroom door and flung herself across the bed. She stared unseeingly at the wall by the door—and then she realized her eyes were resting on Marco's briefcase, the one he opened when he paid bills or filled out tax forms. He had no desk. Could that battered briefcase hold answers?

It seemed a base thing to do—to snoop in Marco's personal stuff—but she had to know the truth. She got up and closed the bedroom door; then she hoisted the heavy leather briefcase to the bed and opened the brass clasp. Papers, bills, check registers, paycheck stubs, receipts. She unzipped a divider and pulled out another cluster of papers and envelopes. She paused, eyeing the Mexican address written on the top envelope, and the name: Yolanda Garcia. She could not remember Marco ever mentioning anyone by that name.

She laid the envelopes on the bed and began unfolding the heavy parchment document she had found tucked behind them. Suddenly her stomach cramped, and a wave of panic and nausea swept over her. She crammed the papers back into the zippered pocket, latched the briefcase, shoved it back along the wall where she had found it, and fled to the bathroom. Perched on the edge of the bathtub, she lowered her head to her knees. *God, please let me find out the truth. Help me get through this. Oh, God, I need you.*

She sat there for a long time, waiting for her stomach to stop churning. At last she returned to the bedroom. This time she locked the door.

Opening the zippered section again, she pulled out the papers. Like a woman opening her own death sentence, she unfolded the parchment. Marco's name and Yolanda's—United in Holy Matrimony. Numbly, she gazed at it for a long time, then laid it on the bed. Hands trembling, she opened one envelope after another, reading letters from Yolanda, letters asking for help with the children, one letter informing Marco that she and the children had moved, others bearing news of relatives and acquaintances and updates on the children—not warm, but civil and businesslike.

Luisa's ears were ringing, and her head felt light. She struggled to breathe. Marco had lied to her.

What had happened to tear him from his family? Why were he and Yolanda no longer together? Why wouldn't she let him see the children—or was that a lie too?

SONG OF THE SHEPHERDESS

A broken home. Fatherless children. A woman struggling to raise a family alone. Her mind traced the outlines of Yolanda's life as if she were gazing into a mirror. She groaned.

Twelve years. And all this time she had lived with their husband and father. *Oh, Lord, what have I done?* Grief and shame washed over her. She, Luisa, was the "other woman," the thief, the mistress.

Oh, God, have mercy. I didn't know.

The conviction she had been shrugging off all this time settled on her shoulders now. She had knowingly chosen to live in sin with a man who was not her husband. She had chosen her actions, but the consequences of those actions were not hers to choose. Her conscience screamed accusations in her tortured soul.

It is not too late, my child. She heard the whisper of the Shepherd. *It is never too late to turn around and live in the light of my truth, my love, my presence.* It was true, she knew. But it seemed impossible.

If this man she had loved was not who he said he was, who was he? If only she could wake up to find this was all a dream—or go to sleep and never wake up at all.

By the time Marco came home, his breath rank with alcohol, Luisa was calm—but still angry.

Right away, he began pleading with her to understand. "Luisa, I'm really sorry about what happened today; it's ridiculous. The lawyer is mixed up. I don't have a wife. I don't know where my children are. You're my wife, Luisa, and we have a son. Why do we need the state of California to say we belong together?"

"I can't marry another woman's husband, Marco."

"Luisa, be reasonable. It's all a mix-up. Believe me, she is not my wife. I don't even know where she is!"

"This game is over, Marco. If you want to know where she is, you should check your briefcase."

Marco's shoulders slumped. He pushed past Luisa and stumbled into the bedroom, slamming the door behind him.

CHAPTER 52

Counting the Cost

In the morning, Marco held Luisa for a long time. "I'm sorry, Luisa," he said. "Please forgive me. I didn't mean to deceive you. In my mind and heart it was true. As far as I'm concerned, she's not my wife. How could she be my wife when I haven't seen her for years? Please believe me, sweetheart. There is no woman for me but you.

"Luisa, if you can forgive me, we can go on together as though it never happened. We have Hamit to think about, and your other children, and the grandchildren. We're a family, and nothing can change that."

Luisa's heart churned like a roiling black storm. She had loved this man for years. His lies had slapped her in the face again as soon as she awoke this morning. But after all, this was little more than the predictable next chapter in a life strewn with disappointment and betrayal. It felt almost normal by now.

But there was more to this than whether she could forgive and go on. "Marco, you don't understand. This isn't about how we feel. It isn't about how things seem to us. God created us, and He makes the rules—not to make us miserable, but to make our lives work the way He designed them to work. God's Word doesn't change, and He gave us His laws to make us free."

Marco would never understand, she could tell. Tears stood in her eyes as she rushed on. "I haven't been faithful to what I knew God wanted for my life. God says it is sin to live together unmarried, and living with someone else's husband or wife is adultery. Sin is bondage, and it separates us from God, no matter how good it feels at the time. I love you, Marco, but I can't go on like this."

"I just don't get it." Marco shook his head as if shaking out cobwebs. "I don't get it, but I know it's important to you, so it's important to me too. I love you, dear. Some way or other we'll work it out."

Hamit tapped on the bedroom door; it was time to leave for school. Marco kissed Luisa again and went to meet Hamit.

As father and son walked along the sidewalk that morning, oblivious to the passing cars and a sky threatening rain, Marco's heavy eyebrows weighed down his brooding black eyes. "Hamit, you know what I've always told you: take care of your mother." Hamit had heard it many times, but Marco seemed extra serious today. "Never forget to take care of your mother, son."

Hamit had felt the negative charge in the apartment when he returned from school the day before. His mother had barely spoken a single full sentence, even during supper, and his father had not come home until after he was asleep. Of course, Dad often came home late—but something was definitely weird in the house. When Mom had walked him to school that morning, she had been as happy as a child. What could have happened?

Whatever it was, Hamit resolved that he would always keep the trust his father was giving him. He would be there for his mother.

That afternoon when Luisa walked Hamit home from school, she was mostly silent once again. She had more teaching to do that day, teaching that would implicate her, and she was not sure how to do it. "Come, Hamit," she said when they reached the house. "Let's read the Bible before I make supper."

Hamit ducked into his room, tossed his camouflage backpack on the bed, and returned to the table. Straddling a dining room chair backward, he hooked his elbows around the backrest and rested his chin on his wrists.

Luisa was leafing through her Bible. "I want to read to you what God says about marriage and divorce, son. The prophet Malachi wrote down the words the Lord wanted to say to His people. This is what Malachi wrote: 'The LORD hath been witness between thee and the wife of thy youth, against whom thou hast dealt treacherously: yet is she thy companion, and the wife of thy covenant. And did he not make one? . . . And wherefore one? That he might seek a godly seed.'[1]

"You see, Hamit," Luisa said, "No matter what happens after a man and a woman marry, they have made a covenant with each other before God, and God has made them one. No one else belongs in that union. If one of them lives with someone else, God calls it uncleanness, and it is against His holy design. Such disobedience cuts people off from the blessing that comes from doing things God's way. Don't ever forget this, son. God designed that one man and one woman should marry and raise their children to love and serve Him."

She picked up the Bible and read on: " 'Therefore take heed to your spirit, and let none deal treacherously against the wife of his youth.'[2] A man or woman deals treacherously when he or she violates that covenant to be true to each other until death. Malachi says God hates divorce. Two verses later it says it wearies God when we do evil and say God is pleased with it.

"I think I've wearied God, Hamit. I have not been living right. I'm not married to your father." She was quiet for a long time, and Hamit waited.

Luisa sighed as she pondered Hamit, this son of her sin, this son of her heart, this beautiful, innocent boy. "I am going to be sleeping in your room from now on, Hamit. It is disobedience to my heavenly Father to keep sleeping with Marco."

Hamit struggled to understand what she was telling him. As far as he was concerned, his parents had always been as good as married. But having Mom in his room was fine with him.

The next time Conrado stopped by, Luisa poured him a cup of coffee and sat down at the table across from him. "Conrado, how would you like to

[1] Malachi 2:14–15
[2] Malachi 2:15

make some money in Guatemala, working at something much safer than playing coyote?"

Conrado laughed shortly. "There is no money like that to be made in Guatemala, Mama. Not safely anyway." As Conrado lifted his coffee cup, Luisa admired his hands, so like Reynaldo's. The capable hands of a man who could do anything he set his mind to—anything but rule his own spirit.

In the hills around La Laguna, Conrado was legendary for his rage and fighting prowess, but also for his engineering skill. He had only to see something once, and he could build it. What could he be with his heavenly Father in control of his life?

"I would like to have a decent house built on my property," Luisa said, watching his face. "It will never be easier than it is now. I want you to build it."

"I could do it, Mama. I finished mine a long time ago."

Luisa knew about Conrado's house: two snug block buildings on concrete foundations, high on the hill above the bean field. By planting the buildings solidly on Leland Seibel's land, Conrado had gained a sense of payback for his humiliation the day he tried to drag Lidia from the churchyard. Trying to reason with Conrado about the house site would only have angered him, so Luisa had done the only honorable thing she could think of: she had bought the land back from Leland for the same price he had paid for it years before.

Luisa pulled her thoughts back to the present. "I want Mama to have a better place to live—and who knows, I might need it someday myself. I want to put it right against the mountain next to her current house." Luisa unfolded a napkin and sketched out a plan. She would have the rooms connected around a courtyard, and there would be an indoor bathroom.

Conrado looked it over, made suggestions, and promised to start as soon as he got back to Guatemala.

Home life was changing for Luisa and Marco. They had always argued, but it was happening much more, and tensions were running high. Luisa had not made a clean break with Marco. Sometimes she was sharply conscious that this man was not hers, but other times it just seemed too complicated and impractical to follow God's standard in this mixed-up world. *Most of my family loves and accepts Marco, and he loves them. Without Marco, what would hold us all together? How could I support myself without his help? What if I separate from him and lose Hamit?*

Whatever shred of trust she had held for Marco was gone. He was the friendliest man in the apartment complex, frequenting every floor in his job as maintenance man and janitor, exchanging pleasantries with tenants wherever he went. His supply closet adjoined the public laundry room in the basement, where ladies, often alone, waited for their weekly wash to slosh, spin, and dry. Often he would stand in the room and chat with one or another of them for half an hour or more while Luisa fumed upstairs.

"Come on, Luisa," he would say. "That woman is nothing to me. You know you're the only one for me."

His reassurances did not comfort her, and when she couldn't stand it anymore, she sometimes stormed down to the laundry room to demand that he come home. Of course, this angered Marco, embarrassed Hamit, and made her miserable. What was she becoming?

One day Marco brought Juana's son Oscar home to live with the family. The relationship between Juana and Oscar's father was going badly, and Marco thought the boys would do each other good. Marco treated Oscar like a son, and he and Hamit, close friends already, soon became like brothers. Despite the trouble between Luisa and Marco, he still spent time with the boys, adjusting their activities and outings to accommodate Oscar, who was younger than Hamit.

Marco set high standards for the boys' behavior at home. "You can eat anything you want when you are on the street. But when food is set on the table at home, you better be hungry, 'cause you're going to eat it." So they ate, whether they liked it or not. They knew better than to argue with Marco.

He also set rules about cell phones. "Phones are for getting in touch with your family when you are away, or calling people sometimes when you are alone. But when you're home, you're *totally* home. No one in the world is more important than the people at home." So Hamit and Oscar kept their cell phones turned off at home. Marco set the example—Hamit rarely saw his father answer his cell phone.

Around this time, the price of rent and groceries increased sharply, and the five dollars Hamit was used to finding on the kitchen counter each morning dwindled to two or three, and then to nothing.

The financial troubles stressed Marco and Luisa's relationship still further. As their relationship deteriorated, the long afternoons Marco spent with the boys became rarer. Still, as long as the boys had each other, Hamit could not be lonely.

For Luisa, though, the loneliness was a yawning void. Sometimes she thought she couldn't take it anymore. Some of the family still came together on Fridays to share supper around Marco's big table, but Marco was often absent, and the good times were getting thinner.

Luisa walked to her jobs each morning. Twice a week she made the rounds of her twenty-seven apartment complexes. Squeegees, vacuum cleaners, trash cans, and dryer lint filled her days. But when she was home in the evenings, Marco usually was not. Marco's weekends, when he wasn't working, were blown in the bars.

In one way Luisa was glad she did not have to encounter Marco much. Yet it galled her to think he might be carrying on a secret life of immorality, then coming back to live with her and Hamit.

Marco would not accept the change in Luisa's behavior toward him. Baffled by her anger and the principles she claimed to embrace, he sometimes tried to force himself on her. On one such occasion, Luisa picked up her sewing machine in desperation and hurled it at him. They ended up in court that time, and the judge ruled in Luisa's favor. "She acted in self-defense," the judge decreed. "She is protected by the laws of the State of California."

Despite the southern coastal warmth that day, the air between them was icy as they climbed into their separate cars to drive home.

Luisa wanted out—with Hamit. But Marco had made it clear he would not give up Hamit without a fight. And he kept reassuring her of his faithfulness. "Luisa, I tell you, you are the only woman in my life," he often said.

Counting the Cost

One rare evening when they were both home, Marco looked at her for a long time before speaking carefully. "Luisa, I wish you would believe me and accept my love. How can I convince you? You are so sure I am unfaithful to you, but you have no proof. Please believe me."

Luisa sat in stony silence. She had mountains of evidence against him, but it was all circumstantial. She could not prove that the ladies who called him on the phone were special to him. She could not prove that he was getting into trouble when he was away for days at a time and failed to answer his phone. And although the older children understood what was happening, they preferred to stay out of the hostility between Marco and Luisa.

"I tell you what, Luisa. If you can ever prove that I am being unfaithful to you, you can leave with Hamit. You can go live wherever you want to live. I mean that, darling. In fact, I will help you move and get settled."

Luisa looked hard at him, and then a trace of a smile softened her eyes. Maybe she was accusing him for nothing. He seemed so earnest.

"Really, Marco?"

"Yes, really, my girl. That very day, you are free. I give you my word." She let him take her into his arms for just a moment. "Do you believe me now?" he asked softly.

CHAPTER 53

Seeking

Luisa felt some satisfaction in knowing she had stuck with Marco against the odds. Her determination had allowed Hamit to grow up with his dad, an opportunity that had doubtless saved him from joining one of the gangs of boys who prowled the local streets, armed with knives.

Her children were all settled in the United States now, except Aide, who had returned to Guatemala. Even Joel had finally come to California. Although he barely knew her as his mother, she was thankful that he was near. Dionel, who had returned to Guatemala for a time, had moved north again and was now living in Oklahoma. Eliza and Benjamín were in Oklahoma too.

In many ways Luisa had what she had hoped and worked for. But Marco was not hers and never could be.

These days another thought troubled her increasingly: the memory of her vow to God. She had promised she would work hard until all the children were in the United States, and then she would find a church. It was past time to pay her vow. She visited several local churches, but each visit left her grieved and confused.

One Sunday morning Luisa went with a relative to a church where she knew the women wore dresses, and some even wore veils during church.

Maybe these people understood holiness.

As the meeting began, a handful of people walked or ran to the front of the building and began praying loudly. A large lady waddled to the piano and began pounding the keyboard, while the congregation shrieked songs at the tops of their voices and the people in front kept praying, twisting their bodies and pounding the floor and walls. After the singing, a preacher stepped up to the pulpit, called for more volume from the sound system, and shouted his sermon at the congregation.

At the close of the meeting, Luisa wept with frustration and disappointment. How could this noisy, chaotic place ever be home for her spirit? How could one even hear the Spirit of God amid such emotional manipulation? *God, please, isn't there some place in this city where people are worshiping you in order and holiness?*

Luisa wanted out of this on-and-off relationship with Marco, with its loneliness, sin, and confusion. If only he would just leave.

Perhaps she could make him *want* to leave.

Arguments broke out whenever Marco walked in the door. Luisa often smelled alcohol on his breath when he came home, and she met him with suspicious questions: "Where have you been? Who were you with?" Her accusations and his defenses flew back and forth until she was throwing things, and sometimes he hit her back. Several times the police were called to their apartment for domestic violence complaints. Once, after Marco split her lip with his fist, Luisa went to court and got a restraining order that barred him from coming within fifteen miles of her. But his absence did not ease the tension and turmoil that raged inside her.

One day a neighbor called Luisa to inform her that Marco had been seen with another woman. The neighbor gave a specific address. Luisa arrived unannounced and confronted Marco and the other woman, fully confirming her suspicions. It was the last straw. Luisa knew the relationship was finally over for good.

That evening Marco called Luisa, begging her to understand, to try again.

"It's over, Marco. You know what we agreed. I'm not trying again."

Seeking

After she hung up the phone, Hamit sat down at the table next to her. "Mama, I think I'm going to leave," he said. "Maybe with me out of the way, you two can decide what you really want from your relationship. I don't want you fighting over me anymore."

"No, Hamit," she said. "You aren't the reason we fight. But I'm so sorry you've had to go through all this. If you need to go for a while, I understand." She knew that she and Marco were still together only because of their mutual fear of losing Hamit to the other.

The next afternoon Hamit walked with his father along the beach, the place where Marco had spent countless happy times with him and Oscar. "I think it's time for me to go, Dad. I can go live with Dionel in Oklahoma. I'm just making more problems for you and Mom by staying here."

"I understand how you feel, son. I guess there's nothing more I can do. It looks like it's over for your mother and me." He paused, gazing out across the ocean. Then he turned to look deep into Hamit's eyes. "Take care of your mother. That'll be your job now. Whatever happens, take care of her."

"I will, Dad, I promise." As they hugged, Hamit found that his dad felt suddenly small in his arms. "And Dad, if you ever need me, you'll let me know, won't you?"

"Don't worry about me, son. It doesn't matter about me." But the catch in his voice and the tightening of his thick arms around Hamit belied his words. "I've failed you and your mother, and you don't owe me anything."

When Hamit left a few weeks later for Oklahoma, Luisa went along to help drive. Though it had been hard to leave Marco, she was relieved to have the pressure and fighting behind her. Now the journey of more than a thousand miles across the Southwest offered her ample time to reflect on her past and her future.

I want God, but I'm afraid I'm still running away from Him. What I would give to feel the peace and comfort of His presence in my life again. If only I could return to Guatemala.

Luisa had stayed in the United States for Hamit, but he was nearly sixteen now, almost a man. Dionel could look out for him if he needed to.

"Do you think you'll be moving to Oklahoma too, Mama?" asked Hamit. "I mean, if things still don't work out with you and Dad."

Luisa smiled crookedly. Hamit refused to give up hope that she and Marco might get back together. "Your dad said he would help me go wherever I want to go. I guess I just need to make up my mind."

As they climbed out of the Colorado River Valley toward Kingman, Arizona, a purple-pink sunset lit the rearview mirror. Darkness descended, and they hummed on through the night. Their 2000 Ford Explorer, a gift from Marco to Hamit when he was only thirteen, seemed lost among the moonlit mountains.

They did not talk much in the night, but traded seats when one or the other got too sleepy.

In the morning a mackerel sky, the clouds like ten thousand tufts of strawberry cotton candy, heralded the sunrise over the Texas panhandle. As they entered Oklahoma a few hours later, thunderheads were unrolling across the sky, and before they reached Oklahoma City, the heavens broke into torrential weeping. Hamit twisted the wiper control, and though the wipers whipped furiously across the windshield, it remained nearly impossible to see the road. Thunder snapped and rumbled, roared and crashed, while jagged lightning pierced the gray blur outside. They pulled the Explorer to the shoulder of the road and waited for the storm to wear itself out.

"We never got storms like this in California," Hamit said.

"No, not like this. We had them at La Laguna, though."

Another bolt of lightning split the sky. Luisa remembered the carcasses of her father's fine sheep sprawled on a mountain. Why was life so rent with pain and loss?

Hamit was pensive. "Dad always told me never to give up, no matter what happens. But I think Dad gave up."

Luisa reached over to squeeze his hand, tears trickling down her cheeks.

Hamit returned the squeeze and held it. "Don't you give up, Mama. Maybe you'll go back to California, but I want you to know, whatever happens, I'll be here for you. Just please don't ever give up."

Another peal of thunder shook the Explorer.

CHAPTER 54

Starting Over—Again

After settling Hamit in Oklahoma City with Dionel and Andrea, Luisa flew back to Los Angeles. Five months later, early in the spring of 2006, she finally made up her mind that it was time to leave Marco for good and start over in Oklahoma. True to his word, Marco helped her move, loading his bright red Dodge Dakota with Luisa's belongings until it squatted. Luisa piled boxes, wall hangings, and pots and pans into her yellow Subaru BRAT until only the driver's seat was clear.

As the two heavily-laden vehicles headed toward Arizona on Interstate 40, Luisa's mind slipped back to the day she had scrambled over a fence with a small bag and a single shoe. Today she felt like the taffy she had seen stretching on merciless steel arms in the window of a candy shop. Aide, Sonia, Juana, Marixa, and Joel were in Los Angeles. Dionel, Eliza, Benjamín, and Hamit were in Oklahoma City. Vicenta was in Guatemala with several great-grandchildren. Following her down the highway was Marco, still under the restraining order. And Conrado? *Oh, Lord, where is Conrado?*

Conrado had not been seen for months. The mountains around La Laguna buzzed with rumors about his disappearance. Some said he was imprisoned in Mexico, but most believed he had been murdered. The police had scoured

La Laguna for his body without result. They had even pumped out the well he had dug behind Luisa's house.

The last time Luisa and Hamit had traveled to Guatemala, she had hiked up to Conrado's house, where his wife still lived. She saw his tools neatly arranged in the secure storage closet he'd built for them. She saw the solid, cozy house she had asked him to build, exactly as she had requested in every detail. *Oh, Conrado, my son, my son.* Alone in the car, her tears fell freely, seen only by the Shepherd, who understood Luisa's pain as she dangled between today and tomorrow, longing with her whole soul for the peace and belonging of the sheepfold.

Once again, the nineteen-hour trip across California, New Mexico, Arizona, and Texas allowed much time for reflection. What had she accomplished in the past seventeen years? She had set out to feed and clothe her family with her own two hands. But had it been worth the price?

She had wanted her family in the United States with her. What for? Now two of her daughters were married, one for the second time and one only after having several children outside marriage. Several who remained unmarried were raising children without their daddies' presence. None of the grandchildren were in Christian schools. Only Eliza's family went regularly to church services, at the Roman Catholic church.

Yet all of them had food to eat, and some were even overweight. All those who lived in the United States had televisions, toys, and electronic gadgets in abundance. They wore the latest styles, whether cute or scandalous.

Luisa groaned inwardly. *What a price!*

She remembered the laughter of little bright-eyed girls in braids and ragged dresses arriving home from school. She remembered little piping voices raised in songs about God and heaven, or quoting memorized passages of Scripture. The innocence of her children's lives in those days, their awareness and dependence on God—looking back on it, it all seemed so precious. They had owned these treasures even amid the turmoil of life with an alcoholic father, even when they had almost nothing to eat—and they had been together.

Today it became crystal-clear to Luisa that Mama Vicenta had chosen the better part. Mama was joyful and trusting no matter what life demanded of her: walking barefoot to beg corn from her neighbors, washing clothes in the river, cooking a sparse meal over a smoky fire, nursing sick children without running water. Though she had never had access to a bathtub in her life, Mama lived with a clean conscience. She understood what mattered most. How had Luisa missed it?

Trinkets, expensive clothes, fine china, extravagant foods—they mocked and taunted her now. Had she sold her birthright for a mess of pottage?

After Marco helped her unload the vehicles in Oklahoma, he announced, "I'm leaving the truck with you. I just paid it off, so it won't cost much to keep. It's a gift." He patted the shiny red hood of his 1999 Dodge Dakota.

"No, no, take it with you. I don't need it," Luisa objected.

"Someday you might. I want you to have it."

Luisa watched Marco enter the terminal to fly home to California. Their sinful relationship was over, she knew. She blinked back tears, knowing that Jesus would be enough. Besides calling her away from the man she loved who was not hers, Jesus had called her away from a steady, dependable income. He had called her to abandon herself to his eternal love and power.

She had obeyed the call.

Dionel and Andrea owned a three-bedroom house with a large fireplace and enclosed backyard at the end of a quiet cul-de-sac. Although they already had two little girls, they welcomed Luisa as they had welcomed Hamit a few months earlier. But Luisa lived out of her suitcase, praying for a place where she and Hamit would not impose on anyone else. Dionel brought her copies of the local ad paper, and Hamit translated the most promising apartment ads for her.

The day they pulled off the highway into the parking area of the Royal Oaks apartment complex, Luisa felt hopeful. Despite their outdated neo-mansard style, with slanted wood-shingled upper walls, the apartments were recently built, the rooms were comfortable, clean, and spacious, and best of all, the rent was only 350 dollars a month. If they were careful, they could afford it. Hamit had landed a job at McDonald's and saved a little money, and for the first three months, a check arrived each month from Marco, enough to cover the payments on Luisa's car.

Luisa and Hamit moved into Royal Oaks within a week. Their apartment was on the first floor next to the swimming pool. The door opened onto a porch between two sections of the building. There were two bedrooms and a living room and kitchen larger than anywhere she had lived in Los Angeles. Luisa was astounded to get so much comfort and convenience for such a price.

Since coming to Oklahoma, Hamit missed the camaraderie of their friends in the San Marino building. Though she hated to do it, Luisa ordered cable television service for him, fearing what Hamit might do with his time if he was not occupied at home.

Though she had never socialized much in Los Angeles, Luisa missed the accepting attitudes of their California neighbors. Here at Royal Oaks, the couple who lived above them always looked away when they met in the parking area or on the steps, and Luisa's attempts to speak to them were met with contemptuous glances.

After Marco quit sending support, Hamit's McDonald's income hardly stretched around to meet all the obligations. When Luisa heard of a cleaning job at Bricktown Hotel and Convention Center, she and Hamit drove fifteen minutes across town and both applied immediately.

A few days later, Luisa was called for an interview. "It's a full-time position, ma'am," her prospective employer told her.

Through the glass door of the office where they sat, Luisa could see the lamps and carpet of the hallway. She remembered the fixtures in the dining room, the big glass windows overlooking the swimming pool, and the guest rooms they had shown her. How could it take eight hours to do that much work?

That night Luisa waited eagerly for Hamit to arrive from work. For one thing, he would probably bring something to eat. Usually he brought several hamburgers, and sometimes flaccid French fries. Sometimes there was a mistake on an order, and if a hamburger waited too long in the warmer,

McDonald's policy prohibited serving the food. Rather than pitch the food in the trash, Hamit stowed it away to take home with him.

As Hamit bounded up the stairs to the apartment, Luisa met him at the door. "They hired me!" she told him.

Hamit's smile broadened, and quick tears of relief pooled in his eyes. "Great! They'll never be sorry." He stooped to kiss her on the forehead, then flourished the crumpled bag in his hand. "I have a McGriddle, two Quarter Pounders, a Big Mac, and even a McFlurry tonight. It has M&Ms and the customer ordered Oreo." He pulled a cup from the bag and sloshed it. "It isn't frozen anymore, but I kept it cold."

"Thank you, God." Luisa bowed her head. God was providing. He would not leave them alone.

She brought a cup from the cupboard and poured in a few inches of the melted McFlurry. Hamit needed most of it; he was young and growing. They had no table, but it didn't matter. Sitting on the living room carpet with their backs to the wall, they devoured three of the sandwiches.

"Did you have enough?" Luisa asked as Hamit picked a scrap of onion off the wrapper.

"Sure, Mom. I've had all I need." Since moving to the Royal Oaks, Hamit was *always* hungry, but he didn't intend to tell his mom; she was doing all she could.

A toilet flushed in the apartment above them, followed by a strange burbling sound from their own toilet that seemed to go on and on. Luisa looked questioningly at Hamit, then rose stiffly from the living room floor, threw the empty wrappers into the waste basket, and hurried into the bathroom.

CHAPTER 55

Getting Settled

Filthy water flowed over the edge of the toilet bowl and across the tile floor. Wadded paper towels floated inside the toilet, caught by the ring. Luisa's heart sank. Twice last week, their toilet had clogged with paper towels and trash from the apartment upstairs, flooding the bathroom floor. Once, it had happened at night, and the mess had flowed into the hall and onto the living room carpet before they found it.

"Hamit, go tell the landlord," Luisa said as she plunged the toilet, trying to free whatever obstructed it.

The landlord arrived and scowled at the mess. "We've never had this problem before. Someone is doing this to make trouble for you." He pursed his lips and ran his hand through his hair, thinking. "Tell you what," he said at last, "you can move into one of the apartments on the other side of the street if you want to. You'll have more room and more privacy over there, and you'll be on the top floor. No toilets above you."

When Hamit translated the landlord's words, Luisa's eyes lit up. She had noticed those apartments, surrounded by large trees and set comfortably apart from each other. They even had carports. Luisa and Hamit moved that very evening and were settled in by bedtime. The landlord had spoken truly. The new place had a bedroom and bathroom for each of them, plus a large private balcony. Best of all, their landlord charged them the same rent as before.

On the day Luisa was to start work at Bricktown Hotel, she walked in the doors right on time. She remembered where the cleaning closet was and went directly to it, dragging out the huge cleaning cart loaded with a mop bucket, brooms, a trash can, paper towels, and squeegees. She polished the long elegant counters in the foyer and vacuumed the carpeted halls. She squeegeed the huge windows at the front of the building and then moved to the breakfast area.

Luisa's stomach constricted at the tantalizing wafts of fresh-brewed coffee, biscuits, and sausage. Before leaving for work, she had drained the last of a rescued McFlurry, while Hamit had eaten a single stiff Big Mac. "Here, Mom, you can have half of it," he had said, cutting the Big Mac in two.

Luisa could not make herself take it from him. "Thank you, Hamit, but I don't need it. You're growing. A fifteen-year-old needs to eat."

She was concerned about Hamit; he seemed restless and lonely. He needed something more to do with his life. Dionel and Eliza worked long hours, so Luisa and Hamit did not see them much. Luisa was thankful that he at least had Dixie, his pit bull pup. Playing with her and training her had filled a lot of lonely time. School and his job took some of his time too, but at home he had nothing but the dog and the television. Luisa sighed, rubbing harder at a stainless-steel drink dispenser. *We really need a church.*

After a quick vacuuming of the floor, Luisa was relieved to leave the breakfast area and its tantalizing smells. She started on the guest rooms, changing sheets and pillow cases, wiping down toilets and tubs, and vacuuming more carpets. In each room she set out fresh coffee packs and cups at each coffee maker and arranged soap and shampoo in the bathroom next to a folded washcloth. Still, she finished all thirty-two guest rooms by 2:30. Her employer had said the work would take until five o'clock. She emptied the mop water, replaced the cleaning rags, and pushed the cart back into the closet. When she punched out at the time clock, it was 2:45 p.m.

Luisa's former employers had raved about her quick, efficient work. Today she wished she could be paid what the job was worth, instead of by the clock. She walked through the wide front doors into the April sunshine. In front of the hotel, water splashed down four levels of an ornate concrete fountain. Daffodils and tulips glowed in large stone planters between stately pillars, and the flags of the United States and Oklahoma snapped in the breeze. Luisa was still hungry.

She started the car, headed out of the parking area, and merged onto El Reno. Maybe when she got her first check she could stop by the Salvation Army store and see if she could afford a decent table for the house. Of course, she thought, a table was little use without food to put on it. It was all they could do to cover rent, car payments, fuel, Hamit's cable TV, and the money she was determined to keep sending to her mother.

Two weeks later, standing in the sunshine beside her Subaru in the parking lot of the Bricktown Hotel and Convention Center, Luisa gazed in dismay at the check in her hand. She had prayed for this job, and she needed every cent. She was thankful that she would have two hundred dollars to send her mother, but this was pitifully skimpy compared to her checks in California. When she thought of the thousands she had blown in Los Angeles, she felt sick.

All that money I earned, and what do I have to show for it? Lord, I know you wanted to bring me here. You said you care for the sparrows, and I know you won't leave me alone. Teach me to trust you.

That evening Hamit arrived home with a thin, shaggy puppy in his arms.

"Where in the world did you get that dog, Hamit?"

"Mama, I couldn't leave him there. He looked so hungry." Hamit scratched the dog's little head. "He was standing beside a homeless man. I gave the guy fifteen dollars for him."

"But isn't Dixie enough?"

Hearing her name, the pit bull looked up at him, her eyebrows raised, her wrinkled jowls hanging sadly around her muzzle. Hamit laughed at her. He loved Dixie. She learned everything he tried to teach her, and they went everywhere together, except to school. They even slept together.

"But this dog is hungry, Mom, and he's going to be beautiful. Once I bathe him, get rid of the burrs, and trim the hair out of his eyes, he'll look just like Benji from the movie. I couldn't leave him there."

"Well, all right. I just hope we can afford to feed him."

Hamit led Dixie to the balcony and closed the door. Then he filled her feed and water dishes and set them on the kitchen floor for the stray pup.

Luisa pulled the day's McDonald's discards from two paper bags: a McChicken sandwich, a McGriddle, three Sausage McMuffins, a Quarter Pounder, and an apple walnut salad. Oh, and here were two thin hash brown patties in a small cardboard package and a baked apple pie. She arranged the gleanings on two plates, dividing the apple pie between them and setting aside the McMuffins for breakfast.

Sitting on the carpet in the bare living room after praying over their supper, Luisa said to Hamit, "I thought this job would be full-time, but I finish easily by three o'clock. That means I get paid only about two-thirds of what I was hoping for."

"You're too good a worker, I guess." Hamit smiled at her. "I'll do all I can to help." He bit into the stiff Quarter Pounder.

"Hamit, you are a great help, and I thank God for you, but I think I'm going back to Guatemala." She tore the corner off the vinaigrette pack and squeezed it onto the lettuce. "Think of all the money I made in California. Where is it? I have my house in Guatemala, of course, and a car, but I'm still making payments on that. We basically have nothing here. But the worst thing is that we have no church. I need to be with the people of God." Luisa was crying now. "It's been so long, Hamit!"

"I thought maybe you would like the church you went to the last couple of weeks."

"I don't feel like I meet God there, Hamit. The people don't seem any different from non-Christians, taken up with themselves and the vanity of the world. I need to go back to our church in Guatemala."

"Do whatever you think you should do, Mom. I would love to see you happy somewhere." The shaggy pup was nosing at Hamit's plate. "No, sit

Getting Settled

Suledi and Vicenta, an inseparable pair.

down," he ordered, gently pushing its hindquarters to the floor.

Luisa continued. "When I went to Guatemala to see Grandma after she broke her hip . . . well, you know Grandma. No matter how much she is hurting, she always wants to know how we're doing, always tells us to get back in church. What if she dies before I find a church? It's hard to stay close to God and keep living right with no other serious Christians around me."

Shortly after Luisa had moved to Oklahoma City, Aide had paid a visit to Guatemala, heading back to La Laguna to take stock of her relatives.

In the sixty-seven years since Vicenta had settled with Bacilio in the high canyon between the peaks of El Paiz and La Laguna, she had loved and cared for three generations of children. Aide's daughter Suledi still lived with her old great-grandmother, giving her all the love, care, and loyalty a faithful fifteen-year-old could give, and the two loved each other deeply.

"Mama," Aide had said, looking into Vicenta's wrinkled face, "you raised me and my brothers and sisters. You've cared for Suledi since she was a baby, and you cared for Ryan while I was in California. I think it is time for me to care for you.

"You're ninety-four, Mama. You have already fallen and broken your hip once. I think you're too old to live back here alone." She glanced across the room at Suledi. "This is a lonely place. It doesn't seem safe to have you and a fifteen-year-old girl here all alone."

So Vicenta had left La Laguna and moved into Aide's house several miles away. Meanwhile, Luisa kept sending financial support to her beloved mother who had taken her place at home all these years.

One month when Luisa's rent came due, there was simply no money to pay it. They had nothing in the house to eat, and only a few minutes remained on her cell phone. They probably wouldn't starve—one good thing about hunger was that it made even cold hamburgers taste good—but how could they live without a house?

Luisa and Hamit prayed and discussed their options. "We don't really need the truck Marco gave us," Luisa said. "Maybe we could sell it."

"Well," said Hamit, "the last time we were at Eliza's house, her husband's friend said he was looking for a truck. You could see if he wants it."

"I'll do that; we have to sell it soon, or we'll be evicted. We are out of money, Hamit. What's left in my purse will buy gas for the rest of the week, and then I won't even be able to get to work. And I haven't even sent Mama her money yet this month. We can't take that truck with us to Guatemala, anyway."

Outside the window, a squirrel raced along the porch rail, its furry cheeks bulging. "That squirrel's been hauling acorns up to a hole in that big maple," Hamit said. "There might be babies there. You leave that squirrel alone, Dixie, you hear me?" He shook his finger at her where she lay on the floor, and she thumped her tail in reply.

"We need seven hundred dollars just to get us through to the next paycheck," Luisa said.

"But, Mom, that truck is worth way more than seven hundred dollars."

"I'm sure it is, but right now I'd be happy for even that much. We have to get that money somewhere, and that truck costs us a few hundred every year for tags and insurance. Which reminds me, the insurance needs to be paid soon."

CHAPTER 56

A Clue

Luisa called Eliza to let her know the truck was for sale. The prospective buyer called back quickly.

"How much do you want for it?" he asked.

"I need seven hundred dollars to pay my bills this month, but it is worth much more than that. It's only seven years old, and it's like new," Luisa said.

"Well, this isn't a good time for me. I'm afraid seven hundred is all I can give you for it, sorry. I do need a truck, but it just isn't a good time for me at all."

Luisa's shoulders drooped. She knew she should insist on more, but what if they lost the sale?

"Let me think about it," she said. "I'll text you in half an hour."

As she hung up the phone, all she could think of was the eviction notice that would surely arrive in a few days. What if they ended up on the street? What if her mother died for lack of her heart medicine? When Marco had given her that truck, he had said she might need it someday. Surely that day had come.

Quickly, before she could change her mind, Luisa typed into her phone, "Will sell for 700. When can you come?"

A few hours later, Luisa gazed with relief at the stack of seven crisp hundred-dollar bills in her hand. Head high, she delivered the rent money to the landlord. Then she went to the bank and sent three hundred dollars to Guatemala for Vicenta.

When Marco heard about the truck sale, he was astonished. "You what?" he shouted at Hamit through the phone. "That truck was worth twelve thousand dollars! Why didn't you tell me you needed money?" But after Hamit explained the crisis they had faced, he calmed down. "Don't worry about it. You did what you thought you had to do. I would have sold it too in your place—but not for seven hundred dollars!"

Once more Marco began sending money each month. He had taken over Luisa's apartment cleaning job when she left Los Angeles, and now he began sending most of those earnings to her. The immediate crisis was over.

Hamit flew to California to visit his father, and when he returned, Oscar was with him. He had missed Oscar, who was more a brother than a nephew. For a few months, until Hamit graduated from high school in the spring, they would be able to attend school together.

Luisa stopped in the produce aisle of the grocery store to examine the tomatoes, wrapped and laid out on Styrofoam trays. She loved to cook, and she hoped never to see another Quarter Pounder in her life. She had found a new job recently, cleaning and stocking supplies at a bank building. Unlike the previous job, this kept her occupied full-time, and the pay was good.

Someone reached past her for a pack of tomatoes, and Luisa glanced back as the other woman added the tray of tomatoes to her cart. She sucked in her breath. How could it be? A pleated, mesh head covering and a long, simple cape dress.

The lady was hurrying after her cart into the next aisle, followed by another Mennonite lady. Luisa stared at them, her tray of tomatoes forgotten. She wanted to run after them, to talk to them, to ask them something—anything

A Clue

to keep them there until she figured out what to do next. But her feet stayed rooted to the spot.

Oh, if I could only talk to them! But they wouldn't understand Spanish.

Luisa kept trying in vain to muster the courage to approach the ladies, even as they made their way to the front, piled their groceries onto the belt, paid the cashier, and pushed their carts out the door.

That evening when Hamit got home, she met him with a shining face. "Hamit, there are Mennonites around here! I saw two of the ladies at the store today."

"Did you talk to them?"

"No, I was afraid they didn't speak Spanish, and besides, I couldn't think of anything to say. They seemed to be in a hurry."

They sat in silence for a while. "Hamit, there has to be a Mennonite church around here somewhere, probably west of the city. I saw those ladies in the store on Rockwell."

"But Mom, what if they were just traveling through?"

"I don't think they were. Their carts were too full. Who would buy three gallons of milk if they were traveling?"

Hamit felt tears pushing at his eyes. "You might be right, Mom. If there is a church around here, I'll do everything in my power to help you find it."

Several days later Hamit had his chance. It was his break time at McDonald's, and no one was using the single computer on the desk at the back of the kitchen. He sat down quickly and pulled up a search page. *Why didn't I ask Mom how to spell "Mennonite"?* His spelling must have been close enough, for the search results included a Mennonite church in Texas. He entered the address and tried to memorize the route to the church from Oklahoma City. Then he closed the browser tab and hurried to wash his hands before the end of break time.

The computer was not for personal use, but he had not used it for long. When he had another free moment, he pulled a pen from his pocket and sketched a map of the route on the back of a discarded meal ticket. *Three hours away. I hope Mom won't be too disappointed.*

Luisa was delighted. "Only three hours! Let's look for it on Saturday when we both have the day off work and Oscar is out of school."

Before they left home Saturday morning, Luisa asked Hamit to lead them in a prayer for success and safety. Hamit prayed a little awkwardly, wondering what his mother would think if she knew the life he lived and the company he kept when he was away from home. It bothered him a little that the good students avoided him and his friends at school. He didn't want to disappoint his mother, but he didn't understand her spiritual journey, and he certainly felt no need of a church. Well, whatever she was looking for, he would do what he could to help her find it.

They pulled into a gas station, filled the Subaru's tank, and set off together to find the church Hamit had located online. It was a pretty autumn day, and a church chase was a welcome adventure for the boys. Luisa tried to put her misgivings out of her mind as they rolled down Interstate 44 toward Wichita Falls, Texas.

"It's almost noon," Hamit said a while later. "I think we have about an hour to go."

"Then let's get burgers and fries here," Luisa suggested. "Somewhere besides McDonald's."

As they pulled back onto the highway a few minutes later, Hamit reviewed the route in his head for the hundredth time. When he thought he recognized the right road, he turned right. They drove west for miles, each new building that rose from the lonely landscape sparking a flurry of fresh hope.

"Look over there!"

"Where?"

"I think it's a barn."

"Wait until we get closer."

"It might be a church, and this is about the right area."

"No, it's a machine shed."

"Well, maybe we're almost there."

For hours they peered down dirt roads at houses, hay barns, machine sheds, loafing sheds, milking parlors, and Baptist and community churches,

A Clue

driving down countless back roads before returning to the main road to continue the search.

"Are you pretty sure it's along this road somewhere?" Luisa asked at last.

"Not really. I think I'm lost. I'm sorry, Mom. I must have written the directions down wrong." Weary and disheartened, they turned around and began the long drive home to Oklahoma City.

One evening a few days later, Luisa and Hamit sat at their table eating tamales with chicken and rice. "Hamit, I know what I saw at the store," she said. "Those women must go to church somewhere."

"We can drive some of the roads outside the city if you are sure there is a church somewhere," Hamit said.

Luisa cleared the table and stacked the dishes in the sink to be washed later. She gave the table a quick wipe and dried it with a towel. Then she pulled a map from the drawer under the toaster and spread it out.

"Let's start here." She pointed to a street running west out of town toward El Reno. "We can follow as many side roads as we have time for. Then we'll try a different highway next week, maybe here somewhere." She traced I-35 northward out of town. "We'll check out everything within an hour or so of the city. They wouldn't likely live more than an hour from their church house, would they?"

The following weekend found them in the Subaru again, going west. As they headed out of town, Luisa felt a confidence unwarranted by the reality of her search. How often she had read that promise: "And ye shall seek me, and find me, when ye shall search for me with all your heart."[1]

Luisa claimed God's promise for herself. She had wasted enough years. Now she would seek until she found His people. It was not God's will for one woman to try to serve Him alone. She wanted to be in the kingdom of God with brothers and sisters, living out God's plan for their lives.

As the suburbs thinned out, Bible verses kept coming to her mind. "Exhort one another daily . . . lest any of you be hardened through the deceitfulness

[1] Jeremiah 29:13

of sin."[2] *Hardened, that was me for sure.* "There, Hamit, try that road. There are buildings down that way, and it doesn't look too commercial."

As noon neared, Luisa pulled out their lunch bag and handed Hamit a pita pocket filled with chicken salad to eat as he drove. She kept her eyes on the countryside as she unwrapped her pocket and began to eat.

"How far are we going today, Mama?"

"Just a little farther. What if it is just a few more miles down the road?"

---

[2] Hebrews 3:13

CHAPTER 57

Two Searches

Roads ran to the left and right each mile, and along each road were scattered houses in clusters of barns and sheds. Electric wires sagged between endless rows of poles, seeming to rise and fall as the yellow Subaru zoomed by.

"Take care of your mother, son. Whatever happens, take care of your mother."

"Yes, Dad, always. I love Mom. Making her happy is the most important thing in my life."

Hamit looked over at Luisa. "Do you think we should go back now?" He really hoped she was ready to turn around. He had invited Sindy to go out with him this evening, and he wanted to get home in time to wash his truck.

Sindy was not the first girl Hamit had dated, but she was the first his mother had approved of. Hamit had known Sindy in school, but not closely; she and her many friends studied hard and behaved themselves, and they had nothing to do with his crowd. It was when he worked alongside her at McDonald's that a remarkable friendship sprang up between them. Sindy was a lovely Latina whose family had come from Honduras, and they had a lot in common. She was the happiest girl Hamit knew, but her idea of fun was respectful and wholesome. Spending time with Sindy made Hamit see himself in a new light.

One morning as Hamit finished shaving, he looked at himself in the mirror for a long time. He didn't like what he saw. "What do you want to do with your life, Hamit?" he asked himself out loud. "Do you want to be a troublemaker? Is that a life?" In that moment Hamit decided to change. From now on he would be a man of honor.

Returning to his room, Hamit surveyed the empty pop cans, candy bar wrappers, scattered socks, and rumpled bed. Glancing at the clock beside the bed, he snatched his backpack off a pile of shoes behind the door and hung it on a hook in the closet. Rummaging through the chaos, he found a couple of plastic bags and started on the trash.

Luisa watched the changes in Hamit's life and thanked God for Sindy. If only Hamit would be interested in the things of God. Sindy attended church faithfully each Sunday—without Hamit.

Spring comes early in Oklahoma, and when Hamit and Sindy were engaged, they began to dream of a Valentine's Day wedding. However, when they began calling pastors, they realized many other starry-eyed couples had had the same idea. They had waited too long to make arrangements. They would have to choose another date. Then, one day in late January, Sindy got a call from an elderly pastor she had called before. "The couple I was gonna marry on Valentine's Day backed out on me," he said. "So if y'all still wanna come down to Chickasha, we can do the weddin' for ya."

"Oh, thank you!" Sindy said. "But we were hoping you'd come to Oklahoma City."

"No, honey, I can't come up there. I'm blind and I got nobody to drive me. But I got a nice little chapel down here where we can fix y'all up."

On February 14, 2009, in Chickasha, Oklahoma, a small group of family members gathered to witness the marriage of Hamit and Sindy. The pastor was gracious, the chapel charming, the setting lovely. Luisa and Marco sat in the front row, side by side. For one day they would be a couple for Hamit's sake. Sindy was beautiful in a simple white dress, and Hamit glowed when he looked at her. But Luisa noticed he often looked at his parents too, with an expression on his face that made Luisa want to cry—a look of wistful hunger.

Two Searches

When the ceremony was over, Marco invited the whole family to the Golden Corral restaurant, where he had reserved space. They feasted from the buffets, and when they were full, they dipped fruit in the chocolate fountain. It was a pleasant day, but being with Marco reminded Luisa how lonely she was, especially when she returned to her apartment that evening.

Still, her resolve to follow the truth was not shaken. "God, you know how alone I am," she prayed, "but I thank you for giving Hamit a good wife. Please help me find your people."

Though Luisa had given up her weekly searches for a church, she never stopped praying and longing. Every time she had a chance to travel a new route, she scanned the landscape, the road signs, and the side roads for any evidence of a Mennonite church. One time some relatives visited and invited Luisa, Hamit, and Sindy to go with them to Eureka Springs, Arkansas. On the way, Hamit and Luisa, by long practice, spotted a couple of hopeful-looking church buildings too far away to read the welcome signs. A sign at the end of a side road read "Mennonite Cheese," but their traveling companions did not want to be bothered chasing churches, so they hummed on down the main road. A billboard loomed before them along the turnpike: "Amish Cheese House," it taunted as they flew past. What if there was a cheese vendor nearby who could help her find a church? Well, nobody else wanted to stop, and they were over three hours away from Oklahoma City anyway.

"Why don't you come to church with me?" Sindy invited Luisa a few weeks later.

"Maybe you'd like it, Mama," Hamit said. "Tell you what, I'll go if you do." Hamit had never been to the church, but Benjamín had been attending there for years and had often tried to get Hamit to go with him.

"Sure, I'll go with you," Luisa promised. She would gladly do that to get Hamit to a place where he could hear the Word of the Lord.

But arriving home from church the next Sunday, climbing the steps to her apartment, Luisa felt tired. She sighed. She should try the church a few more times before giving up, she supposed, but she had no heart for it.

She picked up her Bible and began reading: "For what fellowship hath righteousness with unrighteousness? and what communion hath light with darkness?"[1] She felt her head clear a little. Sometimes it was hard to remember if the Bible really said these things or if she was just hanging on to a personal notion. Luisa remembered when she had read these words forty years ago, and how they had made perfect sense to her and Reynaldo. God was holy, and He wanted a holy people.

"Wherefore come out from among them, and be ye separate, saith the Lord, and touch not the unclean thing; and I will receive you, and will be a Father unto you, and ye shall be my sons and daughters, saith the Lord Almighty."[2]

Unclean things: immorality, greed, and hate. God had said, "Don't touch it." That included divorcing one's spouse and marrying another. That included surrounding oneself with luxury while the poor cried for bread. That included going to war or taking people to court. These things belonged to the darkness of this world, not to Christ's kingdom of light. And what about selling food to people who came to church, as they did at the place she had been that morning? In Luisa's mind, that didn't fit with the example of Jesus who went about doing good—who fed five thousand people for free, just because they were hungry. She looked out the window for a long time. *Is there no one else in Oklahoma City who sees these things?*

Several weeks passed, and each weekend Luisa went to church with Hamit and Sindy.

In the quiet of her Royal Oaks apartment, the Bible was her daily bread. She pondered Ephesians 4:20: "But ye have not so learned Christ."

Luisa had read the passage a thousand times, and she knew the context of the verse well. Paul said people had grown callous and given themselves to lust and uncleanness.

That was certainly one of the things that bothered her. The immodesty of the churchgoers was part of moral uncleanness. Furthermore, she knew many members were no longer married to their first wives. *Lord, I have not*

---

[1] 2 Corinthians 6:14
[2] 2 Corinthians 6:17–18

so learned you, she prayed. *You are a holy God, to be reverenced and loved and obeyed.*

Luisa read on: "If so be that ye have heard him, and have been taught by him, as the truth is in Jesus: that ye put off concerning the former conversation the old man, which is corrupt according to the deceitful lusts."[3] The former way of life—God had called her to put it off. She read on. "And be renewed in the spirit of your mind; and that ye put on the new man, which after God is created in righteousness and true holiness. Wherefore putting away lying, speak every man truth with his neighbour: for we are members one of another."[4]

"Members one of another"? If I keep attending there, am I a partaker of the sins of other church members? She wanted to support Hamit and Sindy, wanted them both to know she was proud of them for going to church. She also wanted to be able to tell her mother she was back in church.

She could still see Vicenta's black eyes pleading with her. Mama had been so thin when they had last seen her. Her voice was thin too—so unlike she used to be. Yet the clarity with which she spoke was undiminished. "Reina, you have to find a church." She had reached out to clutch Luisa's hand. Mama's hand was thin and cool, but surprisingly strong.

"If you don't find a church somewhere, Reina, this will be the last time I see you. Ever." Luisa had thrown her arms around Vicenta then and held her as if she would never let go.

The next time she shook hands with the preacher at Sindy's church, Luisa decided to confide her conflict to him. "I don't feel right here," she said. "The sermons are good, but the people don't seem to understand about following Jesus and obeying His teachings. It seems to me that there is no difference between the people here and the people who don't know Jesus at all. And when we come together to worship, people are selling food, making a profit off their brothers and sisters."

---

[3] Ephesians 4:21–22
[4] Ephesians 4:23–25

The pastor did not hesitate. His voice was kind but firm. "If you don't feel right in this church, you ought to leave. The door is open. No one is keeping you here."

Luisa left with a sinking feeling. She knew she would not be coming back, but where was she to go? *Where are the people of God? Where are the people who understand that there are two roads, one leading to life and one to death? Where are the ones who have chosen the narrow road?*

She tried to keep a cheerful face over lunch that day, but she didn't fool Hamit. "Did something happen, Mama?" he asked.

Luisa told him what the pastor had said.

"I knew you weren't happy there," he said softly. "I'll help you look some more if you want."

What wouldn't he give to see his mother happy? He thought of the day they had piled everything they owned into three pickups and moved from the Oxford Building to the San Marino Building. Luisa had looked so happy that day—she had even walked differently. If only he could see her like that again. "I have Saturday off," he said. "We can keep looking."

Luisa smiled sadly. "I'm not going to bother you with it anymore, son. You have a wife and a life of your own. But that church has to be around here somewhere; I know I saw two Mennonites in the grocery store."

CHAPTER 58

Along a Country Road

Luisa eagerly dialed the phone number someone had given her on a recent visit to Guatemala—the number of her nephew Juan. *Imagine Juan Calderón being right here in Oklahoma City after all these years. Won't Dionel be surprised?*

When a man's voice answered, Luisa smiled. It was Juan alright. Before long they were deep in conversation, filling in the history of their years apart.

"I really want to get back in a Mennonite church, like the one in Guatemala," Luisa said. "I've looked and looked, but there don't seem to be any around."

"You know, that's funny; I just heard about one," Juan said.

"What? Here in Oklahoma City?"

"No, about an hour away. I've never been there, but I have a phone number for someone who goes there. A man named Mike—hold on a minute, let me find it. Okay, here it is. Mike Russel."

"Oh, Juan, I have to talk to him. Does he speak Spanish?"

"No, he doesn't, but some of the preachers at the church do."

"Thanks be to God!" Luisa's hand shook, and tears streamed down her cheeks. She tried not to shout into the phone. "God has heard me, Juan! How did you find them? I have been praying and looking for months and months."

"He just called me one day. He had met Rigoberto's daughter Reina at a Mennonite church in Texas, and she gave him my number and asked him to call me. I guess she was concerned about me living alone here without a church."

"God is good!"

"But Aunt Reina, I need to tell you something else about that church."

"What is it, Juan?"

"It isn't quite like the Mennonite churches in Guatemala. I don't know, maybe it isn't a real Mennonite church at all. Debbie Russel wears her dresses all the way to her shoes, and she wears a veil that covers all her hair."

"I don't think those details would matter, Juan. I am looking for God and His people."

"They also don't have as many rules as we were used to in the Mennonite church. Not everyone wears the same pattern of clothes."

"None of those things matter, Juan. If God is there and His people are worshiping Him with their whole lives, not just with their mouths, it is what I am looking for. The Bible says there are two roads. I've been on the wide road a long time, and now I want to walk with other Christians on the narrow road that leads to life. Juan, I've been to so many churches, and most of them seem to walk with the world and just say some Christian things. I'm sure this is an answer to my prayers."

"Well, if you go, let me know how you like it. Maybe I'll go with you sometime."

Luisa folded her phone, slipped it into her pocket, and dropped to her knees by the chair. "Thank you, thank you, God," she prayed. "Please let this be the answer I seek. Please don't let me be disappointed."

She pulled out her phone again and called to tell Hamit the good news.

As Hamit ended the call a few minutes later, he smiled. He hadn't heard his mom that excited in—well, maybe never. Having recently committed his own life to Christ, he understood her search better than he once had. He looked again at the phone number and address he had scribbled on a napkin, then punched the number into his phone.

After work, Hamit dropped by Luisa's apartment. When he came through the door, his mother was glowing. Tears filled his eyes; how he hoped she wouldn't be disappointed.

"I talked to him, Mom—Mike Russell."

"You did?"

"Yes. He sounded like a nice man. He said several people in his church speak Spanish, including two of the preachers." Hamit walked across the room and gave Luisa a hug. "I gave him your address and told him you'd like to go to church there on Sunday. He wants to come meet you and find out where you live before Sunday morning."

"Oh, son, I am so happy. I knew God would hear my prayer." Luisa looked heavenward and murmured, "Oh, God, I love you!"

On Saturday afternoon, as Luisa sat in her apartment reading her Bible by the window, a car pulled up to the curb outside, and a man stepped out and walked uncertainly toward the neighbor's apartment. He was dark-haired, bearded, and neatly dressed in a long-sleeved, button-down shirt. He hesitated for a bit by the next building, then walked around the side of her building. *What if it is Mr. Russel,* she thought. But she stayed where she was, and after a few minutes the man returned to his van.

As it turned out, the man was Mike Russel. After calling Hamit to confirm where Luisa lived, Mike and Debbie Russel visited her on the following Saturday.

Luisa lay awake all that night, crying and thanking God, basking in the wonder of what was happening to her. Once again she felt like the girl who lay awake at night, eagerly waiting to join the little band of seekers hiking through the dark to the little Presbyterian church house in Sibilia. She rose when the sun was barely up and prepared for church. Finally, at 8:20 a.m., she picked up her Bible from the table, snapped off the light, and stepped outside. She would drive to Mike Russel's house and ride with them to Perkins.

When she arrived at the Russel home, four little children were following their parents down the front steps. Mike and Debbie greeted her with wide smiles and warm handshakes, and Debbie kissed Luisa's cheek in greeting.

Then they introduced her to their row of shy little ones. The Russels' simple clothes, orderly children, and reverent manner reassured Luisa in her conviction that she had found her people at last.

Since Luisa and the Russels did not know each other's language, communication was awkward, but a communion of spirit bound them together as they traveled out of Oklahoma City toward Perkins.

An hour later they turned into a gravel parking lot, where a dozen cars were already parked outside a low brick building—a "Firemen's Hall," according to the sign out front. Tears flooded Luisa's eyes as she watched families climbing out of their vehicles and entering the building.

Next to them a minivan was parked with its side doors open, the mother leaning down to tuck a shirt tail into a small boy's pants while the father unfastened a little girl from her car seat and picked her up, her tiny blue skirt draping over his arm. Luisa followed the Russels into the building, entering a room nearly filled with rows of chairs. Standing in the rear of the room, she watched people greeting each other with hugs and the familiar kiss of peace, and wonder grew in her. *Oh, Shepherd, thank you!*

Luisa sat beside the Russels and opened the hymnal. The singing was all in English, but the pure a capella harmony transported her to heavenly places. When the preaching began, the church's deacon, Steve Shetler, came and sat near her, softly translating the message into Spanish.

The group shared a fellowship meal together afterward, and many people introduced themselves to Luisa. Becky Emerson, from Oklahoma City, spoke Spanish and offered to drive Luisa to midweek ladies' meetings. Luisa also met Gama Aguilar, from El Salvador. He was married to Steve Shetler's daughter and had been in the United States for only a year.

As Luisa climbed into the Russel van a couple of hours later, she was floating. Twenty years had passed since she had last driven away from the Hopewell meetinghouse in Hubbard, Oregon. *Oh, Lord, I think my search is over.*

The next Sunday she told Hamit, "I am going by myself today. I need to know how to get there when someone else isn't available."

"Go for it, Mom. I'm sure glad you've found a place that makes you so happy."

Although the church usually shared a common meal on Sunday, one Sunday a month was reserved for meals at home. This Sunday Joe and Debby Morris invited Luisa to their home for lunch. The Russels would be coming too, and Ernest Strubhar, a pastor in the church, with his wife Ruth, both fluent in Spanish. To Luisa, this was another confirmation that these were the same people of God she had known in El Edén, Guatemala City, and Hubbard, whatever they might call themselves. In all the other churches she had visited over the years, not once had anyone invited her to their home for a meal.

As Luisa walked into the Morris home that afternoon, the welcome and acceptance she felt from Joe and Debbie and their polite, smiling children transcended language. She watched in admiration as the Morris daughters bustled about the kitchen, the sons collected chairs to accommodate the visitors, and the parents gently directed all the activity. When the food was all set out, Debby spoke quietly to Joe, and he called everyone into a circle for prayer.

When everyone had been through the food line, Ernest turned to Luisa. "So, tell us a little of your background," he invited. "You didn't grow up here, I suppose."

"I lived in Guatemala until 1988," Luisa said. "I am a Mennonite."

Ernest raised his eyebrows and smiled good-naturedly. "Is it not a little lie?" he said.

Her claim must sound strange, Luisa realized, considering her circumstances. "But what reason would I have for lying to you?" she asked Ernest. "I am not in need of financial help or anything like that. Here, let me show you." She dug her phone from her pocket, looked up a number, and handed the phone to Ernest. "Here, you can call Leland and Esther Seibel. He will tell you. He was my pastor."

Ernest and his wife exchanged startled glances, and Ernest handed back Luisa's phone, smiling. "We know Leland and Esther. I believe you. So how did you end up here?"

CHAPTER 59

Vicenta Goes Home

It still did not seem real; Mama was gone. Luisa called Ernest, who prayed with her. How kind of God to bring her to a church family before taking her mother home. When Luisa had last visited her several weeks before, Vicenta had been very weary. "I am so sick. I just want to die," Vicenta had said. And now she was gone.

Vicenta had pointed the way for Luisa in her death as in her life. Those who had been with Vicenta reported that shortly before she died, she had sent for Carlos. "Put me in bed," she had instructed Aide when she knew he was almost there. Aide had pushed her wheelchair from the kitchen and gently helped her into her bed, where she was waiting for Carlos when he arrived.

When Carlos had stood by her bed, she had reached out a thin, wrinkled hand to touch his arm. "Carlos. It seems like I am going to die. I just want to ask that God would bless you, and that His blessing would reach you always."

How did Mama do it? Luisa wondered. For decades, Mama had borne the brunt of Carlos's unkindness, yet she had chosen forgiveness and active love. In Luisa's heart, Carlos's wrongs against her and her mother still festered. She had not even tried to be friendly with him for years. *No doubt; I hate him.*

One day, weary of the grudge that ate at her core, Luisa fell to her knees.

God, I need your forgiveness, too, for all the wrongs I've done to Carlos. She was on her knees for a long time, battling her carnal desire to see Carlos suffer for his mistreatment of her and Mama. "Lord Jesus," she groaned at last, "I choose to forgive him, not because he deserves it, but because of you and your great mercy to me. Give me your love for him, and give me grace to tell him I am sorry for all the nasty things I've said and done to him."

Luisa thought of Jesus hanging on the cross, blood streaming down his face. "Father, forgive them," Jesus had said. Could she possibly pray God's blessing on Carlos? "Father, forgive him!" she cried into her hands, and a sweet sense of release washed over her. She was ready to talk to Carlos now.

Luisa made a quick trip to Guatemala for Vicenta's funeral. Aide and her husband killed a cow to feed the four hundred people who came to pay their respects to the revered old grandmother of La Laguna. She had lived among them for a full century, planted decades of corn crops on Bacilio's land, and raised three generations of children. Leland Seibel preached at the funeral, and Frank Martin was there too.

At the cemetery a girl in her teens, a stranger, came up to Luisa and wrapped her arms around her. "You are my grandma," the girl said softly. Looking closer into the girl's sweet face, Luisa saw the features of her firstborn. *Oh, Conrado, my son.* Her eyes welled with tears as she kissed the cheeks of her granddaughter. The girl stayed near Luisa during the graveside service.

With tears rolling down her cheeks, Luisa sang, *"Cuando allá se pase lista, a mi nombre yo feliz responderé"* (When the roll is called up there, I'll happily respond to my name).

Oh, Mama, I will see you again in heaven. Thank you, God.

One thing more needed to be done before Luisa returned home.

"Chilolo, will you go with me to see Carlos?" she asked.

"I can go with you tomorrow," he said. "Carlos needs Jesus."

The next day, Luisa and Chilolo walked to Carlos's house.

"I've come to tell you I'm sorry, Carlos," Luisa said. "I have hated you. I have not treated you kindly. I have lied about you. Can you forgive me? I am a Christian now, and I am so sorry for my bitterness against you."

Vicenta Goes Home

Luisa with her two special older siblings, Yanet and Chilolo, in 2013.

Carlos's eyes narrowed. "I will *never* forgive you," he said. "Never."

Chilolo tried to reason with Carlos, but it was no use. He did not want to reconcile. Chilolo and Luisa turned away with heavy hearts. They would continue to pray.

Luisa returned to Oklahoma City, where she and Andrea planned a memorial service to be held in Dionel's house. Vicenta had been more than a mother to them, and they all felt orphaned by her passing.

CHAPTER 60

Blessed Are the Meek

The church in Perkins began holding a Spanish Bible study each Friday evening in the home of Mike and Debbie Russel. Gama often taught the Bible study, and sometimes Steve or Ernest. Luisa attended faithfully, and occasionally Juan Calderón and one or two others came as well.

A few months after Vicenta's funeral, Luisa received a call from Dionel. "I'd like to go with you to the Bible study on Friday night," he said. "Shall I come and pick you up?"

Luisa laughed aloud and hugged herself as she hung up the phone. *Oh, Lord, are you calling my family back to you?*

She had known Dionel was reconsidering his life lately. One big change was that he had gotten rid of his television. "I don't know what changed," he had told her, "but I see it with different eyes. It is full of lust and covetousness and pride, and I don't want it in my home."

As they drove across town that Friday evening, Dionel smiled at Luisa. "I guess you're wondering why I'm coming to this Bible study. It's hard to explain, but maybe it started with that recorded message Juan Calderón had. It was by Leland Seibel, and he was preaching about meekness. I got him to give it to me, and there was just something about it—I mean, it was weird how it took me back to the church house in Guatemala. But it was more than that. I kept listening to it over and over."

Dionel fell silent, remembering the evening last week when he had flopped across the bed, bone-weary from a hard day of work, and pressed play on that recording yet again.

"These verses, the Beatitudes, hold the secret to the fulfilled, secure, and happy life Christ wants for us," Brother Leland had explained. "Today we will focus on verse five: 'Blessed are the meek, for they shall inherit the earth.'

"To be meek is much more than being humble. It means I no longer say, 'Lord, I don't want to do this,' or 'I can't do this.' A meek horse does not fight against you. It is not rebellious. It lets you direct it wherever you want. So many of our sorrows, brethren, and so many of our worst difficulties come because we resist God's will for us. We want something different from what God wants, so we are sad, stressed, and desperate."

No doubt about that, Dionel had thought. Brother Leland was describing his life.

"But Christ says, 'Blessed are those who give their lives to me, who patiently accept my will for their lives, who obey me without resistance or rebellion.' That is being meek, brethren."

As Brother Leland preached on, Dionel forgot his weariness, overtaken by a deep hunger of soul.

"Meekness is patience when we are treated wrong. Meekness does not seek revenge or justification; it leaves that to God. Meekness is flexible, patient, gentle, tender, and resigned. It is not selfish, proud, or cruel.

" 'Blessed are the meek,' the Lord says. But the world says the way to be happy is to stand your ground, chase your own goals, and not let anyone stand in your way."

Dionel knew all about that. His anger and competitiveness alarmed him sometimes.

"But Christ says, 'No! This is not happiness. The joyful, blessed life is meekness.'

"Is a meek, gentle horse weak? No, it has great strength, but its strength is under control. That is meekness: strength under control, power under discipline. Rebellious horses never win races. The winner responds to his rider. When the rider says, 'Run!' he runs. When he says, 'Turn right,' the horse turns right. Winners are powerful, but under control.

"Remember Gethsemane, brethren. Jesus was facing the cross. He struggled with the price He would have to pay for our salvation, but He prayed, 'Not my will, but thine, be done.'[1] Brethren, this is meekness."

Outside the bedroom window, darkness fell and the streetlights came on as Dionel listened.

After Leland closed his message and prayed, the recording continued as the congregation began to sing: "Have thine own way, Lord, have thine own way. Thou art the Potter, I am the clay."

As always, that song seemed to pierce his soul. He was so far from God. The darkness within him yawned blacker and more terrifying than he had ever felt it. He wept, the soul-wrenching cry of a man who ached to end it all. *If only I could die. What do I need a life for anyway? Oh, God, living without you is not life!* He lay there for a long time, groaning over the empty years of his life, over his sins, over the vast and filthy wasteland of his soul. *I can't live without you, God, but I can't return, either. It's too late, too late. I have sinned too greatly, messed up too much. I can never be clean again.*

In that moment of absolute darkness, something long frozen had broken loose inside him.

Dionel pulled himself back to the present and looked at Luisa again. "You know I've been going to church with Andrea. The people there say they are Christians, but they aren't meek like Jesus taught us to be. They are worldly, carnal, and self-seeking. They sue others in court. I have talked to the pastor and shown him what the Scriptures say about these things, but he doesn't want to hear it.

"I attended there for a year, but I finally decided to quit. And you know what? The pastor never once called or visited me to see why I had stopped

---

[1] Luke 22:42

coming to church. What kind of shepherd is that?" Dionel paused, remembering a lone figure on horseback winding down the steep trail into their high canyon. "Remember Leland? If one of us missed a meeting, if someone was sick, if a rumor was afloat, if our cow died—whatever the need was, he was always there. I know what a shepherd looks like."

The following Sunday, Dionel attended church with Luisa, and the Sunday after that he attended on his own.

"Andrea, I want you to go with me," he said one weekend when she was off work. She agreed, but came away from the meeting distressed. "That is the deadest church I have ever attended. The people are nice, and the preaching is okay, but the Spirit isn't there at all."

"I know what you mean, Andrea," Dionel acknowledged. "It is really different from the churches we've been attending. But that is the way we worshiped God when I was a boy, so it's familiar to me, and it seems quiet and orderly. And you know, the truth is that the Spirit doesn't come just because everyone is screaming and crying and making noise. He comes where people are obedient to Him. The Spirit is in the hearts of the people."

In the weeks that followed, Dionel kept coming to church, sometimes with Andrea, and Luisa could sense the conflict in his soul. *Oh, God, please bring Dionel back to you. Let him understand that it is never too late to return.*

One bright summer day, Luisa received the call she had prayed for. "Mama," Dionel's voice said, "do you want to go with me to Perkins? I need to speak to Brother Ernest."

Later, as they drove toward Perkins, Dionel explained. "I couldn't wait anymore; I had to do something. Let me tell you about the dream I had a few days ago. It was about my son Eli.

"I was walking along the base of a mountain holding Eli's hand and thinking about my life. He let go and ran up the mountain ahead of me. Suddenly I saw this huge snake slithering down the mountain toward him. I called him, but he couldn't hear me. Then I couldn't see him anymore."

Dionel paused, and sweat stood on his forehead.

"I yelled and yelled for Eli. Then the snake came after me. I could see its fangs and its evil eyes. You can't imagine how terrified I was. Eli was gone, and I couldn't save him. I kept calling and calling his name, but nobody answered.

"Just when the snake was about to eat me, a sheet of red flame roared up from the bottom of the mountain and burned the snake to a coal. Then I saw Eli walking toward me, safe.

"I was shaking when I woke up. I knelt right there beside my bed and begged God for mercy for me and my family. Mama, we have to turn our lives around."

Tears sprang to Luisa's eyes. "Dionel, my son, my prayers are being answered!"

That afternoon while Ernest listened kindly, Dionel poured out the dark story of his long years of selfishness and sin. "I have set a terrible example for my siblings and my children," he said. "Sometimes I lie awake at night, wondering why I ever left God. Sometimes I have wanted Him so much."

Dionel sat quietly, remembering. "Sometimes God would touch my heart and I would be very sad. I felt alone, as if no one cared. I didn't know where there was a church to go to. For years now, Satan has been telling me it is too late to change. He says I can never undo all the wrong I have done. But I am coming back; I can't live any longer without God."

After they had prayed together, Ernest smiled at Dionel. "Press on, brother," he said. "God will give you the strength and grace to do whatever it takes to make things right."

Dionel knew freedom would require making restitution for some of his past wrongdoing. The worst was the phone call to Leland Seibel. Dionel wept when he heard Leland's voice on the other end of the line. "This is Dionel Monterroso. I—I need to make some things right with you . . . Conrado paid me to help him steal from your house, two different times. I stood outside the window and took the things and helped him haul them away. I'm so sorry, Brother Leland. I feel terrible every time I remember it. I want to—I'm sorry, Leland, can—can you wait a second?"

Dionel turned away from his phone and blew his nose. How could he have done that, even as a boy? He would never forget the moment when Conrado had handed Esther's sewing machine out the window to him, the same machine that had whirred and rattled over so many dresses for his own sisters. Recovering himself, he picked up the phone again.

"As I am able," Dionel promised, "I will pay back the value of everything we took."

"You don't need to pay any of it back. I am in no need," Leland answered. "This call alone is worth far more than anything you took. It's all forgiven already, brother."

As Leland spoke, the weight of years rolled off Dionel's conscience. He knew that whether Leland needed it or not, he would certainly make restitution.

Over the next year, Leland found several unexpected deposits in his bank account.

CHAPTER 61

This Is My Body

One day in late September, Gwen Hertzler accompanied Luisa to a meeting with the church in Perkins. The Hertzlers lived in Oklahoma now, a couple of hours from Perkins, and had rejoiced at the opportunity to reconnect with Luisa after learning she was in Oklahoma City. As the headlights of the car illuminated the road ahead, a favorite Spanish hymn played on the car's sound system. Luisa wished she could make Gwen understand the joy she felt these days. If only they knew each other's languages better!

But Luisa was bubbling over. She would do her best. "All time I play songs," Luisa said. "I sing all time. I sing, I sing." She looked upward, squeezing her eyes shut briefly. "I love you. I love you. Too much I love you," she murmured. It was an echo of the song the little shepherdess had sung in the Guatemalan highlands: "For my soul is in you, and wants to live in you."

Inside the firemen's hall, a circle of tables filled the room. White plastic folding chairs were set up around the outside of a ring of tables, leaving the space inside the ring open. Half the chairs were already filled when Luisa entered and sat beside Ernest and Ruth Strubhar.

More people entered from the dark outside and took places along the tables. Did any of them feel the sense of family so keenly as Luisa that night? Only God knew the long journey of disappointment, guilt, and frustration that had brought her to this place. Only He knew how many Saturday mornings she had spent straining to spot a church house on the Oklahoma plains. *Oh, Mama, if only you could see your Reina now!*

After the opening hymns were sung, Ernest asked Luisa to testify of God's work in her life. She rose from her chair and scanned the group. "Sisters and brothers," she began, as Ernest interpreted. "I thought I was a Christian when I left the Mennonite church in Guatemala. But I was separated from my husband and children, and we were bad off financially, so I came here to the North to support my family. After I arrived in California, I fell easily into sin, living in fornication. I was wrong. I lived and dressed like the world. I did wrong to one person," Luisa confessed, remembering Carlos, "lying to him and returning evil for evil. But that is all made right. I have asked forgiveness of the one I wronged. In all of this, God always loved me, and He reached out His hand to me. Jesus never wanted to leave me."

Luisa looked down the row of tables to where Mike and Debbie Russel sat with five clear-eyed children. "Thank you, Mike and Debbie," she said, "for coming to me, and for all you have done for me. And thank you to all my brothers and sisters who prayed for me. I have a new life following Christ." As Ernest finished interpreting her testimony, the little group smiled their welcome.

Ernest read a passage from his Spanish Bible and asked Luisa a few questions. His final question was, "Are you of one heart with us to gladly submit to God and follow Him in daily life, obeying His Word?"

Luisa did not hesitate. "I am!" *I've held the reins too long, Lord. I'm coming home!*

Ernest had spoken with Leland, Luisa knew, about her desire to join the congregation at Perkins, and Leland had been entirely supportive. *Who knows,* she thought, *maybe I will even return to El Edén someday. If I do, I will do all I can to bless those who wronged me, and I will lay my burdens on my Father instead of carrying them myself.*

The congregation stood to welcome Luisa to the brotherhood, and Ernest finished, "Be kindly affectioned one to another with brotherly love; in honour preferring one another . . . rejoicing in hope; patient in tribulation; continuing instant in prayer . . . . Bless them which persecute you: bless, and curse not."[1]

The elders broke bread and passed it around the room. As Luisa reached out to receive her portion, her eyes filled with tears. How long had it been since she had shared the body and blood of the Lord, her God of light? Could it really have been thirty-two years? As she swallowed the sacred bread, she felt the arms of the Shepherd around her. Once again, after all this time, she was next to the heart of her Shepherd of light. Through all the tangled paths of her life, His love had never failed her.

---

[1] Romans 12:10, 12, 14

EPILOGUE

On a dark night in January, about thirty friends and relatives gathered at Dionel's house in Oklahoma City, in memory of Vicenta.

The author and her husband were there. They had connected months earlier with Luisa, but this was their first meeting with the rest of the family.

Dionel, still of gentle, gracious manner, with his sweet wife Andrea and their daughter Evelyn, welcomed the guests as they arrived. No one knew then that Dionel was already in a valley of decision.

Benjamín was there. The once scrawny baby had grown into a strong man. And Eliza, the sweet girl with long braids, thoughtful eyes, and capable hands, who could quiet a baby, milk a goat, or show a teacher how to start a fire, who faithfully did whatever was at hand to do—she was now a quiet, middle-aged woman. She seemed sad.

Luisa's youngest son, Hamit, sat beside his young wife, somewhat apart from the memories of Vicenta that filled the thoughts of the others. He alone had been raised by his mother, not by Grandma Vicenta.

Juan Calderón, grand-nephew of Vicenta and son of Benigno and Valeriana, was there, with the same radiant smile of the charming schoolboy. He was now a father of seven children, and his family remained in La Laguna.

Among those not present at the memorial gathering were Sonia, Juana, Marixa, and Joel, who lived in California; and Aide, who remained in Guatemala. Months after this gathering, Aide would say of her grandmother, "I want to forget about the past and follow the example my grandma was for me. She was a great person for me."

All had traveled many roads from Guatemala in 1983 to wherever they found themselves in 2011. But with God, there is no here or there, no now or then. His great father-heart encompasses the whole earth, yearning to bring home every last wandering child.

After a short service and a message of comfort from Ernest Strubhar, the guests filed around the kitchen table, loading their plates with delicious food from two cultures.

The beautiful view from Luisa's house on La Laguna.

At the end of the evening, when Hamit shook hands with Henry and Gwen, he spoke of the change in Luisa's life since reconnecting with the church. "I am so glad you people found my mother," he said gently in slightly-broken English. "She used to cry a lot. She was sad. But now she is so happy."

They looked into his honest eyes and saw tears. And they wondered at the ways of the Shepherd.

In June of 2013, Luisa again visited Carlos in Guatemala. He was in poor health, but he served her a drink and invited her to sit down. "We are family," he said. "We will put the past behind and get along." His kind words were an answer to her prayers. It was the last time she saw him alive.

Luisa has returned to La Laguna, where she once again attends the Mennonite church in El Edén. She lives in the house she commissioned Conrado to build for Vicenta. Fifty yards off is the place, now overgrown with grass, where eighty years ago Bacilio built a home for his bride, its four corners formed by living trees.

AFTERWORD

On May 15, 1980, I worshiped with the church in Chimaltenango, Guatemala. That was also the day the first Sunday meetings were held in El Edén. I was eighteen years old, and like the brothers and sisters gathered in Rigoberto's sala that day, I was brimful of hopes and dreams. I was soon to be married to Henry Hertzler and had come to Guatemala to visit him.

Having grown up in the foothills of the Cascade Mountains of Oregon, I felt at home with the rugged beauty and the narrow, winding roads of Guatemala's hill country. I dearly loved the people, the warm and sensible connectedness of their simple lives, the easy smiles and greetings, the kisses planted gently on each cheek.

I liked the soft lilt of their voices in speech, the depth, energy, and freedom of their voices in song. I loved the direct way they looked at me when I spoke, as though I was pre-approved and accepted. I liked their tickled laughter when I used the wrong Spanish word.

I liked their homes, small, spare, and arranged for service, the poorer homes displaying no ornamentation beyond a riot of flowers—bougainvilleas, massive geraniums, and assorted colorful blooms spilling from cans, pots, and buckets lining courtyard walls.

Though my visit would be only two weeks, I felt I could make my home in Guatemala and love it.

I knew nothing then of the drama playing out in the mountains of Sibilia and El Edén, several hours away, but I would glimpse it occasionally over the next thirty years until it captivated my heart and mind, compelling me to seek to understand and tell the story.

Almost three years after that Sunday morning in May, I would meet Reina for the first time, the day I hiked over the mountains with Norma González and the other ladies to see Reina's day-old baby, Benjamín.

Henry and I had arrived in Guatemala two months before—a quick decision and move. Carl Martin had been recalled to serve his home church in Illinois, leaving the little El Edén school lacking a teacher for the upper grades in the middle of the school term, and Henry's familiarity with the culture and language had led someone to suggest him as a replacement.

On the day of Percy Stauffer's funeral, Leland asked us to take Reina, Conrado, and the baby to the doctor. That was the day she learned her milk was making her baby sick.

I held Benjamín on my lap as we drove to Xela. He wore a grimy oversized shirt, shawl, and damp diaper, and his lips and tongue were blotched with white thrush sores. How precious he was, and how pitiable!

Coincidentally, Reynaldo rode with us to Percy's funeral in La Victoria later in the day. He held our son Anthony on his lap and merrily fed him candy. Little did any of us imagine that six years later Reynaldo's body would be laid to rest in the same cemetery.

In the spring of 1991, Henry and I were traveling through California, visiting various families who were seeking fellowship and encouragement. Back home in Oregon, Ernest and Ruth Strubhar kept our children. The day we parked in front of the Oxford building, where Luisa lived, I was particularly glad the children were not with us.

As we locked the car and looked around us, we felt like foreigners. Cautiously, we opened the door of a massive old building and ascended a long flight of stairs. As we made our way deeper into the bowels of the ancient structure, the long dingy halls and the smoggy city that surrounded the building collided in my mind with memories of a mud hut on a wide, grassy hillside, swept fresh with wind and sun and rain. We knocked on Luisa's door, and it opened to reveal a small room filled with mostly familiar faces and a few items of furniture. Eleven Guatemalans lived there, half of them from El Edén. I remember a bed dominating most of the floor space and a tall armoire or wardrobe on the left, against which Dionel leaned, smiling shyly. Eliza was there, enamored with her new husband. In the glow of early love, she alone looked happy. A tiny kitchen huddled like an afterthought beyond a doorway in the far corner of the room.

We visited for a little while. Henry read a passage from the Psalms and led in prayer. When we said goodbye, Luisa seemed sad—reluctant to let us go.

She assured us she was preparing to return to Guatemala soon.

I kept a journal during this trip through California, recording impressions of people we visited and the circumstances we found them in. It was written like a parable, as if a young apprentice shepherdess were trying to see her experiences from the perspective of the Great Shepherd.

This scene made no sense to me. The grief I felt at seeing Dionel and Eliza and so many others from El Edén in these circumstances, coupled with the knowledge of the prosperous lives many of us led back home in Oregon—all of it became a series of crying questions. What desperation would induce these dear people to trade their families and Guatemala's beautiful countryside for this miserable, concrete cage? What could be done to bring them back to the Shepherd and to help meet their physical needs, and why wasn't it being done? Didn't the church have a responsibility to seek and pursue such sheep? Could the churches here and the churches there work together to find and help them?

I wrote, "How can we retreat into the great walled fold and forget this revelation?"

Though the memory of that visit haunted us, the distractions and busyness of life dried the tears off the worn-out question marks. We thought Luisa returned to Guatemala, and we never went back to Los Angeles. Within two years we moved to Oklahoma.

But the loving Shepherd never forgot.

I did not live most of this story; I only wrote it. I do not claim to have it all right, but I have done my best. I apologize to the Barrios and Monterroso families if at any point my story violates your memories. I have spent hours with some of you, less with others. I have asked a thousand questions, many of them two or three times. I have prayed that my pen would be faithful. Your faces and hearts were in my prayers as I wrote.

Conversations have been reconstructed from journals, letters, and from my memories as well as those of others. Probable details have been added and internal conflicts imagined in a way that reflects the struggles of the characters as I understood them. Some names, details, and relationships have been changed slightly to protect identities.

I pray that Luisa's story may inspire my readers as it has me—to a greater compassion for those whose choices perplex us and to a deeper trust in a Shepherd who understands every journey.

ACKNOWLEDGMENTS

Luisa, thank you for trusting me with your story. Thank you for the many miles you traveled with us to Guatemala and Los Angeles. Thank you for opening painful places. I loved you before, but you have become closer than a sister as I have walked these years with you. I know God will continue to be your Healer, your Strength, and your Light.

Thank you, Chilolo and Yanet, for your kindness and respect toward me, a stranger. Thank you for sharing memories no one else could have known. Thank you for being there all those years for your little sister and her children.

Dionel, Aide, Sonia, Juana, Marixa, Benjamín, and Hamit, thank you for sharing. Without your words and your tears, I could not have understood the story. To all of Luisa's sons and daughters, whether I managed to meet with you or not, you are close to my heart, and wherever life takes you, you will remain in my prayers. Special thanks to Dionel and Hamit for all the time, help, encouragement, and patience you expended on me.

Sonia, the scrumptious meal you prepared for me and my hosts in your home was a highlight of this journey. Thank you for your open-hearted generosity.

Thank you, Andrea and Evelyn, for the blessing of your friendship, for leaving a bed empty for me, and for the tamales when my mother died. You are beautiful women.

Thank you, Leland and Esther, for the journals and notes; for food and clean water in empty guest quarters. Thank you for friendship and prayers. I have long admired your character, and reconnecting over this project has deepened that admiration.

Rosene Burkholder, the detailed record of your short visit to Guatemala, and your rare Monterroso family photo, were priceless.

Thank you, Ed and Ruth Miller, for your hospitality, and for showing me around Los Angeles, praying with me, and venturing with me into places the security guard warned us away from.

Alvin Mast, your patience, your counsel, and your confidence in this fledgling writer helped me immeasurably to coax this book to life. Thank you.

Marita Horst, God used your girlish confidence in me to nudge me into picking up my pen past middle age. Thank you for all the fun.

Sheila Petre, do you have any idea how much I needed your encouragement, wisdom, and critiques? God did. He gave you to me for a niece and a cheerleader. Thank you.

To the beautiful sons in my home, Jeremy, Josiah, Hans, Stephen, Henry, and Raphael: thank you for sharing my time and attention these two long years without complaining. Thank you for listening and making me believe the story was good. You are a joy and blessing to me. I love you.

Grace, it has happened! You are holding the book in your hands—the book in which you have invested as many hours as I, but with broom and mop and skillet. You, darling, are my right arm. You are grace abounding to me.

Esther and Abigail, my precious daughters-in-law, thank you for your patience and support. I hear your sighs of relief. I understand.

Anthony, when I taught you to write, I didn't imagine you would someday be my editor. You believed in my work—I believed in yours. We tried each other's patience, but we persevered. You polished and trimmed my whittlings, and I will always be thankful to you, my son and my brother, for your invaluable help with this manuscript.

Henry, beloved, what can I say? Without you, this book wouldn't be. Thank you for answering God's call to teach thirty-three years ago. Thank you for being my chauffeur, guide, and interpreter in 2013 when we revisited the people and places of this story. Without your confidence and unwavering support in every aspect of this project, I couldn't have completed this. Thank you for being there for me.

And now, Great Shepherd of Love, I am humbled in your presence. Through this story, I felt you shake Panorama, I heard you call Bacilio's children to your heart, I watched your arms reaching out to your wounded, wandering sheep, your steps following them untiringly. I saw eternal love, and I wrote what I saw. I didn't find all the answers I sought, but it doesn't matter. Like Job of old, I finally have put my hand on my mouth.

PRONUNCIATION GUIDE

Adelma	ah DEHL mah
Aide	ahee DEH
Alberto	ahl BEHR toh
Amalia	ah MAH leeah
Andrea	ahn DREH ah
Angela	AHN heh lah
arroz con leche	ah ROHS kohn LEH cheh
atole	ah TOHL
azadón	ah sah DOHN
Bacilio	bah SEE leeoh
Baldomero	bahl doh MEH roh
Benigno Calderón	beh NEEG noh kahl deh ROHN
Benjamín	behn hah MEEN
buenas tardes	BOOEH nahs TAHR dehs
buenos días	BOOEH nohs DEE ahs
Carlos	KAHR lohs
Cerezo	seh REH soh
Chabela	cha BEH lah
Chano	CHAH noh
Chilolo	chee LOH loh
Chimaltenango	chee mahl teh NAHN goh
Conrado	kohn RAH doh
Cornelia	kohr NEH leeah
Corteza	kohr TEH sah
cusha	KOO shah
Dionel	deeoh NEHL
Dios la bendiga	deeohs lah behn DEE gah
Don Feliciano Escobar	dohn feh lee SEEAH noh ehs koh BAHR
Don Leon	dohn leh OHN
El Edén	ehl eh DEHN

Elena	eh LEH nah
Eliza	eh LEE sah
Evelina	eh veh LEE nah
Fuego	FOOEH goh
Gabino	gah BEE noh
Gama Aguilar	GAH mah ah ge LAHR
González	gohn SAH lehs
Hamit	HAH meet
Hola	OH lah
Isabel	ee sah BEHL
Juan Lopez	hooahn LOH pehs
Juana	HOOAH nah
kiosko	KEEOHS koh
La Cumbre	lah KOOM breh
La Laguna	lah lah GOO nah
La Victoria	lah veek TOH reeah
leche	LEH cheh
Lencho	LEHN choh
Lidia	LEE deeah
Magdalena	mahg dah LEH nah
manta cantel	MAHN tah kahn TEHL
Marco Domínguez	MAHR koh doh MEEN gehs
María	mah REE ah
Mariano	mah REEAH noh
Marixa	mah REEK sah
Milagro	mee LAH groh
paches	PAH chehs
El Paiz	ehl PAHEES
Palestina	pah lehs TEE nah
pila	PEE lah
Princesa	preen SEH sah
pupusas de queso	poo POO sahs deh KEH soh

Reina	RAY nah
Reynalda Barrios	ray NAHL dah BAH rreohs
Reynaldo Monterroso	ray NAHL doh mohn teh RROH soh
Rigoberto Ochoa	ree goh BEHR toh oh CHOH ah
Rios Montt	REE ohs mohnt
San Jacinto	sahn hah SEEN toh
San Juan	sahn hooahn
Santiago	sahn TEEAH goh
Sergei	SEHR gay
Sibilia	see BEE leeah
Sonia	SOH neeah
Suledi	soo LEH dee
Susana	soo SAH nah
Tajumulco	tah hoo MOOL koh
Tijuana	tee HOOAH nah
Tío Lolo	TEE oh LOH loh
Valeriana	vah leh REEAH nah
Vicenta	vee SEHN tah
Xela	SHEH lah
Yanet	yah NEHT
Yolanda Garcia	yoh LAHN dah gah SEE ah

ABOUT THE AUTHOR

Gwendolyn Swartzendruber Hertzler grew up in Oregon, the third of nine children in an old farmhouse along Eagle Creek in the foothills of the Cascade Range. After marrying Henry Hertzler and moving to the Willamette Valley in 1980, she became the mother of twelve children and lived in several states across the US. For the past ten years, the Hertzlers have been part of a small Christian community on a wooded acreage in the Ozark foothills north of Tahlequah, Oklahoma, where Henry and Gwen raise their remaining children, grow a large garden, care for the family's livestock, and spend time with their eleven grandchildren.

Gwen loves singing, beautiful gardens, and people. Her highest goal is to emulate Jesus, and she hopes the stories she writes will magnify God's faithfulness amid human failings, inspiring readers to confide in His goodness and delight in His creativity.

Gwen invites you to share your thoughts at gwenhertzler@gmail.com, or write her in care of Christian Aid Ministries, P.O. Box 360, Berlin, Ohio 44610.

The author and her husband stand in front of Luisa's house on La Laguna.

ABOUT CHRISTIAN AID MINISTRIES

Christian Aid Ministries was founded in 1981 as a nonprofit, tax-exempt 501(c)(3) organization. Its primary purpose is to provide a trustworthy and efficient channel for Amish, Mennonite, and other conservative Anabaptist groups and individuals to minister to physical and spiritual needs around the world. This is in response to the command to ". . . do good unto all men, especially unto them who are of the household of faith" (Galatians 6:10).

Each year, CAM supporters provide 15–20 million pounds of food, clothing, medicines, seeds, Bibles, Bible story books, and other Christian literature for needy people. Most of the aid goes to orphans and Christian families. Supporters' funds also help to clean up and rebuild for natural disaster victims, put up Gospel billboards in the U.S., support several church-planting efforts, operate two medical clinics, and provide resources for needy families to make their own living. CAM's main purposes for providing aid are to help and encourage God's people and bring the Gospel to a lost and dying world.

CAM has staff, warehouses, and distribution networks in Romania, Moldova, Ukraine, Haiti, Nicaragua, Liberia, Israel, and Kenya. Aside from management, supervisory personnel, and bookkeeping operations, volunteers do most of the work at CAM locations. Each year, volunteers at our warehouses, field bases, Disaster Response Services projects, and other locations donate over 200,000 hours of work.

CAM's ultimate purpose is to glorify God and help enlarge His kingdom. ". . . whatsoever ye do, do all to the glory of God" (1 Corinthians 10:31).

THE WAY TO GOD AND PEACE

We live in a world contaminated by sin. Sin is anything that goes against God's holy standards. When we do not follow the guidelines that God our Creator gave us, we are guilty of sin. Sin separates us from God, the source of life.

Since the time when the first man and woman, Adam and Eve, sinned in the Garden of Eden, sin has been universal. The Bible says that we all have "sinned and come short of the glory of God" (Romans 3:23). It also says that the natural consequence for that sin is eternal death, or punishment in an eternal hell: "Then when lust hath conceived, it bringeth forth sin: and sin, when it is finished, bringeth forth death" (James 1:15).

But we do not have to suffer eternal death in hell. God provided forgiveness for our sins through the death of His only Son, Jesus Christ. Because Jesus was perfect and without sin, He could die in our place. "For God so loved the world that he gave his only begotten Son, that whosoever believeth in him should not perish, but have everlasting life" (John 3:16).

A sacrifice is something given to benefit someone else. It costs the giver greatly. Jesus was God's sacrifice. Jesus' death takes away the penalty of sin for everyone who accepts this sacrifice and truly repents of their sins. To repent of sins means to be truly sorry for and turn away from the things we have done that have violated God's standards (Acts 2:38; 3:19).

Jesus died, but He did not remain dead. After three days, God's Spirit miraculously raised Him to life again. God's Spirit does something similar in us. When we receive Jesus as our sacrifice and repent of our sins, our hearts are changed. We become spiritually alive! We develop new desires and attitudes (2 Corinthians 5:17). We begin to make choices that please God (1 John 3:9). If we do fail and commit sins, we can ask God for forgiveness. "If we confess our sins, he is faithful and just to forgive us our sins, and to cleanse us from all unrighteousness" (1 John 1:9).

Once our hearts have been changed, we want to continue growing spiritually. We will be happy to let Jesus be the Master of our lives and will want to become more like Him. To do this, we must meditate on God's Word and commune with God in prayer. We will testify to others of this change by being baptized and sharing the good news of God's victory over sin and death. Fellowship with a faithful group of believers will strengthen our walk with God (1 John 1:7).